Voices
of
Five Counties

**A guide to writers of Herefordshire, Shropshire,
Staffordshire, Warwickshire and Worcestershire**

To the members, past and present, of the Bredon
and Bromsgrove literature classes

Rosemary Toeman

Voices
of
Five Counties

A guide to writers of Herefordshire, Shropshire, Staffordshire, Warwickshire and Worcestershire

Illustrated by
Judy Hadley

ℍ Halfshire Books

Halfshire Books
6 High Street, Bromsgrove
Worcestershire B61 8HQ

First published in Great Britain
by Halfshire Books 1994

ISBN 1 899062 00 9

Typeset in Times by Myst Ltd, Weobley, Hereford, and printed in Great Britain
by Cromwell Press Ltd, Broughton Gifford, Melksham.

Contents

Acknowledgements

Rosemary Arthur (Mrs D M Partridge), M and M Baldwin, Hazel Beese, Mr F W Billington, Birmingham and Midland Institute, Birmingham City Library, A L Boon, Bredon Literature Class, Bromsgrove Literature Class, Bromsgrove Library, Burton-on-Trent Library, Cannock Library, Mr L Cooper, Coventry City Library, George Cowley, Roy Crompton, Mary Croxson, Chris Davies, Brenda Dean, Miss Wendy Dedicott, Droitwich Library, Stephen Drucker, Dudley Libraries, Dudley Local History & Archives Department, Hazel Edwards, Miss A J Farnol, Roy Fisher, Ivan and Joyce Forward, Mrs Olga Fox, Jane Fraser, Mrs Marjorie Green, Mr Stephen Guy, Mr H Jack Haden, Joan Hall, Halesowen Library, Shirley Ann Hankins-Symonds, Hanley Library, Miss Marilyn Harris, Mrs T Harris, Mrs Dorrie Hedges, Hereford Library, Alan Holden, Janet Hope, Hilde Hunt, Joe Hunt, John F Jenkins, Jim William Jones, Mrs Jim William Jones, Maureen P Jones, Phil Jones, Mrs Beverley Juggins, Kidderminster Library, David Knowles, Gary Lanham, Leamington Spa Library, Lichfield Library, Madeley Library, Malvern Library, Geoffrey Mason, Doreen Mitchell, Brigit Morton, Newcastle-under-Lyme Library, Mrs Muriel Paine, Mrs Ruth Parker, Mrs Karen Priest, Mrs Pat Purcell, Nuneaton Library, Jon Raven, Miss Vera Rawlings, Redditch Library, Dave Reeves, Ken Rock, Ross-on-Wye Library, Elizabeth Schafer, Shrewsbury Library, Solihull Library, Stafford Library, Staffordshire Libraries, Arts and Archives Headquarters, Stoke-on-Trent Library, Stourbridge Library, Stratford-upon-Avon Library, Anna Toeman, David Toeman, Harriet Toeman, Chris Upton, Walsall Local History Centre, James Warner, Mrs G R Wilson, Wolverhampton Library, Worcester Library, Eileen Wright.

Preface

This book is concerned with writers of fiction, especially the less well-known and long forgotten, who are in some way associated with the west midland counties of Herefordshire, Shropshire, Staffordshire, Warwickshire and Worcestershire.

In 1974, among many other boundary changes in Britain, the short-lived metropolitan county of the West Midlands was created. In order to avoid confusion between the county of the West Midlands and the counties of the west midlands, it was decided to use the pre-1974 county names and boundaries when placing an author geographically.

Having made this decision it seemed appropriate to adopt 1974 as the cut-off date for the inclusion of authors. Only those who have published, broadcast or been performed before the end of 1974 are listed. Brief reference is made to the work of those who have continued to publish after 1974, if such information has been available, but the focus is necessarily on their pre-1974 work.

It was less easy to define exactly what is meant by a west midland counties' author. In the end, it was decided to include all those who have lived in the area – for however short a period – even though this meant making reference to authors such as Vera Brittain who was a mere infant when she left Newcastle-under-Lyme. Decisions as to whether or not to include visitors were even more difficult to make. If authors, such as Richard Corbett or George R Windsor, are known to have been influenced by the people or places of the west midlands, they are listed. Some distinguished writers are listed – for interest's sake, rather than to make any clearly untenable claim to them. If, like Nathaniel Hawthorne or Mark Twain, writers came to the area on literary pilgrimages to the homes of the famous, they are listed. And if they are known to have been guests at literary gatherings in the great houses, such as Hagley Hall, Abberley Lodge, Polesworth Manor or the Leasowes, they are listed.

Some early historians and chroniclers, Tacitus and Layamon for example, have also been included – mainly to give the guide some sort of chronological perspective. It was decided also to include essayists, diarists and letter writers whose work so often exhibits the figurative, the poetic and the anecdotal – not to say the fictional.

When it was discovered how large a number of authors are associated with the west midland counties it was decided to list as many as possible at the expense of comprehensive lists of work or detailed literary commentary and analysis. Most of the entries are therefore very short – though it is hoped not insultingly so. And for well-known authors whose details are readily accessible in any national literary guide the emphasis in this book has been on charting their associations with the area.

Where only a little information is available – inevitably so with the less well-known and long forgotten authors who are the especial interest of this guide – it was nevertheless decided to include an author so long as a date of birth, of death or of publication adequately places him or her historically and there was reasonable certainty of a connection with the area.

When and how and to what effect an author came to be associated with the west midland counties were the questions the guide aimed to answer. This association is therefore the first concern of each entry. The formula 'believed to have' – to be found in entries such as those for C Goodall or Elizabeth Jenkins – represents hearsay evidence that it was not possible to verify, but which was considered sufficiently convincing to justify a listing. The presence of further commentary is no indication of an author's literary status – it merely reflects the compiler's own interests and tastes.

There are, unfortunately, sure to be omissions – of individual authors, as well as of relevant details. These are also the compiler's responsibility; as are any factual mistakes and idiosyncrasies of literary interpretation and evaluation.

Begun in the autumn of 1992, in an attempt to satisfy an identified curiosity about authors of the west midland counties, this guide may turn out to be most valuable as a stimulus to interest and to further research. Herefordshire, Shropshire, Staffordshire, Warwickshire and Worcestershire possess an extraordinarily rich seam of literary achievement that, to labour the metaphor, waits only for the scholar and the enthusiast to take up pick and shovel.

This guide is only a beginning.

Introduction

It is difficult to know quite how to introduce a book which is in itself little more than an introduction – to the variety and quantity of fiction to be found associated with the counties of the west midlands. Only the reader can decide whether or not it is worth exploring further the bookshops, the libraries and the local record offices of the area in order to follow up the books and authors listed in this guide. What I would like to do is to draw your attention to those characteristics unique to the area which seem particularly to have prompted writers into prose or verse.

To begin with, the type of industry to be found here has inspired much work specific to the west midland area. Arnold Bennett, Frederick Harper and Noah Heath have written about the Potteries; G A Henty about the coalmines of Cannock Chase; L P Jacks, Silverpen, Vera Oram and Boswell Taylor about Birmingham's heavy industry; Nellie Kirkham about the leadmines of Staffordshire; John Petty about the scrapmetal industry of the Black Country; and many more.

The rivers of the area have readily found admirers – among many others John Huckell for the Avon, James Henry James for the Wye, Alfred Rowberry Williams for the Severn and George Wakefield for the Dove. The scenery of Shropshire inspired A E Housman, David Rudkin and Mary Webb. Sutton Park prompted Edwin Edridge and Harry Howells Horton into verse. The Shrawley area prompted W P Hodgkinson into prose.

Often cities, towns or villages provide the inspiration. Ludlow on its hill caught the imagination of Donald Herbert Barber. Robert W Thom's civic pride was aroused by Coventry; Harrison Corbet Wilson's by Leamington Spa. Leek numbers among its admirers Nellie Birch, Muriel Hope Brown, William Challinor, Elijah Cope, A L Gee and Ralph de Tunstall Sneyd.

Some of the great houses were chosen as models for fictional counterparts – among them Alton Towers for Benjamin Disraeli's Muriel Towers and Calwich Abbey for George Eliot's Donnithorne Chase.

Of the area's most famous sons and daughters, William Shakespeare inspired John Brophy, John Jordan, Peter Whalley and others to write. Alfred Lord Tennyson wrote about Lady Godiva; Michael Drayton and Richard Corbett about Guy of Warwick; William Hazlitt about Joseph Priestley; and Mrs G Linnaeus Banks about William Hutton. There are many more.

Historical events in the west midland counties have frequently been a source of inspiration. To give only two examples – Jan Weddup described how the bloody battle of Edgehill and its aftermath still seem to pervade the place and Sir Walter Scott used Kenilworth's part in the tragic story of Amy Robsart for the central scenes in his historical novel.

And lastly, the language of the west midland counties has often prompted writers to try to reproduce its range of vocabulary and versatility of tone in order to capture the essence of place and time. O'd Hedgefud, the creation of J Eric Roberts, who told the Bilberry Pie tales, speaks the language of Cannock Chase. It is the Black Country dialect which Walter J Morgan, David Bailey, Harry Harrison, T Gough, Henry Bull and Jim William Jones have used to such effect – both comic and serious – in their poems and short stories. The vernacular voice of Coventry is used by A E Feltham to express his everyday experiences. John Audelay chose the Salopian vernacular in which to declare his religious commitment.

And no doubt the literary gatherings at the hospitable homes of such as William Shenstone, Lord Lyttelton or Sir Henry Goodere, and the writing groups similar to the one Fanny Burney's uncle joined in 18th-century Worcester or the present-day Walsall Writers' Circle, have also fostered and still foster writing that has its roots in and draws nourishment from the soil of the west midlands counties. And this soil is very rich.

Of course it would be a nonsense to suggest that every book written by every west midlands author mentioned in these pages is a literary master-piece. But if you can find the time to read at least some of the books associated with the five counties, you will find much to take pride in and a great deal to please.

I hope this guide will tempt you irresistibly.

A

ABERCROMBIE Lascelles
1881–1938 poet and critic. Educated at Malvern, in 1930 he published a collection of his poetry in the editions of work by contemporary writers produced under the title, *Oxford Poets*. He also wrote a critique of Thomas Hardy (1912) and several studies on poetics, including *The Theory of Poetry* (1924) and *The Idea of Great Poetry* (1925).

ADAMS Geoffrey Pharaoh
b.1921 novelist. Born at Lye in Worcestershire, he draws on his own experiences as a Japanese prisoner during the Second World War in his novel, *No Time for Geishas* (1973).

ADAMS Gerald
mid-20th C novelist. His novel, *Red Vagabond; Story of a Fox* (1951), is set in the south Shropshire countryside near Bishop's Castle where he lived for several years.

ADDISON John
d.1911 short story writer. Editor of the *Brierley Hill and Stourbridge Advertiser* from 1860 to 1870, he then for a short time joined the staff of the *Birmingham Daily Gazette* and in 1888 was elected to the Staffordshire County Council. His short stories, collected under the titles of *A Dudley Quakeress* (1900), *Palace and Borough, a Tale of Bewdley the Golden* (1901) and *The White Canon of Halesowen, a Tale of the Suppression of the Abbey* (1902), first appeared in the *Dudley Advertiser*.

ADDISON Joseph
1672–1719 poet, politician and essayist. The son of the Dean of Lichfield, he lived in the town from 1683 to 1698 and was educated at the grammar school. He frequently visited his friend, William Walsh*, at Abberley Hall, where a tree-lined path is named Addison's Walk; and he also spent time at Hagley Hall, the home of Lord Lyttelton*. In 1713 he bought the country estate of Bilton Hall where he planted avenues of trees and planned and developed extensive vegetable and fruit gardens. He is best known for the poem, *The Campaign* (1705), which celebrated Marlborough's victory at Blenheim, for his tragedy, *Cato* (1713), and for his essays in *The Tatler* (1709–11) and in *The Spectator* (1711–12 and 1714).

ADKINS Geoffrey
late 20th C poet. He is believed to be living in Stafford. *Doorkeeper* (1974), his only known collection of poems, is mainly to do with the trials and disappointments of modern life.

AGNEW Rev A T
1886–1961 poet, playwright, novelist and essayist. From 1912 to 1916 he was curate at St Mary's in Shrewsbury; from 1916 to 1923 he was curate at St Mary's in Walsall; and in 1923 he returned to Shrewsbury as vicar of St George's. His collection of verse, *The Tyrant, and Other Poems*, appeared in 1916. *The Disguised Lady* and *The Last Farewell* are his most successful comedies. *Madman's Island*, a compilation of prose and poetry, contains two of his short novels, as well as essays, verse and short stories.

AINSWORTH William Harrison
1805–82 novelist. He was a frequent visitor to Boscobel House, Brewood and Chillington Hall, researching among family papers and tracts on

which are based his historical novel, *Boscobel, or The Royal Oak, Tale of the Year 1651* (1872). His other publications include *Rookwood* (1834) and *Old St Paul's* (1841).

ALDIS James A
late 19th C poet. He taught at Queen Mary's Grammar School in Walsall from 1879 to 1897. Much of his work, which was published in *Punch* and *The Spectator*, concerns local scenes and people.

ALEXANDER Evelyn Mary
early 20th C children's writer. She was a pupil at Barr's Hill School in Coventry. *The Fairy Boat Race* (1927), her only known work, is perhaps rather too sentimental a tale for modern tastes.

ALINGTON Rev C A
1872–1955 novelist. From 1908 to 1916 he was headmaster of Shrewsbury School. His only known novels, *Strained Relations* (1922) and *The Evans* (1927), are concerned with family life.

ALLBEURY Ted
b.1917 novelist. Born in Manchester, he was brought up in Birmingham. His best-known novels published before the end of 1974 are *A Choice of Enemies* (1973) and *Snowball* (1974). He continues to write, mostly in the thriller genre, and his popularity grows yearly. *Line-crosser* (1993) is his latest work.

ALLBUT Thomas Henry
b.1842 poet. Born at Hanley, the son of the following, he was educated at Shelton Hall. His poems, many concerned with pastimes and topical events of the Potteries, were published in several periodicals including *The Argosy* and the *London Morning Post*.

ALLBUT William
1809–79 short story writer. Born in Hanley, in 1859 he published two short stories, entitled *Anna, a Tale* and *Look to the End*. *Compendium*, a collection of miscellaneous facts and information, was devised specifically for use in schools for girls.

ALLCOCK Florence B
mid-20th C novelist. She belongs to the Redditch Allcock family, manufacturers of fishing tackle. The author of several novels, in 1934 she published her best-known, *Facts and Fiction – a Historical Romance of the Midlands*, which is set in the fictional Worcestershire town of Richdale. Other work includes *What's In a Laugh?* (1936) and *Crikey* (1938).

ALLEN T S
mid-19th C poet and essayist. He lived in Dudley. His only known poem, *A Trip to Paris in Verse*, was published in 1831. Other work includes essays and local and historical guides.

ALLEN Walter E
b.1911 novelist, journalist, children's writer, critic and broadcaster. Born in Aston in Birmingham, the youngest son of a silversmith, he was educated at King Edward's School and the University of Birmingham where he was a friend of Louis McNeice* and Henry Reed*. He worked in the aluminium industry in the city before becoming a journalist for the *Birmingham Post and Gazette* and a broadcaster on BBC Midlands. Later he obtained a post as a schoolmaster in Birmingham. His novels include *Innocence is Drowned* (1938), *Living Space* (1940), *Rogue Elephant* (1946), *All in a Lifetime* (1962) and, arguably the best, *Blind Man's Ditch* (1939) which details the violent repercus-

sions in Birmingham of the industrial depression. Part of this novel is based on the trial of two murderers, Ridly and Betts. It was only by accident that he discovered R D Smith to be broadcasting his children's stories in Jerusalem during the Second World War. *The English Novel* (1954) and *Six Great Novelists* (1955) are examples of his literary history and criticism. He was a member of the Birmingham Group which included Walter Brierley*, Peter Chamberlain*, Leslie Halward* and John Hampson*. His fiction is deeply evocative of time and place and always reveals his fascination with ordinary life.

ALLESTREE Richard
1619–81 essayist. He was born at Uppington near the Wrekin in Shropshire, and with Richard Baxter* attended the endowed school at Wroxeter. His chief work, *The Whole Duty of Man* (1658), a treatise on all the duties due to God and man, was popular for more than one hundred years. According to William Thackeray, it was much read by those members of the servant classes – such as Miss Crawley's maid, Hester, in *Vanity Fair* – who aspired to greater things.

ALLWOOD Arthur
b.1893 poet. He lived in Minsterley and Shrewsbury. The autobiographical *Wanderings of a Shropshire Lad* appeared in 1964. A collection of his shorter poems, *Our Beautiful Shropshire*, was published in 1968.

ALMA Roger
mid/late 20th C poet. He lives at Hanley Swan near Malvern and is a principal lecturer in the English Department at Worcester College of Higher Education. Though also

known for his non-fiction work, which includes studies of Thomas Hardy (1979) and Molly Holden* (1974 and 1978), he was a winner of the annual poetry prize in the *Critical Review* (1965) and has had poems published in the *Critical Quarterly* (1966 and 1974), in *Bitteroot* (1975) and in *Poetry Now Metric Muscles* (1994).

ALMEDINGEN E M
1898–1971 novelist, poet and children's writer. She fled from her native Russia in 1923 and settled in Shropshire – first in Worfield, then in Church Stretton and lastly at the Attingham estate. A prolific writer, especially of historical novels, she is perhaps best known for her children's books – such as *Little Katia* (1966) and *A Candle at Dusk* (1967). A gentle determination to succeed motivates most of her central characters.

ALSOP George Philip Ranulph
b.1890 poet. Born at Bednall vicarage in Stafford, he contributed poems, mostly inspired by nature, to several periodicals. He is the grandson of the following.

ALSOP James Richard
1816–80 poet. Born at Bonehill near Tamworth, he returned to his native county when he became vicar of Acton Trussell-with-Bednall in 1867. His thoughtful, kind-hearted poetry, much of it based on classical and biblical stories, was published posthumously in 1880 as *The Prayer of Ajax and Other Poems*.

AMPHLETT James
1775–1860 poet, novelist and journalist. Born near Stafford, he was educated at Brewood Grammar School. Though he published two

volumes of poetry, *War Offerings* (1803) and *Invasion* (1804), and a novel in three volumes, *Ned Bentley* (1809), he is best known as the editor of the *Staffordshire Advertiser*, the *Lichfield Mercury* and the *Shrewsbury Journal*. He spent his last years in Shrewsbury.

ANDERSON Patrick
b.1915 poet, playwright and novelist. He is Canadian by adoption. From 1952 to 1957 he was lecturer in English at Dudley Teachers' Training College. He wrote several volumes of poetry, travel books and the autobiographical, *Snake Wine* (1955). In 1957 a novel, *Search Me*, was published and his radio play, *A Case of Identity*, was broadcast on the Third Programme. For a time he was book reviewer for *The Spectator*. He is believed now to be living in Canada.

ANDREW Stephen
See LAYTON, Frank G

ANSTICE Joseph
1808–36 hymn writer, translator and essayist. Born at Madeley Wood Hall in Shropshire, the son of a local mine owner, he wrote more than fifty hymns, most of them in a tremendous burst of creativity during the last year of his life. In his last weeks he dictated his work to his wife. William Ewart Gladstone, a fellow student at Oxford, wrote of him, 'I bless and praise God for his presence here'. A translator of the Greek poets, he also wrote the treatise, *Influence of the Roman Conquest upon Literature and Arts in Rome*.

ARCHER Fred
b.1915 writer and farmer. Born and bred in Ashton-under-Hill in the Vale of Evesham, he has lived there all his life. His first book, *The Distant Scene*,

was published in 1967. *Secrets of Bredon Hill* appeared in 1971. Later work includes *Poacher's Pie* (1976) and *By Hook and By Crook* (1978). He continues to write about rural life. *Country Twelvemonth* (1992) is his latest work.

ARKWRIGHT Sir John Stanhope
1872–1954 poet and politician. He was MP for Hereford from 1900 to 1912. His most well-known poem, *The Supreme Sacrifice*, has been set to music and is still frequently sung at Remembrance Day services.

ARLEN Michael
1895–1956 (pseudonym of Dikran Kouyoundjian) novelist and short story writer. Born in Bulgaria of Armenian parents, he was educated at Malvern College. He became naturalised in 1922. His most famous novels are *The Green Hat* (1924) and *Flying Dutchman* (1939); and he also wrote several volumes of fashionably cynical short stories, amongst them *The Romantic Lady* (1921) and *These Charming People* (1923).

ARLETT Vera Isabel
b.1896 poet. Born in Penn near Wolverhampton, she remained in the Black Country until the age of twelve. In 1927 she published a selection of her lyrical poems, some of which seem to have been inspired by her childhood.

ARNOLD Matthew
1822–88 poet, essayist and critic. He was educated at Rugby School where his father, the historian, Thomas Arnold, was headmaster from 1828 to 1842. In 1845 he himself taught for a term at Rugby. His poem about the school chapel, 'Rugby Chapel', and his most famous poem, 'Dover Beach', were published in *New Poems*

(1867). Earlier collections include *Empedocles on Etna and Other Poems* (1852), *Poems* (1853), *Poems Second Series* (1855) and *Merope* (1858). The most important of his critical writings is *Essays on Criticism* (1865 and 1888). *Culture and Anarchy* (1869) includes many of his views on educational reform as well as a critique of English social and political life.

ASH Charles Bowker
1781–1864 poet. He was born at Adbaston in Staffordshire, the son of a farmer. During his adult life he travelled widely, within and beyond the boundaries of the west midland counties – living for a while in Hodnet, Eccleshall and Hinstock. His poetry is somewhat pedestrian, and often trite, but there is something appealing in its good nature. The collection, *Poetical Works of C.B.Ash of Adbaston*, was published in two volumes in 1831.

ASHMOLE Elias
1617–92 poet and antiquarian. Born at Lichfield, the only son of Simon Ashmole, saddler, he was educated at Lichfield Grammar School. In 1644 Charles I appointed him commissioner of excise in Lichfield; and a year later he moved to Worcester in the same capacity. Best known as the founder of the Ashmolean Museum in Oxford, he wrote several poems in celebration of worthy friends such as Francis Witwicke and William Lilly, the astrologer.

ASTLEY Philip
1742–1814 equestrian theatre manager and writer. Born in Newcastle-under-Lyme, he became known as the founder of the modern circus and wrote about his military, riding and theatrical experiences.

Natural Magic; or Physical Amusements Revealed, inspired by his enthusiasm for his life's work, was published in 1785.

ATKINSON Canon J A
d.1914 playwright and essayist. From 1900 to 1907 he was vicar of St Michael's Church in Coventry. Though primarily a religious writer, he also wrote plays including *Hang Out the Broom* and *Sixes and Sevens*, both published in the 1880s. In 1894 he edited his father's translation from the original Persian of *Laili and Majnun* which had first appeared in 1836.

ATTENBOROUGH Frederick
1887–1973 poet. He lived in Burton-on-Trent. His only known collection, *Cities in Sonnets*, was published in 1926.

AUBREY John
1626–97 essayist and enthusiast. He owned property in Herefordshire; and in his *Miscellanies* (1696) wrote about instances of folklore to be found in Holme Lacy, Ross-on-Wye, Pembridge and Stretton Sugwas. He is perhaps now best known for the anecdotal volume, *Brief Lives*, which was published posthumously in 1813.

AUDELAY (or AWDELAY) John
fl.1426 poet and divine. An unworldly and devout man, he was canon at Haughmond Abbey near Shrewsbury. Reputed to be both blind and deaf, he wrote his religious poems in a representation of the Shropshire dialect.

AUDEN W H
1907–73 poet and playwright. He was brought up in Birmingham where his father was a schools' medical officer employed by the city's education department. In 1937 the

Birmingham Post reported his being awarded the King's Medal for Poetry. Bristol Street is mentioned in the poem, 'As I Walked Out One Evening', published in *Collected Shorter Poems 1927–1957* (1966). A major literary figure in pre-war Britain, he published among other collections, *Poems* (1930) and *Collected Longer Poems* (1968). His plays include *The Dog Beneath the Skin* (1935) and *The Ascent of F6* (1936). Though his poetic reputation is none too steady, the power and insight of much of his 'social' verse is undeniable.

AUSTIN Muriel
mid-20th C children's writer. She has lived in Lichfield. Her published work includes *Reading and Making, My Little Writing Books* and *Stories Read in BBC Children's Hour*.

AUSTIN Richard
b.1926 poet and short story writer. Believed to have lived in Shropshire, he wrote the verse narratives, *Carnival* (1972), *Nocturne* (1973) and *The Hour Before Twilight* (1974).

AVERY Harold
1867–1943 children's writer. The son of William Avery JP, the well-known local historian and author of *Old Redditch*, he was born at Headless Cross near Redditch in Worcestershire. He spent the last years of his life living in Evesham. Many of his novels and short stories, none of which are now in print, have a school or historical setting. They include, among many others, *The Forbidden Room* (1911), *A Fifth Form Mystery* (1923) and *No Surrender* (1933).

AYSCOUGH John
1858–1928 (pseudonym of Francis Browning Drew Bickerstaffe-Drew) novelist. He was educated at Lichfield. Most of his novels, perhaps in consequence of his conversion to Roman Catholicism in 1877, contain a strongly religious element. *Gracechurch* is set in Ellesmere.

B

BACON Admiral Sir Reginald
1863–1947 novelist. He was the managing director of Coventry Ordnance Works from 1910 to 1915. Most of his books, including *The Jutland Scandal* (1925), have a naval flavour; though *A Social Sinner* (1928) belongs more to the murder/mystery genre.

BADNALL Richard
1797–1839 poet. Born at Leek in Staffordshire, he completed his education at Chaddesley Corbett in Worcestershire. His only poem of note, *Zelinda, A Persian Tale in Three Cantos* (1830), was dedicated to Mrs Littleton of Teddersley Park, Staffordshire.

BAGOT Bishop Lewis
1740–1802 poet and essayist. He was born in Blithfield, Staffordshire. Although his 1761 verses on George II and George III appeared in one of the editions of the *Oxford Poets* (see ABERCROMBIE, Lascelles), he is believed to have published only one book, in 1780, which contained his Warburtonian Lecture on the 'Prophesies'.

BAGSTER Hubert
1902–75 (pseudonym of Dr H B Trumper) novelist. Born in Birmingham, the son of a doctor who practised in the city from 1872 to 1932, he later lived in Herefordshire where he wrote two novels – *Country Practice* (1957) and *Doctor's Weekend* (1960). His third, *Exhumation of Murder*, the result of ten years' research into the life of the poisoner, Herbert Rowse Armstrong, was published posthumously in 1975.

BAILEY David
1834–1917 poet. Born at Broad Lanes, Sedgley, he began his education at James Penrose's private school in Bilston where the poor sight which was eventually to result in blindness first began to make itself apparent. His poems appeared in various publications, including the *Black Country Magazine*, and, though not especially profound, they show the Black Countryman's understanding of the music of language – a skill reflected in his interest in phonetic spelling.

BAKER Dorothy
mid-20th C novelist. She lived in Walsall. *The Street* (1951) is set in the Black Country, in the fictional town of Wallgrove. It tells the story of its heroine's struggles to sustain certain standards of decency in the dreadful poverty of urban industrialisation.

BAKER E
mid-20th C short story writer. He is believed to have lived in Darlaston. He published a volume of local interest tales called *Black Country Stories* (1952), of which the best known is 'Martha Toddles Visits the Bull Ring'.

BAKER Sir Henry William
1821–77 hymn writer and editor. The eldest son of Sir Henry Loraine Baker, he was vicar of Monkland in Herefordshire from 1851 until his death. As well as writing thirty-seven of its hymns, among them the popular 'O worship the King, all glorious above' and 'The King of love my shepherd is', he also helped to edit *Hymns Ancient and Modern* in 1861. This book, intended to supersede the local and sectional collections in use at the time, was renamed by one irritated author as 'Hymns Asked For and Mutilated'.

BAKER Rev Thomas
b.1804 poet. Born in Burslem, he was the author of the collection, *Leisure Hours* (1837), which celebrates local scenery and the delights of reading and writing poetry.

BAKEWELL Thomas
1761–1835 poet. Born in Cheadle, he went to work as a boy in the local tape mill where he later became foreman. His study, *The Domestic Guide to Cases of Insanity*, appeared in 1805 and he later founded a lunatic asylum at Trentham. He is buried at Stone. Volumes I and II of his *Moorland Bard or Poetical Recollections of a Weaver in the Moorlands of Staffordshire* were published in 1807.

BALL Richard
b.1919 poet. Born in Clun, he was brought up in Maesbury near Oswestry. He attended the village school before going to Oswestry High School. *Avalon One* was published in 1968, *Chain* in 1974. He continues to write poetry of lyrical imagery and energetic thought.

BALLARD Ernest
1869–1952 poet, short story writer,

essayist and horticulturist. He is a member of the Ballard family which has lived in Ledbury and Colwall for several generations. He wrote three volumes of essays, some poetry and verse, and gained a worldwide reputation for his work in developing new strains of Michaelmas daisies. His short stories, *The Little Man in Blue and Other Stories*, were published in 1930.

BANCROFT G P
1868–1956 playwright. He was clerk of assize for the Midland Circuit from 1913 to 1946. The success of his play, *The Ware Case* (1913), is celebrated in *Stage and Bar* (1939), a collection of anecdotes and commentary.

BANKS Edward
1849–84 poet. Born in Merridale, Wolverhampton, and educated at Brewood School, he later became an architect. A collection of his poems, *Waifs of Rhyme*, was published posthumously in 1885.

BANKS George Linnaeus
1821–81 poet, newspaper proprietor and playwright. He was born at the Bull Ring in Birmingham, a descendant of Richard Penderel of Boscobel who is reputed to have concealed Charles II in an oak tree (see AINSWORTH, William Harrison). For a time he was editor of the *Birmingham Mercury*. His published work, mainly of a distinctly worthy nature, includes *Spring Gatherings* (1845), *Staves for the Human Ladder* (1850) and, perhaps the best-known, *Life of Blondin* (1862). In 1852 he organised a public dinner and presentation for Charles Dickens* in Birmingham. The poems and songs in *Daisies in the Grass* (1865) are alternately by himself and his wife. His later work is rather less

lachrymose than his earlier efforts.

BANKS Mrs G Linnaeus
1821–97 novelist and poet. She married G L Banks* in 1846 and came to live in Birmingham. Her verse appears in *Ivy Leaves* (1845), in *Daisies in the Grass* (1865, see above) and in *Ripples and Breakers* (1870). In 1887 she published the novel, *In His Own Hand*, which was based on the life of the writer and bookseller, William Hutton*. All her prose work takes a fervently moral stance.

BANTOCK Gavin
b.1939 poet. He lives in Barnt Green near Birmingham, and has published several volumes of poetry including *Christ* (1965), *A New Thing Breathing* (1969), *Anhaga* (1972) and *Isles* (1974). He has also won several awards for his poetry, much of which confirms that 'the world of men is a dark place'. *Dragon* appeared in 1979.

BARBER Donald Herbert
b.1907 novelist. He lived for a while in Ludlow which provided settings for several of his books including ... *And Ludlow Fair Again* (1963) and *God and Tony Clee* (1964). He describes *David's Day of Glory* (1962) as 'a grateful tribute to the fair ancient town set on a hill in a Shropshire Valley'.

BARCLAY Florence L C
1862–1921 novelist. Though a visitor only to the region, several of her novels, including *The Mistress of Shenstone* (1911) and *The White Ladies of Worcester* (1924), have local settings. Her best-known work is *The Rosary* (1909), one of the sunniest stories ever to have been written, which sold over 1¼ million

copies. Her two visits to Worcester Cathedral, when she was six years old and forty years later, provided her, she claimed, with vivid and inspiring memories.

BARCLAY Vera C
mid-20th C novelist. Believed to have lived in Birmingham, she wrote a novel relating to life in her home city called *Knave of Hearts* (1933).

BARFORD Dora
b.1904 novelist. A member of a well-known Coventry family, she has lived all her life in the city. She was first published in 1931 with *Mr Corrington*, which was followed by many others including *Captain Lucifer* (1931), *The Golden Cargazon* (1932) and *Greek Fire* (1935). She is generally described as belonging to the Farnol* school of novelists whose members specialised in historical thrillers.

BARING-GOULD Sabine
1834–1924 novelist, hymn writer and folklorist. He is associated with Kinver and several of his novels, including *Bladys of the Stewponey* (1897), *Guavas the Tinner* (1897) and *Perpetua* (1897), are set in the area. Most of his work reveals an attractively romantic fervour; though *Virgins, Saints and Martyrs* (1900) exhibits an undeniably gothic ring. The well-known 'Onward Christian Soldiers' is numbered among his many hymns.

BARKER Sarah
mid-20th C poet. Her only known publication is a collected edition of her poems which appeared in 1937. Much of her work is concerned with the county of Shropshire where she lived and worked as a teacher in Ironbridge.

BARLOW James
b.1921 novelist. Born at Leamington Spa, he began his education in the town and later attended a school in Stoke-on-Trent. From 1939 to 1940 and from 1941 to 1960 he worked as a rating inspector for Birmingham Corporation – during which time he wrote for *Punch* and published his first novel, *The Protagonists* (1956) – a job he left in order to devote all his time to writing. Of his many novels, *The Patriots* (1960) and *Term of Trial* (1961) have been filmed.

BARNARD A Sedgwick
b.1868 poet. Born in Walsall, while working for the town's corporation he published his only known work, a small volume of verse entitled *Ragged-staff Rhymes*.

BARNETT Anthony
mid/late 20th C poet. Believed to have lived for a time in Shropshire, he has published several volumes of poetry including *A Marriage* (1968), *Poems for the Daughter of Charles Lievens* (1970) and *Fragile and Lucid* (1973). His work is abrupt and imagist, with few concessions to narrative or coherency.

BARNFIELD Richard
1574–1627 poet. He was born at Norbury in Shropshire at the home of his maternal grandparents, but was brought up by his sister at Edgmond Manor House near Newport. *The Affectionate Shepherd* appeared in 1594. His last work, *The Encomion of Lady Pecunia*, a satire on the influence of money, was published in 1599. The rest of his life was spent at Darlaston. For all its sentimentality, his work achieved the undeniable honour of being for a time mistaken for Shakespeare's.

BARROWS Harold M
1861–1913 poet and essayist. Born in Walsall, he lived there all his life practising as a solicitor. The six essays published as *True Friends* (1889) first appeared in the weekly journal, *Books*. Some of his poetry is included in Alfred Moss's* *Songs from the Heart of England* (1920).

BARTLETT Fred R
late 19th C poet. A native of Bilston, he was a worker 'mid the din and smoke of the Black Country'. The collection, *Flashes from Forge and Foundry* (1886), his only known work, demonstrates his delight in painful puns and amazing rhyming schemes.

BASELEY Godfrey
b.1904 radio playwright. He was born in Alvechurch in Worcestershire, the son of a butcher. An active member of the Birmingham Rep, he joined the BBC when permanent studios were set up in the city before the war. The effect of his rural upbringing greatly contributed to his most famous radio creation, *The Archers*, which, originally envisaged as a sort of farming Dick Barton, was first broadcast on the BBC Light Programme in 1950. He now lives in Bromsgrove.

BATHER Lucy
1836–64 children's writer. After her marriage to Arthur Henry Bather she lived at The Hall, Meole Brace near Shrewsbury. Though most of her work for children is contained in short stories, she also wrote *Footprints on the Sands of Time: Biographies for Young People* (1860).

BATIGAN Bernard
1832–1908 poet, critic and elocutionist. Born in Hanley, he produced about a dozen books of original poems, many of them intended specifically for recitation. Other publications include *Pen Pictures of Great Actors* and *Pen Portraits of Famous People*.

BAXTER Richard
1615–91 Puritan divine and hymn writer. Born in his mother's family home at Rowton into an old Shropshire family, he was baptised at High Ercall and, in the company of Richard Allestree*, attended the endowed school at Wroxeter. Ordained at the age of twenty-three, he taught in Dudley before becoming assistant Presbyterian minister in Bridgnorth, to whose people is dedicated his most famous work, *The Saints' Everlasting Rest* (1650). (This was written while he was staying at Rous Lench in Worcestershire, the home of Sir Thomas Rous. It was Lady Rous who nursed him during a serious illness in 1647.) He lectured in Kidderminster in 1641, before becoming chaplain to the Parliamentary troops, and returned to the town in 1650 to live in retirement for about ten years, during which time he made extended visits to Coventry. A statue of him, commemorating his ministry, now stands in a garden next to Kidderminster parish church. His numerous writings include *A Call to the Unconverted* (1658), the affectionate tribute to his wife, *A Breviate of the Life of Margaret Baxter* (1681), and an autobiography, *Reliquiae Baxterianae* (1696).

BAYLEY Barrington J
b.1940 novelist. Born in Birmingham, he was a coalminer before becoming a civil servant and now lives in Shropshire. *The Star Virus*, his first novel, was published in 1972;

and was followed by *Empire of the Two Worlds* (1972), *The Soul of the Robot* (1974), and many others. Later work is also in the science fiction vein.

BAYNARD James B
late 19th C novelist. Born in the USA of English parents, he was brought up in Coventry. His work includes a novel in three volumes, *The Rector of Oxbury* (1870), and *Lord Galford's Freak* (1880) which is set in Coventry.

BAYNES Robert Hall
1831–95 poet and short story writer. He was vicar of St Michael and All Saints in Coventry from 1866 to 1879. Most of his poems and stories, which include the collections, *Autumn Memories* (1869) and *Songs for Quiet Hours* (1878), reveal a strongly religious – and not altogether patient – concern for human frailties.

BEAMISH Josiah Smith
late 19th C short story writer. He was a member of a Coventry family of printers. Most of what he called his 'sketches' were inspired by Biblical stories (*Mordecai and Haman* [1875], for example) or by religious leaders (such as Martin Luther in *The Brave Saxon* [1895]).

BEARDMORE George
b.1908 (also publishes as Cedric Stokes) novelist and children's writer. The nephew of Arnold Bennett*, he was born in Stoke-on-Trent and educated at Orme Boys School in Newcastle-under-Lyme. His published novels include *Madame Merlin* (1946), *A Tale of Two Thieves* (1947), *A Lion Among the Ladies* (1949), which is set in Trentham, and *A Thousand Witnesses* (1953), whose heroine comes from Bilston.

BEDDOME Benjamin
1717–95 hymn writer and poet. Born in Henley-in-Arden, the son of a Baptist clergyman, he wrote over 830 hymns. Though described as 'always impressive, always striking and sometimes ingeniously brought about', few of these are still sung in chapels today.

BEDDOW Bruce
1897–1976 novelist and short story writer. He lived in Cannock and set most of his work, including *The Golden Milestone* (1925), *A Man of the Midlands* (1928), *The Coal Merchant* (1929) and *Coals from Newcastle* (1929), in Staffordshire.

Cuthbert Bede

BEDE Cuthbert
1827–89 (pseudonym of Edward Bradley) novelist, essayist and illustrator. Born at Kidderminster, the son of a surgeon, he was educated at Kidderminster Grammar School and after ordination in 1850 held the benefice of Bobbington. His published work includes *Nearer and Dearer* (1857), *Happy Hours at Wynford Grange* (1859) and *Mattins and Muttons* (1866). The hero of his best-known novel, *The Adventures of*

Mr Verdant Green (1853), came from Warwickshire. This perhaps first example of the now popular 'campus' genre contains illustrations by the author. As Shelsley Beauchamp, a pseudonym derived presumably from the Worcestershire village of the same name, his brother, Waldron, wrote local history pieces for the county newspapers.

BEEDING Francis
See PALMER, John Leslie

BELL Josephine
b.1897 (pseudonym of Doris Bell Ball) novelist. She wrote a large number of novels, most of them in the detective mould, but only one, *Trouble at Wrekin Farm* (1942), which is set in rural Shropshire, belongs to the west midland area.

BELL Robert Stanley Warren
1871–1921 short story writer and playwright. He was born in Henley-in-Arden. His schoolboy stories appeared in several magazines before being collected and published in book form. The comedy, *A Companion for George* (1921), was successfully produced in London.

BELLAIRS Rev H W
1819–64 poet. Believed to have lived in Warwickshire, he wrote a collection of poems entitled *Traditions of Nuneaton and the Neighbourhood* (1860) which contains celebrations of Arbury, Mancetter, Nuneaton and several other local places.

BELLOC Hilaire
1870–1953 poet, novelist, historian and politician. His mother's family lived in Birmingham, where for a time he attended the Cardinal Newman Oratory School. It is perhaps unlikely that his short stay in the area inspired any of his work. In his poem, 'The South Country', he describes the Midlands as 'sodden and unkind'. Other work includes *The Bad Child's Book of Beasts* (1896) and *Sonnets and Verses* (1923).

BENNET Georgiana
mid-19th C poet and short story writer. A prolific writer, believed to have been born in Staffordshire, she manages to combine sympathy with an uncompromising sincerity. Among her published books are *Fancy Sketches; or, Tales for Leisure Hours* (1838) and *The New Year's Eve and Other Poems* (1865).

BENNETT Enoch Arnold
1867–1931 novelist and short story writer. Born in Hanley, the son of a solicitor, he was educated at schools in Burslem and Newcastle-under-Lyme, and worked in his father's office for three years from the age of eighteen. Most of his novels and short stories, including *Clayhanger* (1911), *Hilda Lessways* (1911) and *These Twain* (1916), are set in the Five Towns – fictional representations of the six towns which make up the Stoke-on-Trent conurbation. The character of Darius Clayhanger was inspired by Charles Shaw (1832–1906), a worker in the pottery industry who published his autobiography, *When I Was a Child*, in 1903. Though Bennett's work is no longer so popular as previously, his evocation of the spites and resentments of family life and of the hazards of social aspiration is unmatched.

BENNETT Herbert
d.1918 poet. Born in Walsall, he was educated at Croft Street Council School and Queen Mary's Grammar School and later attended the

A Potteries scene

University of Birmingham. He was killed in the First World War. His poems appeared in the *School Magazine* and in Alfred Moss's*, *Songs from the Heart of England* (1920).

BENSON George

mid-20th C novelist. Brother of Stella Benson* and nephew of Mary Cholmondeley*, he was born and later lived at Lutwyche Hall on Wenlock Edge. He wrote only one novel, *Brother Wolf*, which was published in 1933.

BENSON Stella

1892–1933 novelist, poet and short story writer. Born at Lutwyche Hall, the sister of George* and niece of Mary Cholmondeley*, she left Shropshire in 1913. She began publishing in 1915 with *I Pose* but apart from *Tobit Transplanted* (1930), which won the Femina Vie Heureuse Prize, most of her novels are now forgotten. Her name though lives on in Vera Brittain's* *Testament of Experience*, which includes an account of the effect the news of her death had on the writer. She describes herself as 'editor' of her last book, *Pull Devil –*

Pull Baker (1933) (see SAVINE, Nicholas de Toulouse). *Hope Against Hope and Other Stories* appeared in 1932. A volume of her poems (1935) and *Collected Short Stories* (1936) appeared posthumously.

BENTLEY Samuel

1722–1803 poet. Born in Uttoxeter, the son and grandson of hairdressers 'in comfortable circumstances', he was educated at Uttoxeter Grammar School. His poems, characterised by 'sweet reasonableness of argument ... with an easy flowing style', were collected and published in 1774.

BERGONZI Bernard

b.1929 poet, critic and academic. From 1971 to 1992 he was Professor of English at the University of Warwick. His first collection of verse, *Descartes and the Animals*, appeared in 1954 and another collection, *Memorials*, was published in 1970. His later work, which includes *Exploding English* (1991) and *Wartime and Aftermath* (1993), is mainly non-fiction.

BERNE Keri

early 20th C (pseudonym of Edward Paterson) poet and playwright. He lived at Wellington in Shropshire. A collection of his verse, *Poems*, appeared in 1900. Other publications include *Gleys* (Parts 1 and 2), *Daily Studies of Life*, and *His Acre*. His work tends to be narrative and urbane.

BERNERS Lord (Gerald Hugh Tyrwhitt-Wilson, 14th Baron Berners)
1883–1950 novelist and composer. The first volume of his memoirs, *First Childhood* (1934), mentions that he was born in Bridgnorth. His generally good-humoured, though by no means unsatirical, work includes *The Camel* (1936), *Count Omega* (1941) and *The Romance of a Nose* (1941).

BERRINGTON Bramley
late 19th C short story writer. His only known collection, *In After Years: a Sketch* (1884), relates to the city of Birmingham where he lived all his life.

BERRINGTON Julia
b.1851 poet. Born in Bilston, the elder sister of Emily Edridge*, she remained in Staffordshire all her life – living for several years in Wolverhampton. In 1906 she married R E W Berrington, one-time mayor of the town. Her poems, many of them religious in theme, appeared in several local publications.

BERRY Arthur
b.1925 poet, playwright, painter and broadcaster. The son of a colliery bricklayer and a publican's daughter, he was born in the Potteries' village of Smallthorne. After studying art in London and working in Manchester, he returned to the area to live in Biddulph where he farmed a smallholding and continued to teach. Some of his plays are included in the repertoire of Stoke-on-Trent's

Victoria Theatre. His work is invariably concerned with 'his own rut' and, though free of nostalgia, is evocative of a passing world.

BETJEMAN John
1906–84 poet and essayist. Two of his poems – 'A Shropshire Lad' and 'Pershore Station, or A Liverish Journey First Class' – confirm his links with the area. He also wrote *The Shell Guide to Shropshire* (1951). His work, combining accessibility with vision, has often been underestimated. It is doubtful whether the work he produced during his poet laureateship (1972) advanced his reputation. *Collected Poems* (1958, revised 1962) ran to several editions and sold almost a million copies. The recent publication of his letters has prompted an even more searching reappraisal of his work.

BETTANY Jeanie Gwynne
late 19th C novelist. She lived in the Black Country, possibly in Bilston, which provides the setting for *The House of Rimmon* (1885).

BETTS Frank
early 20th C poet and playwright. He was a member of a well-known Coventry family of agricultural merchants. His work includes two volumes of poetry, *The Western Isles* (1903) and *The Iron Age* (1916), and a collection of dramatic pieces, *Saga Plays* (1917).

BEVAN J
mid-20th C poet and editor. He was for a time head of the General Studies Department at Wolverhampton Technical Teaching College. Many of the poems in the collection, *My Sad Pharaohs* (1968), explore and deplore the sadness of human relationships. He was one of the editors of the

Penguin Modern European Series.

BIERCE Ambrose
1842–1914 journalist and short story writer. An American, he stayed in Leamington Spa in 1874 where he edited and wrote for *The Lantern*. This short-lived magazine, supported by the Empress Eugenie because of its efforts to answer attacks aimed at the Emperor and the Russian aristocracy, was mainly of a satirical nature. He is perhaps best known in this country for the collection of short stories, *In the Midst of Life* (1891), and for *The Cynic's Word Book* (1906).

BILLINGHAM Edgar
mid-20th C poet and short story writer. He lived in Worcester. The collection, *Midland Poems* (which includes 'Brummagem Fair'), in which he aimed 'to give interest to a wide variety of readers', was published in 1944. His short stories appeared in several periodicals.

BINDER Pearl
b.1904 (pseudonym of Lady Elwyn Jones) novelist. She was born in Staffordshire. Her work includes *Muffs and Morals* (1950) and *The Peacock's Tail* (1952).

BINDMAN Jeremy
b.1951 poet. He was born in Coventry. The short collection of verse, *Marcato*, was published in 1973. His work shows a clarity of expression and an uncompromising vision of the futility of much human aspiration.

BIRCH Nellie
early 20th C poet. She lived in Leek. Her best-known work, *Sunbeams and Shadows: A First Book of Poems* (1926), contains verse about Leek and other local places.

BIRCH William Thomas
b.1846 poet. Born in Uttoxeter, he lived there all his life. Much of the work in his collection, *Armageddon and Other Poems* (1920), deals with the heroism, pathos and tragedy of war.

BIRD Kenneth
b.1916 children's writer. He has lived in Church Stretton and is associated with Kidderminster and Droitwich. *Bishop Must Move* (1967) was his first novel. Other work includes *Smash a Glass Image* (1968), *The Mozart Fiddle* (1969) and *The Rainbow Coloured Hearse* (1970). His most popular series of books concerns the talking dog 'Himself' who was first introduced in *A Dog Called Himself* (1968).

BISHOP Les Gurney
mid-20th C novelist and journalist. He was born in North Staffordshire. His first novel, *Paper Kingdom* (1936), was described in the *Times Literary Supplement* as Dickensian. Much of his work is set in the world of journalism and newspaper production.

BISSELL Thomas F
1843–1910 poet. Born in Wednesbury, he was organist at the parish church for thirty-eight years. Music often forms the theme of *Poems*, the only known collection of his work.

BISSET James
1760–1832 poet. When he was sixteen he came from Perth to live in Birmingham. *The Poetic Survey and Magnificent Directory of Birmingham* is perhaps his best-known work. Reputed to have had a very good opinion of himself, he enlivened many a gathering of his fellow citizens with his songs and fiddle-playing. In 1812 he moved to

Leamington Spa where he was chosen to lay the foundation stone of the Royal Pump Rooms in 1813. In 1814 he published his *Guide to Leamington* which included many references to his beloved Birmingham, punctuated by snippets of verse.

BLACK William
1841–98 novelist. A Scottish writer of several historical novels including *A Princess of Thule* (1881) and *Judith Shakespeare* (1884), he set his miscellany of fiction and fact, *The Strange Adventures of a Phaeton* (1892), in the west midland counties.

BLOOMFIELD Robert
1766–1823 poet. In the summer of 1807 he stayed at the Swan Hotel in Ross-on-Wye while visiting the town with friends. The result of his tour of the Wye Valley was the verse tale, *The Banks of the Wye* (1811). During his last years he became ill, and died in extreme poverty.

BODEN Hilda
mid-20th C novelist. She is believed to have lived in Birmingham. Her only known novel, *Family Affair: a Midland Chronicle* (1948), details the lives and loves of the Lloyd family.

BONAR John
mid-19th C poet. He lived in Leamington Spa. His prize-winning poem, 'Venice', recited at Leamington Speeches, the annual celebration of the town's history, was later published in 1853.

BOOKER Rev Luke
1762–1835 poet and essayist. Ordained in 1785, he became successively lecturer of St Peter's in Wolverhampton, curate at Dudley, rector of Tedstone-de-la-Mere in Herefordshire in 1806 and vicar at Dudley in 1812. His best-known

works, all of which have a religious theme, are *Malvern, a Descriptive and Historical Poem* (1798) and *The Springs of Plynlimmon* (1834).

BORLASE James Skipp
late 19th C novelist. He lived in Worcester. In the 1880s *The White Witch of Worcester*, a piece of lurid Victorian gothic set during the thirteenth-century Barons' Wars, was especially written for the *Worcestershire Chronicle* and published in serial form. His other mystery tales include *Who Murdered John Cameron?*, *Nina the Nihilist* and *The Black Hand*.

BORROW George
1803–81 novelist and traveller. In 1825 he visited Stafford and stayed at the Swan Hotel. In *Romany Rye* (1857), the best known of his delightful literary mosaics of fact and fiction, he wrote: 'The inn ... was a place of infinite life and bustle ... Often ... when lonely and melancholy, I have called up the time I spent there, and never failed to become cheerful from the recollection.'

BOUCHER Ben
1769–1851 poet. Born at Horseley Heath in Staffordshire, he was a collier by trade who spent most of his life in Dudley and became known to the Black Country frequenters of taverns as the 'Dudley Poet and Rhymist'. He celebrated every local event in rhyme – from a hanging to a dog fight. Some of his work can still be found in the broadsheets and pamphlets of his day. He died in great poverty in Dudley Workhouse.

BOULTON Marjorie
b.1924 poet, playwright, critic and translator. The family home is at

Burslem in Stoke-on-Trent and she was educated at Barton Grammar School. Best known as an expert in Esperanto, she has also written poems in English and Esperanto and translated two detective novels into Polish. A volume of poetry, *Eroj*, and her play, *Virino Ce La Landlimo*, were both published in 1959.

BOURNE Hugh
1772–1852 hymn writer and poet. Born at Fordhay Farm near Tunstall, the son of a wheelwright, he was the principal founder of the Primitive Methodist Connection in 1810. For organising open meetings at Mow Cop near Burslem he was excommunicated by the Wesleyans. Though he is now best remembered for his revivalist hymns – noted for their simplicity, rather than for their literary merit – a poem, *The Creation, Fall and Redemption of Man*, was published in the *Methodist Magazine* in 1822.

BRADBY G F
1863–1947 novelist and poet. Educated at Rugby School, he returned there as assistant master and housemaster from 1888 to 1920. No doubt his schoolmastering experiences inspired him to write his most famous novel, *The Lanchester Tradition* (1913), a school story involving a great deal of esprit de corps.

BRADLEY Harold Frank
b.1904 poet. Born in Worcester, he was educated at Worcester Royal Grammar School and St Peter's College in Birmingham. He has taught in schools in both Coventry and Worcester. His work includes the collections, *Poems of the Worcester Area* and *The Jongleur*. In 1951 he won the James Howard Gilmore

Award.

BRADY Nicholas
1659–1726 poet and playwright. He was vicar at Stratford-upon-Avon from 1702 to 1705. Best known for his part in compiling a new version of the Psalms in 1699, he also translated Homer's *Aeneid*, wrote a tragedy, *The Innocent Imposter*, and published three volumes of sermons.

BRAIN Charles Lewton
1863–1919 poet. He was successively curate of St Patrick's in Walsall, in charge of the mission at Chasetown (1897), attached to St Francis's in Handsworth (1898) and parish priest at Brewood. A collection of his poems, *Eucharist and Other Verses*, was published posthumously in 1923.

BRASSINGTON Michael
b.1942 poet. He was born in Birmingham and attended local schools and Moseley College of Art. The managing director of an advertising agency, he now lives at Anslow near Burton-on-Trent. *Profile of the Poet Brassington* and *A Head of Our Time* were published in 1974 and have recently been reissued (1991).

BRAZIL Angela
1868–1947 children's writer. She lived for a time in Coventry. Almost all of her fifty or so novels, which include *A Fourth Form Friendship* (1911), *The School By the Sea* (1914) and *The Madcap of the School* (1917), are to do with boarding-school life where virtue is always properly rewarded.

BRENNON Nicholas
late 20th C children's writer. Born in Coventry, he was educated at Coventry Residential School in Cleobury Mortimer and at Coventry College of Art. His only known work

is the adventure tale, *Olaf's Incredible Machine* (1973).

BRETTELL Mrs
early 19th C novelist and poet. She was born at Burslem. Her books include the novel, *Meriden; or the Memoirs of Matilda* (1819), and the verse collection, *Susan Ashfield and Other Poems* (1820).

BRETTELL Noel H
1908–91 poet. Born at Lye in Worcestershire, he was educated at the village school, at King Edward VI Grammar School in Stourbridge and at the University of Birmingham. A volume of poems, *Bronze Frieze*, was published in 1950 and several of his other poems, many with an African theme, have been included in anthologies. He lived for many years in Zimbabwe.

BRIAN Havergal
1876–1972 songwriter and composer. He was born in Stoke-on-Trent and educated locally. His work includes the vocal orchestral piece, *By the Waters of Babylon* (1903), an opera cantata, *Vision of Cleopatra* (1907), and the burlesque opera, *The Tigers* (1916).

BRIDGES John Affleck
1835–1925 poet. The elder brother of the poet laureate Robert Bridges, he lived in King's Norton in Birmingham. His work, though not of great distinction, found ready publication in periodicals.

BRIERLEY Walter
mid-20th C novelist. A member of the Birmingham Group (see HAMPSON, John), which included Walter E Allen*, Peter Chamberlain*, Leslie Halward* and John Hampson*, he lived for a while in the city before moving to Derby. Of his five published novels, the best, *The Means Test Man*, is based on his own experiences as an out-of-work coalminer during the depression. *Sandwichman* was reissued in 1990 by the Merlin Press in a series called Radical Fiction.

BRIGHT Geoffrey
pub.1948 poet. He lived in Leominster. The collection, *Hereford is Heaven and Other Verses*, which contains poems 'in serious mood' and 'not so serious', was published in 1948.

BRINDLEY Thomas Bardel
mid-19th C poet. He lived in Stourbridge. His only known collection, *The Omnipotence of the Deity and Other Poems*, appeared in 1843.

BRINKLEY Matilda
mid-20th C novelist. She lived in the village of Pinley in Warwickshire. Her only known work, *Tell the Bees* (1935), is subtitled 'A Warwickshire Romance'.

BRITTAIN Vera
1896–1970 novelist. The daughter of a wealthy paper manufacturer, she was born and stayed for eighteen months in Newcastle-under-Lyme. Her most famous novels, *Testament of Youth* (1933), *Testament of Friendship* (1940) and *Testament of Experience* (1957), are autobiographical. (see BENSON, Stella)

BRITTON Herbert E
early 20th C poet. He lived in Shipston-on-Stour in Worcestershire. Many of the poems in *Visions of a Dreamer* (1912), which was dedicated to his wife, first appeared in the *Kidderminster Shuttle*. Another collection, *Twelve Poems* (1915), published in aid of Kidderminster Infirmary and Children's Hospital,

includes several verses about Birmingham.

BRITTON John James
1832–1913 poet, novelist and short story writer. Born at Handsworth, he was educated at King Edward's School, New Street in Birmingham. After several years in the south of England and abroad, he returned to the west midland area – to live first at Alcester and then at Halford Bridge. A collection of short stories, *Tales for a Cosy Nook*, appeared in 1859. He also published a novel, *Flight*, and three books of poetry, *Carella* (1867), *The Lay of the Lady Ida* (1882) and *Sheaf of Ballads* (1884).

BROCKHURST Arthur
b.1858 poet. Born in Walsall, he often visited his aunt at Tuck Hill in Shropshire, a place which was to be the inspiration for much of his poetry. He became a student at Saltley College in Birmingham. His first teaching post was at Queen Mary's Grammar School in Walsall, after which he became headmaster at several of the local council schools. It was in *New Age* that his first poem, a sonnet, was published. He is well represented in Alfred Moss's*, *Songs from the Heart of England* (1920). The two booklets, *Christmas 1907* and *Christmas 1919*, are collections of sonnets and other verse.

BROMLEY Josephine
mid-20th C poet. She lived in the village of Byton. The collection, *Herefordshire Ballads of Byton*, 'based on memories of my father', was published in 1968.

BROMLEY Mary
mid-19th C poet. Born at Abberley Hall, she lived there until its sale in 1836 when with her four older

unmarried sisters she moved to Bewdley. The small volume of sacred poems, her only known work, was published in 1861.

BRONTE Patrick
1777–1861 poet. The father of the three novelists, Charlotte, Emily and Anne, for a few months in 1809 he was curate at All Saints' Church in Wellington in Shropshire before moving to Haworth. While there he published two small volumes of poetry, *Cottage Poems* and *The Rural Minstrel*.

BROOK Peter
b.1889 (pseudonym of A H Chovill) novelist. Born in Warwickshire, he later lived in Birmingham. *Rick and Dick* (1929) and *Arden Vales* (1934) are set in the rural Warwickshire of Liveridge, Henley-in-Arden and Wootton Wawen.

BROOKE Rupert
1887–1915 poet and playwright. Born in Rugby, he was educated at Rugby School where his father was one of the masters. The collection, *Poems*, appeared in 1911; *1914 and Other Poems* in 1915. He is now best remembered for his poem, 'The Old Vicarage, Granchester'. *Collected Poems*, edited by Edward Marsh, was published posthumously in 1918.

BROOKES Arthur Heybeard
mid-20th C poet. He lived in Selly Oak in Birmingham. His only known work, the collection, *Love Songs and Poems*, appeared in 1932.

BROOKS Charles William Shirley
1816–74 playwright, novelist, journalist and essayist. He often wrote under the name of Shirley Brooks. Although he was articled to his uncle, a solicitor in Oswestry, and eventually qualified, he did not practise his

chosen profession. Instead he wrote for the *Morning Chronicle*, the *Illustrated London News* and *Punch*. Several of his plays were performed in the West End. But he is perhaps chiefly remembered for the autobiographical *The Gordian Knot* (1858) which was illustrated by Tenniel.

BROOM Herbert
1815–82 novelist. He was born in Kidderminster. Though best known for his books on law, he also wrote two mystery novels, *The Missing Will* (1877) and *The Unjust Steward* (1879).

BROPHY John
1899–1965 novelist. *Gentleman of Stratford* (1939) – the story of Shakespeare's life – was inspired by the author's researches in the Stratford-upon-Avon district.

BROWN John Lewis
early 20th C poet. He lived in Coventry. His only known work, the collection, *Istar and Tammuz and Other Poems*, was published in 1907.

BROWN Muriel Hope
late 19th C poet. She lived in Leek. She is best known for *Lays and Lyrics*, a collection of poems mainly concerned with Leek and its surroundings.

BROWN Thomas
1663–1705 poet, Tory pamphleteer, sketch writer and hack writer. Reputed to have been born at Shifnal, the son of a tanner, he was educated at Newport Grammar School in Shropshire. He is now chiefly remembered for the immortal lines 'I do not love thee, Dr Fell. / The reason why, I cannot tell; / But this I know, and know full well, / I do not love thee, Dr Fell.' – lines inspired by John Fell (1625–86) a prebendary at Worcester Cathedral in 1660. *Amusements Serious and Comical*, his sketches of London life, appeared in 1700.

BROWNE Emily A
1845–1939 artist and poet. She lived in Leamington Spa and was art mistress at the art college in Beech Lawn. A copy of her *Marvellous Tales*, a translation for children of well-known stories, was given to Leamington Library.

BROWNE Isaac Hawkins
1705–60 poet. Born in Burton-on-Trent and educated at Lichfield, he settled at Badger Hall in Shropshire and was elected MP for Much Wenlock in 1744 and 1747. *Design and Beauty* (1734) and *A Pipe of Tobacco* (1736) brought him literary renown, but his best-known work is *De Animi Immortalite* (1754). In 1768 his collected poems, under the title of *Poems Upon Various Subjects; Latin and English*, were published in two volumes by his son (see below).

BROWNE Isaac Hawkins
(1745–1818) essayist. Sheriff of Shropshire in 1783 and MP for Bridgnorth in 1784, he published *Essays, Religious and Moral* in 1815.

BROWNING Elizabeth Barrett
1806–61 poet, translator and essayist. The eldest of the Barrett children, from the age of three she lived at Hope End until it had to be sold in 1832. This house, built to her father's somewhat bizarre design, was situated between Colwall and Ledbury. It was while living here that she fell from her horse and sustained the serious injuries which were to make her a semi-invalid for so long. Described by her as 'Dimpled close with hill and valley, / Dappled very close with

shade' ('The Lost Bower'), the Herefordshire countryside often inspired,
influenced and informed her poems.
Collections include *The Seraphim and
Other Poems* (1838), *Poems* (1844)
and *Poems* (1850).

BRYANS Sibella E
early 20th C novelist. *A Tale of a
Country Village*, subtitled *A Story for
Mothers' Meetings* and published by
the Society for Promoting Christian
Knowledge, is set in the village of
Coverley in Worcestershire.

BUCHANAN Robert Williams
1841–1901 poet, playwright and
novelist. He was born in Caverswall
in Staffordshire, the son of a Scottish
journeyman tailor. His first novel, *The
Shadow of the Sword*, appeared in
1874. Beginning in 1880 he wrote and
produced many popular plays, such as
Lady Clare (1883) and *The Charlatan*
(1894). A prolific writer of flour-
ishing verse, which included the
volumes, *Undertones* (1864) and *The
Book of Orm* (1870), he also
published *Collected Poetical Works* in
1880. Although the novel, *God and
the Man* (1887), is dedicated to Dante
Gabriel Rossetti, he is now chiefly
remembered for his attacks on the
Pre-Raphaelites, especially Algernon
Charles Swinburne, whom he satirises
in the poem, 'The Session of Poets'
(1866).

BUCKLEY Rev William
?1520–?1570 poet, obituarist and
mathematician. Born at Lichfield, he
was a prebendary at Upton Decanii in
the city. He wrote verses 'On the
Death of Bacon' and 'On the Death of
the Dukes of Suffolk'.

BUDD Horace
mid 20th C poet. Believed to have
lived in Birmingham, in 1952 he

published *"Midland" Measure With
Variations 1941–1951*, a collection of
poems mainly to do with the people
and places of the area. His work is
respectful, without becoming fulsome
or sentimental.

BULL Rev Henry
b.1859 poet, hymn writer and sketch
writer. Born in Wolverhampton, he
wrote many Black Country sketches
in dialect, such as *That's Him to a T*
(1890). He also contributed dialect
poems to the Wolverhampton
newspapers.

BULLOCK-WEBSTER Violet
early 20th C poet and short story
writer. She lived in Ludlow. *Sweet
Scented Leaves* (1913), a collection of
stories 'of conduct and character', is
her only known work.

BURBURY Mrs E J
mid-19th C children's writer. She
lived in Shrewsbury. *The Grammar
School Boys: a Tale of School-boy
Life* (1854), which is dedicated to
Benjamin Hall Kennedy*, the then
headmaster of the Royal Free
Grammar School of Shrewsbury, is
based on her knowledge of life at the
school.

BURLEIGH Florence
mid-20th C poet and short story
writer. Born in Wolverhampton, she
returned from the USA to her native
town following a breakdown in
health. Visits to Germany inspired her
collections of stories, *Three Days in
Ringen* and *Goethe in Ringen on the
Rhine*.

BURNE Charlotte Sophia
1850–1923 linguist, essayist and
folklorist. She was born at Morton
vicarage near Oswestry. As assistant
to Georgina Jackson*, she worked on
dialect studies, but her main interest

was in the myths and legends of Shropshire. Her book, *Shropshire Folk Lore* (1883), was the inspiration for some of Mary Webb's* work.

BURNEY Fanny (Madame d'Arblay)
1752–1840 novelist and diarist. She frequently visited her uncle Richard, an enthusiastic though unpublished writer who lived at Barbourne Lodge in Worcester. Here her cousin Edward is reputed to have fallen in love with her, but to have been too shy to declare himself. She is now best known for her first novel, Evelina (1778), an amusing and delightful romance written in the form of letters.

BUSBY Roger
b.1941 novelist and journalist. From 1966 to 1973 he worked on the staff of the *Birmingham Mail*. *Main Line Kill* (1968), the first novel he wrote with Gerald Holtham*, is set in Birmingham.

BUSHNELL Mrs Bertha M
early 20th C short story writer. She is believed to have lived in or near Birmingham. *The Sailing of the "Friendship"* (1923) relates to the city.

BUTLER Michael Gregory
b.1935 poet. A one-time teacher in Worcester and lecturer in Birmingham, he now lives in Catshill near Bromsgrove. The collection, *Nails and Other Poems*, was published in 1964. He has also contributed work to various periodicals including *Migrant* and *Universities Poetry*.

BUTLER Richard
See ALLBEURY, Ted

BUTLER Samuel
1612–80 poet. He was born in Strensham in a house leased by his father from Sir John Russell of Strensham Court for whom Mr Butler

worked – possibly as secretary. Educated at King's School in Worcester, in 1630 he went to Earl's Croome to become Thomas Jeffrey's secretary. While steward to the Earl of Carbery in 1661–62, he wrote part of his most famous poem, the satire, *Hudibras* (1663), in his rooms above the castle gateway in Ludlow.

BUTLER Samuel
1835–1902 novelist. Educated at Shrewsbury School, while there he visited his aunt and uncle, the Bathers*, at Meole Brace. His school experiences are to some extent reflected, none too flatteringly, in the semi-autobiographical novel, *The Way of All Flesh* (published posthumously in 1903).

BUTT George
1741–95 poet, novelist, playwright and religious writer. Born at Lichfield, the son of a physician, he was educated at Stafford. As a boy he met Dr Johnson* and became a friend of Isaac Hawkins Browne* the younger. He was the father of Martha Sherwood* and Lucy Cameron*. After ordination in 1763, he became successively curate of Leigh in 1765, the tutor to Sir Edward Winnington's son at Stanford Court in Worcestershire, vicar of Clifton-on-Teme in 1771 and rector of Stanford-on-Teme in 1773. A frequent visitor to Lichfield, where he stayed with his sister, the mother of Henry Salt*, he was married in Warwick in 1773 and then went to live in Stanford-on-Teme. Part of his library there derived from the sale of William Walsh's* collection of books at Abberley. His last living, in 1787, was at Kidderminster, though he remained in his house at Stanford. His daughter, Martha, arranged publication of his

novel, *Felicia*; but his best work is his poetry which appeared in 1793 as *Poems, In Two Volumes*. His four tragedies, deemed unactable by David Garrick*, were never published.

BUTT William
mid-19th C poet. He was born in Staffordshire. *Private Monody on the Death of Thomas Campbell – Written Shortly after the Poet's Decease at Boulogne on the 15th June 1844* is his only known work.

BUTTERS Paul
b.1908 novelist and playwright. A solicitor, he was born in Stafford and educated at King Edward's School in Birmingham. He lived most of his life in Rowley Park in Stafford. His first play, a 'psychological thriller' called *Search No More*, was successfully produced in 1950. The novel, *Price of Admission*, appeared in 1965.

BUTTON P
short story writer. He is believed to have lived in Birmingham where his story, *Brummagem Love*, is set.

BYFORD-JONES Wilfred
1907–77 essayist, short story writer and journalist. He worked for the *Express and Star* and the *Shropshire Star* and lived for some time at Lower Hall in Beckbury. His most popular book was a collection of essays, *Both Sides of the Severn* (1933). Some of his articles and short stories were collected in *Severn Valley Stories* (1967).

BYNG John, Viscount Torrington
1742–1813 diarist. In 1781 he visited Halesowen. In the *Torrington Diaries* (edited and published in 1934) he writes enthusiastically about William Shenstone's* estate, the Leasowes, which was situated a mile or so north-east of the town on Mucklow Hill. He writes less enthusiastically about Bromsgrove.

C

CAINE Jeffrey
b.1944 novelist. He has lived in Shropshire and taught at Shrewsbury Secondary School as head of English. His first novel, *Hamlet My Boy* (1972), is very much concerned with the absurdities of human behaviour. Later work, which includes *The Cold Room* (1976) and *Heathcliff* (1977), continues to 'combine psychological insight ... with ... tension and drama'.

CALCUTT David
b.1950 poet. He was born in Wednesbury and now lives in Walsall. Though no collection of his poems appeared before 1974, work that was later published in *Savage Portrait* (1975) and *Outlaws* (1979) had already appeared in several magazines, including *Midland Read* and *New Headland*. *Terrible Fate of Humpty Dumpty* (1992) was written with Alan Bleasdale.

CALLOW Philip
b.1924 novelist and poet. Born in Birmingham, he was a toolmaker at the Coventry Gauge and Tool Company Ltd from 1940 to 1948. His books include *A Pledge for the Earth* (1960), *Clipped Wings* (1964), *Going to the Moon* (1968), *The Bliss Body* (1969) and *Yours* (1972). Considered to be one of the most interesting twentieth-century novelists, he has

been compared to D H Lawrence by
John Betjeman* and to George
Gissing* by Richard Church. He
continues to write and now lives at
Bidford-on-Avon. The novel,
Magnolia Tree (1993), is his most
recent work.

CALVERLEY C S
1831–84 poet and parodist. Born at
Martley in Worcestershire, he was the
son of Henry Blayds, the curate in
charge who resumed the Yorkshire
family name of Calverley in 1852. He
is most famous for his verse perora-
tions on the delights of beer and
tobacco and for his parodies of poets.
Verses and Translations appeared in
1862, *Fly Leaves* in 1872.

CAMDEN William
1551–1623 antiquarian, essayist and
historian. He journeyed throughout
the west midland counties researching
for his survey of England, *Britannia*
(1586, in Latin; 1610, in English).
The medicinal well at Leamington
Spa is mentioned in the book, though
he regretfully refrains from describing
Hereford Cathedral on account of not
having found the time personally to
visit it.

CAMERON Lucy Lyttelton
1781–1858 short story writer. She
was born in Stanford-on-Teme,
daughter of George Butt* and
younger sister of Martha (Mrs
Sherwood*). In 1806 she married Rev
C R Cameron and went with him to
work among the colliers in the
Donnington Wood district of
Shropshire. Dr Arnold praised her
stories and allegories, among them
Amelia, Two Lambs and *Flower Pot.*

CANAWAY W H
b.1925 novelist, children's writer and
short story writer. He is believed to be

living in Staffordshire. His first novel,
The Ring-Givers, published in 1958,
retells the dramatic story of Beowulf.
The children's book, *Sammy Going
South* (1961), describes the travels in
Africa of a ten-year-old orphan.

CARR J L
1915–94 novelist and publisher.
During his teaching career, which
involved twenty-five different
schools, he taught for a while in
Birmingham. He is perhaps best
known for *A Day in Summer* (1963),
The Harpole Report (1972) and *A
Month in the Country* (1980). A later
novel, *What Hetty Knew* (1988), set
partly in the city, is dedicated to the
memory of the Birmingham printer,
John Baskerville.

CARROLL Lewis
1832–98 (pseudonym of C L
Dodgson) children's writer and mathematician. Author of *Alice in
Wonderland* (1865) and *Alice
Through the Looking Glass* (1871), he
was educated at Rugby School during
the headmastership of Thomas
Arnold.

CARTLAND Barbara
b.1904 novelist, biographer and
playwright. She also writes under the
name of Barbara McCorquodale. The
family came originally from Worcestershire, but she was born and brought
up in Birmingham. Her brother
Ronald, MP for King's Norton from
1935 to 1940, was the first MP killed
in action in the war – at Dunkirk.
Cartland Road in King's Heath, and
the Cartland Arms on Parson's Hill in
King's Norton, are named after the
family. Her books, all in a romantic
vein, are phenomenally popular and
have frequently been adapted for
television – the most successful being
Hazard of Hearts (1988).

CARY Henry Francis
1772–1844 poet and translator. As a child he came to live in Cannock, beginning his education at Rugby School before moving to grammar schools at Sutton Coldfield and Birmingham. At the age of fourteen he contributed poems to the *Gentleman's Magazine* and as a young man he became a member of Anna Seward's* coterie. After ordination he was appointed vicar at Abbot's Bromley in Staffordshire, later moving to Kingsbury near Coleshill. *Sonnets and Odes* appeared in 1788, but it was his translation of Dante's work in 1812 that established his literary reputation. In 1824 his translation of Aristophanes' play, *The Birds*, was published. He is now probably best known for his additions to Dr Johnson's* *Lives of the Poets*.

Edward Cave

CAVE Edward
1691–1754 (known as Sylvanus Urban) publisher, printer and essayist. Born in Rugby, the son of a cobbler, he is now chiefly remembered as the founder of the *Gentleman's Magazine*. In Birmingham in 1735 he was approached by Dr Johnson* and, after the failure of Dr Johnson's school in Edial, took him into his service in London in 1737.

CHADBURN Paul
mid-20th C poet. A teacher in Shropshire, in 1965 he published his narrative poem, *The Cricket Match*, which tells of the mighty battle between the villages of Clun and Flint.

CHALLINOR William
1821–96 poet and critic. He was born in Leek and married a Miss Mary Elizabeth Pemberton from Birmingham. His poems, mostly set in Leek and its surroundings, were published in several periodicals. An incident reported in his *Chancery Reform* is reputed to have inspired the character of Grindley in Charles Dickens's*, *Bleak House*.

CHAMBERLAIN Peter
mid-20th C novelist. He was born in Birmingham into the family who owned the furnishing business, Chamberlain, King and Jones. During the Second World War, as a sergeant in the army, he was mainly occupied in teaching staff to ride motorcycles. *Sing Holiday* (1937) is related to the industrial life of Birmingham. He was a member of the Birmingham Group (see HAMPSON, John), which included Walter E Allen*, Walter Brierley*, Leslie Halward* and John Hampson*.

CHARLTON Geoff
b.1943 poet and editor. Born in Birmingham, he was educated in the city and from 1963 to 1968 worked at menial jobs to support himself while writing. From 1968 to 1972 he studied for his B Ed at Birmingham College of Education before going to teach at Lichfield. Although his

collection of verse, *Words Flowing Won't Be Still*, and a volume of short stories, *Claire and Elizabeth*, did not appear until 1976, he was already well known for poetry readings at universities and in poetry circles in the west midland area and had published work in pamphlet form.

CHARQUES Dorothy
1899–1976 novelist. Born in Alcester, she was educated at Stratford-upon-Avon Grammar School and later settled in the town. The first novel she wrote without collaboration, *The Tramp and his Woman*, appeared in 1937. Other work includes the trilogy, *Time's Harvest* (1946), and the novels, *Men Like Shadows* (1952), *The Nunnery* (1959) and *A Wind from the Sea* (1971).

CHATTERTON Stephen
1753–95 poet. A teacher, he was born at Willenhall and spent his entire life there. His poems, which often dwell on his native Black Country, were published in a collected edition in 1795.

CHETWOOD Knightley
1652–1720 poet and religious writer. Born in Coventry, he was the author of several poems and sermons that were published in local periodicals and pamphlets.

CHETWYND T H
mid-20th C poet and novelist. In 1937 he published the collection, *Poems of the Wye and Herefordshire District*, which was inspired by the area – its legends, its people, its scenery.

CHILTERN H Herman
early 20th C novelist. He lived in Wolverhampton. His work includes *The Mind of the Mark* (1924) and *The Main Chance*.

CHITHAM Edward
b.1932 novelist and children's writer. Born in Birmingham and educated at the city's university, he now lives in Harborne. He taught at Dudley College of Education in 1977 before becoming a lecturer at Wolverhampton Polytechnic. His first book, *Ghost in the Water* (1973), is set against a background of the streets and canals of the Black Country.

CHOLMONDELEY Francis G
b.1850 poet. Born at Hamstall Ridware in Staffordshire, he was educated at Rugby and became vicar of Leek Wootton in Warwickshire. He won the Newdigate Prize in 1872 for his poem, 'The Burning of Paris'.

CHOLMONDELEY Mary
1859–1925 novelist. Born in Shropshire, daughter of the rector at Hodnet, she used the pseudonym 'Pax' for her first two novels, *Her Evil Genius* (1886) and *The Danvers Jewels* (1887). Her paternal grandmother, who inherited Hodnet Hall, figures largely in her autobiography, *Under One Roof* (1917). For a brief time in 1896, after her father had retired, the family lived in Condover Hall which had been left to them by Reginald Cholmondeley, the frequent host of Mark Twain*. *Red Potage* (1899) is her most famous and her most interesting work. Aunt to Stella* and George Benson*, she was a semi-invalid throughout her life.

CHRISTIAN Jill
See DILCOCK, Noreen

CHURCH Alfred John
1829–1912 novelist. His only known book, *Chantry Priest of Barnet* (1885), is set in the west midland counties.

CHURCHYARD Thomas

1520–1604 poet and essayist. Born in Shrewsbury, he lived there until he was nineteen. Later he contributed his best-known work, a verse story called *The Legend of Shore's Wife*, to the 'Drab Age' compilation, *Mirror for Magistrates* (1563), in which famous men and women described the less happy aspects of their lives. His main work, *The Worthiness of Wales* (1587), includes a lively and enthusiastic description of Shrewsbury.

CLARK Muriel

early/mid-20th C children's writer. She lived in Coventry. All her work, which includes *The Wonderful Island* (1927), *The Council of Kandy* (1930), *Long Ago in Galilee* (1937) and *The Gates of the Kingdom* (1947), has a religious emphasis – as the titles suggest.

CLARKE Ethel M

early 20th C novelist. She lived in Coventry. Only one of her books, *The Potter's Vessel* (1907), is still remembered.

CLAYTON John

1885–1939 (pseudonym of Henry Bertram Law Webb) essayist and novelist. The husband of Mary Webb*, he was the nephew of Captain Matthew Webb of Dawley, the first man to swim the English Channel. He was working on a book of essays, *The Silences of the Moon* (1911), when he met his future wife. They lived for much of their married life in Pontesbury in Shropshire. His historical novels, which include *The Gold of Toulouse* (1932) and *The Silver Swan* (1939), were written under his pseudonym.

CLEE Florence Alice

early 20th C poet and hymn writer. Born at Cradley Heath, she later became a teacher. Her poems, which are chiefly to do with nature and the simple life, have been published in several periodicals including *The Philomath*.

CLIFFORD Arthur

1778–1830 poet and antiquarian. He was born at Tixall in Staffordshire. To what extent he actually wrote the poetic contributions in the antiquarian literary collection entitled *Tixall Poetry* (1813) is not known, but most of the voluble and ponderous notes are his. More puzzling is why Sir Walter Scott* allowed this literary curiosity to be published by the reputable Ballantyne Press.

CLIVE Caroline

1801–73 (frequently used the pseudonym 'V') novelist and poet. She was the daughter and co-heir of Edmund Meysey Wigley of Shakenhurst, MP for Worcester from 1784 to 1802. In 1840 she married Archer Clive, rector of Solihull, who later took the living in Whitfield near Kingstone and became chancellor of Hereford Cathedral. Although she wrote several slim volumes of verse, the first being *IX Poems By V* (1840) which was admired by the *Quarterly Review*, it was her prose romances, especially the gothic and sensational, *Paul Ferroll* (1855) and *Why Paul Ferroll Killed His Wife* (1860), which were the most popular of her many publications. She was accidentally burnt to death.

CLOUGH Arthur

1819–61 poet. He was educated at Rugby School during Thomas Arnold's headmastership. The doubts he felt concerning the irreconcilability of Arnold's 'Broad Church' views and the reactionary Oxford Movement, which he encountered as an undergraduate, helped to inspire his thoughtful and sympathetic poetic voice. 'Say not the struggle nought availeth' is the most anthologised and the best-known example of his work. *The Bothie of Tober-na-Vuolich* (1848) and *Ambarvalia* (1849) are among his other works.

CLOWES Gertrude
early 20th C poet. She lived in Coventry. *Bluestones Daughter and Other Poems* appeared in 1923.

COCKAIN Sir Aston
1605–83 poet and playwright. He lived at Pooley in Warwickshire, the friend of John Donne* and Michael Drayton*. Now almost forgotten – owing perhaps to the 'objectionable lack of refinement' in much of his work – he was the author of four plays and of poems on several subjects which were published in the collection, *Love's Elegie*.

COCKERILL Helen
mid-20th C poet. Born in Wolverhampton, she invests much of her poetry, published in various periodicals, with a morbid awareness of life's struggles. Her work includes 'Pictures from Memory' and 'Waiting Days'.

COKE Desmond
1879–1959 novelist and children's writer. He was educated at Shrewsbury School. *The Bending of a Twig* (1906), a parody of the conventional school story, relates what happens to one Lycidas Marsh during his schooldays at Shrewsbury. His other work includes *The Call* (1907), *The Cure* (1912) and *Helena Brett's Career* (1913).

COLDWELL Charles Simeon
1837–1920 poet and editor. He was born at Stafford, and is best known for his editorship in 1860 of *College Rhymes Contributed by Members of the Universities of Oxford and Cambridge*, which included work by Samuel John Stone* as well as several of his own poems.

COLE Alfred A
1821–93 poet. He was minister of the Goodall Street Chapel in Walsall for thirty-three years. During that time he became the first chairman of the Walsall Philharmonic Union and the chairman of the Walsall Science and Art Institute. A sample of his verse appears in Alfred Moss's*, *Songs from the Heart of England* (1920).

COLE G D H
1889–1958 novelist, sociologist and academic. A visitor to the west midland area, he is co-author with his wife of *The Bolo Book* (1923) and of *The Brothers Sackville* (1936), a detective novel which has a Birmingham setting. His biography of William Cobbett appeared in 1924.

COLE Dame Margaret
1893–1980 novelist and sociologist. The sister of Raymond Postgate, she lived in Birmingham and was co-author with her husband of *The Bolo Book* and *The Brothers Sackville* (see above). The biography of her husband, *Life of G D H Cole*, appeared in 1971.

COLE Thomas E
late 19th/early 20th C poet. He lived in Worcester. As well as the poem, 'Love Story of 1646', the compilation entitled *Bronsil Castle* (1920) contains 'Miscellaneous Poems Praising the Beauties of Worcestershire and Herefordshire Scenery'. Two other collections – *The Love Songs of Podd* (1884), which includes a section entitled 'Sonnets of

Worcester', and *Cader Idris* (1935) – were written under the pseudonym of 'Podd'.

COLEMAN Walter
d.1645 poet. He was born in Staffordshire. His long 262-stanza poem, *La Dance Macabre, Death's Duell*, an ingenious and shrewdly expressed version of the subject, was published in 1632.

COLEMAN-COOKE Major John
b.1915 (pseudonym of Langridge Ford) editor, scriptwriter and critic. He was born in Burton-on-Trent and educated at the town's grammar school. The film, *The Harvest That Kills*, appeared in 1967.

COLERIDGE Samuel Taylor
1772–1834 poet and philosopher. He stayed at the King's Arms in Ross-on-Wye during his tour of Wales in 1794. From December 1797 he visited Shrewsbury several times – to preach as Dr Rowe's locum in the High Street Unitarian Church. It was in January 1798 that William Hazlitt* walked from Wem to hear him. He returned the visit to Hazlitt's home in Noble Street a few days later. A complicated writer and personality, he reveals a strong spiritual dimension in his most successful work. He is perhaps now best remembered for the long narrative fable 'The Rime of the Ancient Mariner', published in *Lyrical Ballads* (1798), which he is reputed to have first read at a literary gathering in Mardol in Shrewsbury.

COLES Elisha
1640–80 linguist and poet. Born in Wolverhampton, the son of a schoolmaster, he compiled an *English Dictionary* (1676). He also wrote *Metrical Paraphrase on the History of Our Lord* (1671) which is reputed

to contain the most appalling doggerel ever to get itself into print – an accolade perhaps none too easily won, except of course in the west midland counties.

COLLIGAN Aimee M
early 20th C poet. She lived in Coventry. The verses in *Hazel Leaves* (1929), many of which are to do with the natural world and ordinary life, first appeared in the *Birmingham Weekly Post*, the *Coventry Herald* and the *Coventry Standard*.

COLLINS Wilkie
1824–89 novelist. In 1852 he stayed at the Lion Hotel in Shrewsbury with his friend and fellow writer, Charles Dickens*. He is now known chiefly for his novels, *The Woman in White* (1860) and *The Moonstone* (1868).

COMBE (or COOMBE) William
1741–1823 poet. Like Fanny Burney's uncle, Richard, he was a member of a distinguished writing circle in Worcester. The verse parodies, written to accompany Rowlandson's coloured plates and drawings, *The Tour of Dr Syntax in Search of the Picturesque* (1809), *The Second Tour of Dr Syntax in Search of Consolation* (1820) and *The Third Tour of Dr Syntax in Search of a Wife* (1821), are his best-known work.

COMPTON Henry
1632–1713 poet, translator and letter writer. The sixth and youngest son of the Earl of Northampton, he was born at Compton Wynyates in Warwickshire. He published a variety of 'useful and learned works', most of them exhibiting a distinctly religious flavour – fervour, even, on occasions.

COMPTON Henry
1872–1943 poet. He was born and lived in Coventry where after leaving

school he joined the staff of the *Coventry Evening Telegraph*. A collection of his poems, *Kindred Points*, appeared in 1951.

COMYNS Barbara
b.1909 novelist. Born in Bidford-on-Avon, she was educated mainly by governesses until she went to art school in Stratford-upon-Avon. Her various occupations have included dealing in old cars and breeding poodles. She is the author of several novels, the best known being *The Vet's Daughter* (1959), which has been both read aloud and dramatised on BBC radio. She continued to publish during the 70s and 80s.

CONGREVE William
1670–1729 playwright. In 1689, after leaving Trinity College in Dublin, he went to stay with his paternal grandfather, Richard, at Stretton Hall in Staffordshire. It is thought that while sitting under an oak tree on the estate he wrote *The Old Bachelor* (1693), the comedy that set him on the road to fame. This he revised while staying with his friend, Robert Port, at Ilam Hall in Dove Dale. His later work includes *The Double Dealer* (1693), *Love for Love* (1695) and arguably his best, *The Way of the World* (1700).

COOK Thomas
mid-19th C poet. He was for a time curate at Kidderminster. His collection of verse, *Miscellaneous Poems*, many of them debating the concerns of the spiritual life, appeared in 1832.

COOKE Anthony
mid-16th C poet. He lived at Hartshill Manor near Burton Dasset, an estate in Warwickshire left him by his maternal uncle. *The University* (1550–51), an anthology of poetry published in memory of Dr Martin Bucer, includes some of his verse.

COOKE Arthur O
early 20th C novelist and children's writer. Of over forty publications, mainly to do with the countryside and nature, his novel for children, *Five Hundred Pounds Reward* (1927), is set in a fictionalised Shropshire. His natural history study, *A Book of Dovecotes* (1920), makes reference to Worcester, Warwick, Herefordshire and Shropshire.

COOKE Noah
1831–1919 poet. Born in Kidderminster, the son of a journeyman weaver, he was educated at Old Church School. For a time he was employed in the clay works at Brierley Hill. Known as the 'weaver poet', he published the collection, *Wild Warblings*, in 1876.

COOKSEY Richard
late 18th C poet. He lived in Malvern. Much of his work in the collection, *Miscellaneous Poems* (1796), is about places in the Malvern area.

COOMBES Joyce
b.1906 (pseudonym of Joyce Hales) novelist. She was born at Tettenhall in Staffordshire and educated at Wolverhampton High School. Her work includes *George and Mary Sumner, Their Life and Times* (1965), *Judgement on Hatcham* (1969) and *One Hundred Years on the Hill* (1970).

COOPER George
1786–1860 poet and antiquarian. Born in Newcastle-under-Lyme, he was educated at the local grammar school. Later he became lessee of the town's gas works. Many of his poems are about Newcastle and its surroundings and history. *Some Loose Leaves From My Portfolio* appeared

handsomely printed and illustrated in 1842.

COOPER John Dunning
b.1852 poet. Born in Wolverhampton and educated at the town's grammar school, he dedicated *Prometheus Bound and Original Poems* (1890) to his headmaster.

COPE Elijah
1842–1917 poet, folklorist, essayist and short story writer. Born at Ipstones in Staffordshire, he moved to Leek when very young and remained there all his life – working as a woodcarver and becoming a leading authority on local folklore. The author of many poems about Leek, Rudyard and other local places, he also wrote articles and short stories for the *Leek Times*.

CORBETT (or CORBET) Richard
1582–1635 poet and divine. He visited Warwick Castle in 1619. In his poem, 'Iter Boreale', published in *Certain Elegant Poems* (1647), he mentions the story of Guy of Warwick – a legendary knight of immense size who confronted and overcame several foreign and home-grown monsters. 'Farewell, Rewards and Fairies' is probably the best-known example of his fictional work.

CORELLI Marie
1885–1924 (pseudonym of Mary McKay) novelist. Born in Birmingham, in 1901 she went to Stratford-upon-Avon to live in Mason's Croft (now the University of Birmingham's Shakespeare Institute) where she continued to write and to pursue a career devoted to eccentricity and the preservation of ancient buildings. She is buried in the town's cemetery. *Memoirs of Marie Corelli* (1930), written by Bertha Vyver, her compan-

ion of the Stratford years, records faithfully her contributions to the life of the town. A prolific writer of romantic fiction, she is probably best known now for *Barabbas* (1893) and *The Mighty Atom* (1912).

CORNFIELD John
?1827–1873 poet. He was born in the village of Can Lane, in Sedgley, now known as Hurst Hill. A brick manufacturer and pawnbroker, he published *Allan Chace and Other Poems* in 1877. His poetry veers determinedly towards the melancholic.

COTMAN A
late 20th C poet. He lives in Bishop's Castle in Shropshire. *A New Shropshire Lad*, a collection which celebrates 'a love of England' especially of west Shropshire, was published in 1972.

COTTERELL Constance
late 19th/early 20th C novelist. She lived in Walsall. Her work, which includes *Love is not so Light* (1898) and *The Honest Trespass* (1911), has a tendency to be a little overheated.

COTTERELL George
1839–98 poet and editor. He was born in Walsall. His speech on William Shakespeare*, delivered at the banquet of the Walsall Amateur Corps Dramatique in 1878, was published by popular request. Though somewhat sentimental, his three volumes of verse, *Constantia* (1870), *Yesterdays and Todays* (1887) and *Poems: Old and New* (1894), show a gentle lyricism – and some experimentation with rhyme and metre. *The Banquet*, a political verse satire on Ireland, was published in 1885. He is well represented in Alfred Moss's*, *Songs from the Heart of England* (1920).

COTTERELL Mrs Matilda
1831–1917 poet. Born in Walsall, she lived there all her life. Her work, which though a little naive is fresh and pleasing, appeared in Alfred Moss's*, *Songs from the Heart of England* (1920).

COTTERILL Edith
late 20th C novelist. Born in Tipton in Staffordshire, she lives and works there still. Her experiences as a district nurse were the inspiration for her novel, *A Black Country Nurse at Large* (1973).

COTTERILL Thomas
1779–1824 hymn writer. Born in Cannock, the son of a woolstapler, he was educated at a grammar school in Birmingham. After his ordination, he became curate of Tutbury in 1806 and later the rector of Lane End in Longton. He published *A Selection of Psalms and Hymns* and some of his work can also be found in the anthology, *Gleanings from the Sacred Poets.*

COTTON Charles
1630–87 poet and translator. The son of a gentleman farmer and literary enthusiast, he was born and lived at Beresford Hall on the Staffordshire/Derbyshire border. A friend of Izaak Walton*, he wrote one of the dialogues in *The Compleat Angler* (1676). His love of the locality is expressed in his topographical poem, *The Wonders of the Peake* (1681), as well as in a number of his poems in *Poems on Several Occasions* (published posthumously in 1689). He has been described severally as 'bibulous and reckless' and 'courteous and urbane'.

COTTON John
1844–1934 poet, architect, historian and artist. Born, brought up and educated in Bromsgrove, he later trained as an architect in London. On returning to the town, he designed a number of public buildings, including Droitwich Brine Baths, and became an accomplished landscape artist. His publications include the illustrated collection, *Song and Sentiment* (1891), *Midland Musings* (1910) and *Gleanings* (1922). Local elections were enlivened by his lampoons and skits on prospective candidates.

COTTON Roger
late 16th C poet. Born at Alkington near Whitchurch, he was almost certainly educated at the free school in the town. He is now chiefly remembered for his religious poems, *An Armor of Proofe* (1596) and *A Spirituall Song* (1596).

COVENTRY Lady Anne
1673–1763 essayist. In 1691 she married Thomas, 2nd Earl of Coventry, and from 1710, apart from an absence of seventeen years at the beginning of her widowhood, lived at Snitterfield in Warwickshire. *Meditations and Reflections, Moral and Divine* appeared in 1707. Richard Jago*, who was at the time vicar of Snitterfield, published the sermon he preached at her funeral.

COXHEAD Elizabeth
mid-20th C novelist. *The Midlanders* (1953), not unsurprisingly set in the west midland area, details the lives and loves of people living in several adjacent villages 'in the shadow of industry'.

COXON William
mid-19th C poet. He is believed to have lived in rural east Staffordshire. His volume, *Sacred and Moral Poems* (1831), was printed and sold by a

Burton-on-Trent firm.

CRAIK Mrs
1826–87 (pseudonym of Dinah Maria Mulock) novelist, poet, short story writer, children's writer and essayist. She was born in Longfield Cottage in Hartshill where her father was minister, but preferred to think of Newcastle-under-Lyme as her 'native place'. It was in 1831 that the family went to live there, first in a house in Lower Street and then in Mount Pleasant. When she was only twenty, she took her mother and two sisters away from the unhappy family home to London where she managed to support them on the proceeds of her writing. Longfield Cottage appears in her most famous novel, *John Halifax, Gentleman* (1857). Many of her characters, though wholly confined to the domestic situation, reveal loyalties and inclinations of the most passionate kind.

CRAKE Augustine David
1836–90 novelist. He visited the area in order to research for those parts of *The House of Walderne* (1891) and *The Camp on the Severn* (1900) which have a west midland counties' setting.

CRAMP J F
1868–1952 poet. A member of a well-known family of Coventry ribbon makers, she lived all her life in the city. Much of her work is about the Warwickshire countryside. A collection entitled *Poems* appeared in 1930.

CRANE John
1750?–1820? poet. Born in Bromsgrove where he became a clock maker, bookseller and dealer in fancy goods, he wrote many 'topical rhymes in racy vein' which were originally published in pamphlet form. They were later collected together in a volume called *Poems Dedicated to John Bull, by a Bird of Bromsgrove*. This volume seems to have caught the public's imagination and ran to seven reprintings.

CRAYON Geoffrey
See IRVING, Washington

CRISPIN Edmund
1921–78 (pseudonym of Bruce Montgomery) novelist and composer. During the 1940s he taught for two years at Shrewsbury School. Encouraged by his friend, Philip Larkin*, he began to write detective novels. *Love Lies Bleeding* (1948), set in a public school, almost certainly derives from his own teaching experiences. His work is always intelligent – and often hilarious.

CROPPER Eustace Burton
b.1894 poet. The son of an ironmonger, he was born in a house near Dudley Castle. At the age of eleven he won a scholarship to the grammar school where he was encouraged to train as a teacher. Later he taught at Sedgley Council School and Bent Street School in Brierley Hill. His poetry reflects his Black Country upbringing and his experiences in the First World War.

CROSBIE Marjorie
1892–1971 poet. Born at Worcester Lodge, Penn Fields in Wolverhampton, the daughter of Councillor Adolph Crosbie, she later lived in Codsall. She wrote several volumes of poetry, the first being *Life's Changes* (1912). Her work is lyrical and sincere, if not especially profound.

CROSS Fred W
early 20th C short story writer. *Tarvey: a Tale of the Midlands*

(1921), which describes and contrasts town and country life, is dedicated to the then Lord Lieutenant of Staffordshire.

CRUMP John F
1835–1909 essayist. He lived in Walsall. His work, which is generally in hortatory vein, includes *Greetings in the Market, Essays of a Philosophical Bent* (1894), *Light and Leading, Essays of an Uplifting Type* (1903) and *Changes, a Peroration on Discipline* (1908).

CUSHING Paul
b.1854 (pseudonym of Richard Wood-Seys) novelist. He was born in Stourbridge. His work includes *A Woman with a Secret* (1885) and *The Shepherdess of Treva* (1895).

CYMBELINE
See KILLMINSTER, Abraham K

CYNFYN
late 20th C (pseudonym of Bryan Walters) poet. Born in the Black Country, he was brought up in Bridgnorth where he now lives. Among his several volumes of poetry are *Images of Stone* (1972), *Tir-an-nog* (1973), *To Remember* (1973), *From the Welsh* (1974) and *Prehistoric Forest* (1981). He is regarded as an expert on, and exponent of, Welsh poetry.

CYPLES William
1831–82 poet and novelist. Born in Longton, he published two volumes of poetry, *Miscellaneous Poems* (1857) and *Satan Reformed* (1859), and, anonymously, several novels, the last being *Heart of Gold* which appeared in 1883 after his death. Sentimental though his poems are, they show a delicately figurative quality.

D

DAKEYNE Miss J
mid-19th C poet and folklorist. The author of *Legends of the Moorlands and Forests of Staffordshire* (1860), a compilation which includes some verse, she lived at Quarnford in Staffordshire.

DALEY G C
mid-20th C editor and poet. He was born and lived in Bilston. With F Sherwood*, he edited *Some Bilston Poets* (1951), a selection of work by writers who had been born in Bilston and district and which includes some of his own work.

DALTON Gilbert
mid-20th C children's writer. Born and brought up in Coventry, he was on the staff of the *Midland Daily Telegraph* for sixteen years. He is best known for his Children's Hour radio serials, but he also wrote adventure novels including *The Spider's Web* (1949) and *Operation Catapult* (1951).

DANGERFIELD John
See FREEMAN, John

DANIELL David Scott
mid-20th C novelist. His book, *Fifty Pounds for a Dead Parson* (1960), is based on events which took place in the Worcestershire village of Oddingley in the years 1805 and 1806.

DARBY Paul
b.1949 poet and songwriter. A school teacher, he lives in Brierley Hill. His poems have been broadcast on BBC

Radio WM in his own 20-minute poetry programme. Much of his work has a most uncomfortably surreal quality. *Masque* (1975) reveals the underbelly of city life.

DARKE Marjorie
b.1929 children's writer. Born in Birmingham, she was educated at Worcester Grammar School for Girls and now lives in Coventry. *Ride the Iron Horse*, set in Victorian Warwickshire, appeared in 1973, to be followed in 1974 by its sequel, *The Star Trap*, where the action moves to Birmingham. She continues to write children's fiction, much of it set in the west midland area. *Emma's Monster* appeared in 1992.

DARLING Edward Moore
1884–1968 short story writer. Educated at Lichfield Theological College, he worked in several parishes in the west midland counties, including Walsall, Shrewsbury, Lichfield and Oswestry, and from 1958 was a canon emeritus of Coventry. For thirty years he wrote as agricultural correspondent of the *Birmingham Daily Post* which published several of his short stories that were later collected under the title of *Nathan the Verger*.

DARLINGTON W A
1890–1979 playwright, journalist, critic and novelist. He was educated at Shrewsbury School – as is mentioned in his autobiography, *I Do What I Like* (1947). The play, *Alf's Button*, was successfully produced in London in 1924.

DARWALL Elizabeth
1779–1851 poet. Born at Walsall, she was the daughter of John and Mary Darwall (see below). *The Storm and Other Poems* (1810) was dedicated to the Prince of Wales. She died at Shrewsbury and was buried there.

DARWALL Rev John
1731–89 poet and hymn writer. He was born at Haughton in Staffordshire. Husband of Mary Darwall* and father of Elizabeth*, from 1769 until his death he was vicar of St Matthew's in Walsall. Although *Political Lamentation in Verse* appeared in 1776 and *Discourse on Spiritual Improvement* in 1789, he is probably best remembered as the composer of the popular hymn tune, 'Darwall's 148th'.

DARWALL Mary
mid-19th C poet. She lived in Walsall. The wife of John Darwall* and mother of Elizabeth*, she was encouraged in her writing by William Shenstone* who considered her style to be truly classical. Her work, mostly written before her marriage and under her maiden name, Whateley, was eventually published in 1794 in two volumes entitled *Poems on Several Occasions*. A sample of her poetry appears in Alfred Moss's*, *Songs from the Heart of England* (1920).

DARWIN Erasmus
1731–1802 poet, botanist and physician. From 1756 to 1781 he lived in a house at the west end of Lichfield Cathedral Close (commemorated by a plaque). While here, he established the experimental garden which inspired his poem, *The Botanic Garden* (1789–91). This long treatise in heroic couplets introduces an inchoate theory of evolution not unlike that of his famous grandson, Charles Darwin. In 1804 Anna Seward* published a collection of memoirs of him.

DAVENPORT John
1799–1862 poet. Born at Burslem, he was the son of a potter who later became MP for Stoke-on-Trent. Literature occupied only the leisure moments of his busy life as a barrister. *The Death of Comanchet Chief of the Narraganset Indians and Other Poems* appeared in 1832.

DAVIDSON Gladys
mid-20th C children's writer. Born in Leamington Spa, she lived there all her life. Most of her books are to do with nature and animals and include *Much Ado About Monsters* (1939) and *Animal Adventures* (1945). The collection, *Stories from the Operas*, was published in three volumes.

DAVIE Donald
b.1922 poet, essayist, critic and linguist. *The Shires*, which contains poems about all the west midland counties, was published in 1974. Earlier collections include *Brides of Reason* (1955) and *New and Selected Poems* (1961). *Purity of Diction in English Verse* (1952) and *Articulate Energy* (1955) expound his poetical theory which much influenced the Movement poets (see FISHER, Roy) such as D J Enright*, Philip Larkin* and John Wain*. He continues to write. Later work includes *Collected Poems 1920–1983* (1983) and *To scorch or freeze, poems about the sacred* (1988).

DAVIES Andrew
b.1937 novelist, children's writer, playwright, television adaptor. He lives in Kenilworth. A teacher training lecturer, latterly at Warwick University from 1963 to 1986, he began his very successful writing career with radio plays and children's stories. *The Fantastic Feats of Doctor Boox* appeared in 1972. He now writes mainly for television, both original drama and adaptations which include *A Very Peculiar Practice* (1986) and *Middlemarch* (1994). The 'Marmalade Atkins' children's books, about 'the worst girl in the world', were very popular.

DAVIES Gwyn
mid-20th C novelist. *Hugh the Blacksmith* (1946), set under the Black Mountains at Longtown in Herefordshire, tells a charming story of the friendship between three young and talented men.

DAVIES John
1560–1618 poet and caligraphist. Born in Hereford, he was educated at the grammar school. He wrote several volumes of verse, epitaphs and epigrams, including *Microcosmos* (1603) and *The Scourge of Folly* (1610); and was also a master writer. It is generally agreed that his caligraphy was superior to his poesy. He called himself John Davies of Hereford to distinguish himself from others of the same name, especially the following.

DAVIES Sir John
1569–1626 poet, philosopher and barrister. He was MP for Newcastle-under-Lyme in 1614, though this was many years after he had produced most of his verse. The collection, *Epigrammes and Gullinge Sonnets* (1590), which reveals his strong interest and unsentimental attitude to contemporary society, was banned in 1599 by order of the Archbishop of Canterbury. Other work includes *Orchestra, or a Poem of Dancing* (1596) and *Hymns of Astraea* (1599).

DAVIES O H
1883–1962 novelist. At one time part-owner of a drapery shop in Small

Heath, he set his two novels, *Smite the Rock* and *This Great City* (1924), in Birmingham.

DAVIOT Gordon
See TEY, Josephine

DAVIS Mary
early 20th C poet. She lived in Walsall. Her only known work is entitled *Divine Songs*.

DAVIS Mary A
mid-19th C poet. She lived in Birmingham. A collection of 'Miscellaneous Poems' entitled *The Wild Flower Wreath* – a tender celebration of God's gifts – was published in 1835.

DAWSON Mitchell
mid/late 20th C children's writer. The story, *The Queen of the Trent* (1961), set in the waterways of the midlands, was adapted for BBC television's Jackanory in 1974.

DAY Eric Roland
1892–1966 poet and journalist. Born at Walsall, he published a paper called *The Amateur* in which his poems, often to do with local places and events, appeared regularly.

DAY Thomas
1748–89 novelist. The bestselling morality tale, *A History of Sandford and Merton* (1783–89), is set in Shrewsbury School. His other association with Shropshire is less literary, but possibly more interesting. Disappointed in love, he selected from Shrewsbury Hospital two female foundlings, one with fair hair, one with dark, and arranged for them to be trained up to wifehood. He favoured the fair one, but in the event both refused his offer of marriage. The best laid plans ...

DEACON Edward A
late 19th C poet. He was a native of Leek. *The Widow*, his only known work, was published in 1874.

DEARDON Harold
1883–1962 novelist, playwright, physician and psychologist. Educated at Bromsgrove School, he refers to his schooldays in his autobiography, *The Wind of Circumstance* (1938). Other work includes the novels, *Such Women Are Dangerous* (1933) and *Death in the Lens* (1934), the plays, *Interference* (1927) and *Two White Arms* (1928), and the non-fiction study, *A New Way With the Insane* (1923).

DEFOE Daniel
1660–1731 novelist and political journalist. He visited Great Malvern to enjoy the mineral waters and to test the political climate for the Tory politician, Harley; but while there found more to interest him in a rumour of unmined gold in the town. In 1723 he journeyed throughout Herefordshire and Shropshire – from Leominster and Hereford to Ross, sampling a good deal of Herefordshire cider on the way, and then veered northwards through Shrewsbury to Whitchurch. These travels were recorded in his *Tour Through the Whole Island of Great Britain* (1724–27). Considered by many to be the first English novelist, he is best known for *Robinson Crusoe* (1719), *Moll Flanders* (1722) and *Journal of the Plague Year* (1722).

DEHN Paul
1912–76 poet and film critic and playwright. He was educated at Shrewsbury School. His first volume of poetry, *The Day's Alarm*, appeared in 1949. In 1952 he won an Oscar for his film script of *Seven Days to Noon*. *Collected Poems* was published in 1965.

DEKKER Thomas
?1570–1632 playwright and essayist. Believed by some scholars to have been born in Coventry, he collaborated with John Webster, William Rowley, John Ford and Ben Jonson* to produce plays 'of wit and realism' – including *The Shoemaker's Holiday* (1599), *Westward Ho* (1604) and *The Roaring Girl* (1611).

DELANEY Mrs Mary
1700–88 diarist and letter writer. She often visited her brother, Bernard Granville, at Calwich Abbey near Ellastone in Staffordshire, which is thought to be the model for George Eliot's* Donnithorne Chase. The collection, *Autobiography and Correspondence* (1861–2), edited by Lady Llanover, vividly describes contemporary literary and social life.

DENNIS Geoffrey
early 20th C novelist. He was born and brought up in Walsall. His work includes the historical novel, *Mary Lee* (1922), and a mystery novel, *Harvest in Poland* (1925), which is set in Birmingham, Lichfield and what he describes as 'the other side'.

DENNY Ernest
1888–1917 poet. He was brought up in Redditch, where his father was headmaster of the Wesleyan School, and was educated at King Edward's School in Birmingham. The collection of his poems entitled *Galleys Laden* appeared posthumously in 1918.

DEVANEY Pauline
b.1937 playwright. She was born in Stoke-on-Trent. Her work includes the two television situation comedy series, *The Bishop Rides Again* (1966) and *All Gas and Gaiters* (1966–70).

DEVEREUX Robert, Earl of Essex
1567–1601 occasional poet. He was born, according to Thomas Blount in his *Collections for a History of Herefordshire*, at Netherwood near Thornbury, on the Worcestershire/Herefordshire border. Some of his poems, often appended to his large correspondence, are preserved in Ellis's, *Specimens of Early English Poetry*.

Charles Dickens

DICKENS Charles
1812–70 novelist, short story writer and playwright. He was a frequent visitor to the counties of the west midlands. It is known that he stayed at the Lion Hotel in Shrewsbury three times – in 1838 with 'Phiz', the illustrator of some of his books, in 1852 with Wilkie Collins* and in 1858 when he gave one of his readings in the town and went to view the Roman excavations at Wroxeter. He also stayed at Tong and Newport. Both Shifnal and Tong are mentioned in *The Old Curiosity Shop* (1841). A sign outside the south door of Tong church marks 'the reputed resting place of Little Nell'. The original of Miss Havisham in *Great Expectations* (1861) is supposed to have lived in Newport. Visiting Stafford sometime

in the 1840s, Dickens referred to the Swan Hotel as 'a Dodo of an inn' (*Household Words*, 1858). In 1851 he stayed for a time in Malvern – a setting he used in his play, *Mr Nightingale's Diary*. He gave readings at Leamington Spa in 1855 and 1862, attracting large audiences – as the local paper predicted. Birmingham and Worcester are known also to have been included in his lecturing itinerary. In 1867 he met his biographer, John Forster, in the Royal Hotel in Ross-on-Wye (commemorated by a plaque). They discussed the 1867–8 American tour – which was to contribute to Dickens's breakdown in health. In 1869 he was president of the Birmingham and Midland Institute. It is impossible to say which of his novels is the most popular – the characters and stories are now so much a part of our national heritage, as well as of our literary tradition.

DIGBY Sir John, 1st earl of Bristol
1580–1652 poet. He was born at Coleshill in Warwickshire. Though better known for his political activities in the Royalist cause, he also wrote 'tracts, pamphlets, speeches and poems' – some of which were set to music by Henry Lawes in his *Ayres and Songs*. His published work includes *Speeches* (1647) and *Poems* (1653).

DILCOCK Noreen
1907–85 (also used the pseudonyms Norrey Ford and Jill Christian) novelist. A most prolific writer, she lived in Walsall for several years. Her work, which is chiefly in the romantic/historical/gothic vein, includes *Bid Me Love* (1952), *Harvest of the Heart* (1955), *Master of the House* (1970), *Someone Different* (1970) and *A Scent of Lemons* (1972).

DILKE Thomas
late 17th C playwright. He was born in Lichfield and wrote a comedy, *The Lover's Luck* (1696), and a tragi-comedy, *The City Lady* (1697).

DISRAELI Benjamin
1804–81 statesman and novelist. The MP for Shrewsbury from 1841 to 1847, while preparing for the election he stayed at the Lion Hotel. In his novel, *Lothair* (1870), he used Alton Towers in Staffordshire for Muriel Towers, his hero's chief domain, and Trentham Gardens for Brentham, the ducal home of the college friend, Lord Bertram. In 1979 the Disraeli Project in Ontario, Canada, discovered the novel, *A Year at Hartlebury, or the Election* (1834, authors 'Cherry' and 'Fair Star'), to have been written by Disraeli and his sister, Sarah. He would probably have preferred this melodrama of murder, passion and adultery in a Worcestershire village to have been forgotten. Though better known for his political career, he believed that his novels, especially *Coningsby* (1844), *Sybil* (1845) and *Tancred* (1847), could, and would, influence public opinion.

DIXON Joseph
1836–1913 poet. He was born and lived in Walsall. Little is known about him except that his origins were lowly and he was self-taught. His work, which has a winning simplicity and sincerity, appeared in Alfred Moss's*, *Songs from the Heart of England* (1920).

DIXON Richard Watson
1833–1900 poet and historian. He was educated at King Edward's School in Birmingham. The collection, *Last Poems*, many of them concerned with 'man and his Maker', was edited by Robert Bridges and

appeared posthumously in 1905. He also wrote *History of the Church of England.*

DOBELL Sydney
1824–74 poet. A frequent visitor to Great Malvern to drink the waters, on one occasion he and his wife had 'a charming stroll on the hills with Thomas Carlyle'. The composition entitled *Balder* (1854) is an extreme example of the Spasmodic School of Poetry, of which Dobell was a pioneer – a type of writing much ridiculed by contemporary as well as later generations for its inarticulateness.

DODD Arthur Edward
b.1913 poet and playwright. Born in Stoke-on-Trent, he was educated at Newcastle-under-Lyme High School and has lived in Longsdon and Ellastone. He has worked in the potteries industry as an information officer and librarian. His volumes of poetry include *Poems from Belmont* (1955), *Words and Music* (1963) and *The Fifth Season* (1971). Among his plays are *The Flower-Spun Web* (1960), *To Build a Bridge* (1965) and *Gold in Gun Street* (1973).

DODGE Edward
See LEE, Ernest George

DONNE John
1571–1631 poet and divine. He often visited Polesworth in Warwickshire, the home of Michael Drayton's* patron, Sir Henry Goodere, and officiated at the marriage of his host's daughter, Lucy, to Francis Nethersole (there is a memorial in the church). In 1613, on leaving Polesworth for a visit to Montgomery, he is reputed to have written the poem, 'Good Friday'. He would also have visited Sir Henry's elder daughter, Anne, who had married Sir Henry Rainsford and

was living at the manor house in Clifford Chambers. He was best known as a metaphysical poet, but he published much scholarly, sometimes vituperative, religious exegesis and commentary. *Collected Poems* appeared in 1633.

DORA Sister
1832–78 (honorary title of Dorothy Pattison) nurse and poet. She came to work as a nurse in Walsall Hospital in 1865. Spoken of by Florence Nightingale as 'the world-honoured Sister Dora', she is commemorated by a statue which was erected in the centre of the town in 1886. A sample of her verse appears in Alfred Moss's*, *Songs from the Heart of England* (1920).

DOUGLAS Lord Alfred
1870–1945 poet. Born near Worcester, he is known chiefly for his association with Oscar Wilde and for his propensity to litigation (in 1923 he was sent to prison for libelling Winston Churchill). But he has been admired for two of his many volumes of verse, *Sonnets – I Excelsis* (1924) and *Sonnets and Lyrics* (1935).

DOUGLAS Lady E K
mid-19th C children's writer. She lived near Leamington Spa. *Alick and Janey, the Shepherd's Children* appeared in 1857.

DOVASTON John F M
1782–1854 poet and naturalist. Born at The Nursery, West Felton, he was educated at Oswestry School and Shrewsbury School. *Fitz-Gwarine* (1812), a rewriting of the Fitzwarine legend, is the only one of his works now remembered.

DOVER John
1644–1725 playwright. He was born at Barton-on-the-Heath in Warwick-

shire, the grandson of Captain Robert Dover who promoted the Cotswold Olympick Games which are celebrated in William Somervile's* poem, *Hobbinol, or the Rural Games.* While studying for the law he wrote the tragedy, *The Roman Generals, or the Distressed Ladies* (1667?). This was followed several years later by another play, *The White Rose* (1679).

DOYLE Sir Arthur Conan

1859–1930 novelist. For four months in 1878 he lived in Ruyton-of-the-Eleven-Towns as medical assistant to a Dr Elliot. Later in the same year he went to live in Aston Road North in Birmingham, where he stayed until 1881 while continuing his medical training. He is now best known for the Sherlock Holmes stories.

DRAPER Brenda Murray

early 20th C poet. She lived for a time in Newton Road in Burton-on-Trent. The collection, *Dales of Derbyshire and Other Poems*, was published in 1920.

DRAYTON Michael

1563–1631 poet. He was born at Hartshill Green in Warwickshire (commemorated by a granite shelter on the village green). At the age of seven he went to Polesworth Manor as page to Sir Henry Goodere. Brought up and educated there, he wrote many poems to Anne, the younger daughter, eight years his junior, whom he described as his 'Idea' and whom he loved all his life. He dedicated *Ideas Mirrour* (1594) to Anthony Cooke* who lived at Hartshill Manor. After Anne's marriage to Sir Henry Rainsford, he often visited her at Clifford Chambers Manor. In his long topographical poem, *Poly-Olbion* (1612–22), he mentions the legends of Coventry's Lady Godiva and Guy of Warwick, the beauty of the Rivers Wye and Lugg at Mordiford, Herefordshire's Golden Valley and several places of interest in Shropshire. A prolific poet, he wrote on a multitude of subjects and in 1626 became poet laureate.

DRINKWATER John

1882–1937 poet, novelist, critic and playwright. Employed as an insurance clerk in Birmingham, in 1907 he founded The Pilgrim Players – the company that was to become Birmingham Repertory Theatre in 1913 and of which he later became manager. His play, *Abraham Lincoln* (1918), first produced in Birmingham and then in London, was a critical success. *Inheritance* (1931) and *Discovery* (1932), his two-volume autobiography, details the undeniable catholicity of his artistic enthusiasms and spirit. For instance, in his novel, *Robinson of England* (1937), he describes with great vivacity a football match played in Birmingham between Aston Villa and Arsenal.

DRUCKER Andre

1909–87 novelist, radio playwright, children's writer and master pastrycook. He came to England in 1939 via Prague and Poland. Having spent two years in a prisoner-of-war camp as an undesirable alien, he wrote a commentary on the idiosyncrasies of the English in *Ach! To Be In England* (1950s). Founder of the Vienna Patisserie cafes in Birmingham, he lived in Harborne, writing articles for the *Birmingham Gazette* and radio plays for the BBC's Children's Hour. His novel, *Little Men in a Blind Alley* (1973), is set in one of the city's streets. His children's books include *Don Dorian* (1973), a story about a double-decker bus which plies its trade in the not-too-difficult-to-recognise town of Brumby.

DRYDEN John
1631-1700 poet, playwright and critic. A prolific writer, who visited William Walsh* several times at his home in Abberley, he is now best known for his plays, *Marriage à la Mode* (1672) and *All for Love* (1678), and for his criticism, *Essay on Dramatic Poesy* (1668) and *Preface to the Fables* (1700). It was probably the poem 'Annus Mirabilis' (1667) which won him the poet laureateship.

DUDLEY A E
mid-20th C poet. He lived in Cannock where in 1962 he became secretary of the newly formed Cannock Chase Literary Society which numbered amongst its members J Eric Roberts*. The collection, *A Family Tree and Other Poems*, was published in the magazine, *Poet and Printer* (Spring issue 1968).

DUDLEY Ernest
b.1918 (pseudonym of Vivian Ernest Coltman-Allen) novelist, playwright, children's writer and biographer. He was born in Dudley. Among many other books for children and some historical fiction, the 'Dr Morelle' mysteries are perhaps his best known. They include the first, a play, *Dr Morelle, A Comedy* (1954), and nine novels, most of them published in the late 1950s. He also wrote a biography of Lillie Langtry.

DUDLEY Sir Henry Bate
1745-1824 poet, lyricist and playwright. He was born at Fenny Compton in Warwickshire. Of a quarrelsome disposition, on one occasion he spent £28,000 refuting an accusation of simony. He was a great lover of the arts, a friend of David Garrick* and an admirer of Sarah Siddons. Among his many operas are *The Flitch of Bacon* (1779) and *The Woodman* (1791). His plays include the tragi-comedy, *Passages Selected by Distinguished Personages on the Great Literary Trial of Vertiger and Rowena*, an octavo work in four volumes, written with the help of his wife, which went through at least five editions; *The Rival Candidates* (1775); and *The Travellers in Switzerland* (1793). During the first performance of *The Blackamoor Washed White* (1776), members of the audience became involved in so serious a conflict, drawn swords and bloody noses resulted.

DUGARD Thomas
1607-83 poet. Having been master of King Henry VIII's School in Warwick from 1633 to 1648, he then became rector of Barford – remaining there until his death. His poems are included in Clarke's two anthologies, *Morow* (1675) and *Ecclesiastical Martyrologie*.

DUGGAN Alfred
1903-64 novelist and children's writer. He came to live in Ross-on-Wye in 1956. His books include *Knight With Armour* (1950), *Leopards and Lilies* (1954), *Three's Company* (1958) and *Lord Geoffrey's Fancy* (1962).

DUKES G Robert
mid-20th C poet. He was a schoolmaster and WEA lecturer in Stourbridge. His only known collection, *Poems from the House of the Winds*, was published in 1937.

DUNCUFF Albert Henry
mid-20th C poet. Born and brought up in Birmingham, he became a cellist in

the city's Philharmonic Orchestra. He published a collection, *Poems*, in 1964 in which much of the verse describes people and places in the west midland counties. A copy of this book was presented to Birmingham Central Library 'in celebration of the ordinary'.

E

EADES George A H
mid-19th C poet. He lived at High-field near Bilston. The collection, *The World's Charity and Other Poems*, appeared in 1858.

EAGER Frances
1940–78 children's writer. She lived at Ingram's Hall, The Schools in Shrewsbury. Her books, many of them to do with mysteries and adventures, include *Dolphin of the Two Seas* (1973) and *Midnight Patrol* (1974).

EARLE John
1601?–65 essayist. Bishop of Worcester from 1662 to 1663, in 1628 he published *Microcosmographie*, a witty and sympathetic collection of 'sketches' describing and postulating a variety of social and moral types.

EARP R W
mid-20th C playwright. He lived in Coseley. His dialect play about life in the district, *A Country Called Black* (1950s), was written for the children of Mount Pleasant Secondary Modern School.

EASTAWAY Edward
See THOMAS, Edward

EASTVALE Margaret
late 20th C (also uses the pseudonym Barbara Scott) novelist. She lives in Staffordshire where, encouraged by the Walsall Writers' Circle, she wrote her first novel, *Feathers in the Wind* (1973), which won the Romantic Novelists' Association's Netta Muskett Award. Her later work continues in the romantic vein.

EDELMAN Maurice
1911–75 novelist. In 1945 he became MP for Coventry – representing in turn the N, W and NW constituencies. He wrote several novels, including *A Trial of Love* (1951), *Who Goes Home* (1953) and *The Minister* (1961).

EDES Richard
1555–1604 playwright and translator. Successively a prebendary of Hereford Cathedral (1590), treasurer (1596) and Dean of Worcester (1597), he was one of those selected to translate the Bible from Latin. When younger he had composed several tragedies which are now entirely forgotten.

EDGAR David
b.1948 playwright. He has lectured in drama at the University of Birmingham; and from 1974 to 1975 was resident playwright at the Birmingham Rep. *Dick Deterred* (1974) was a forerunner of his later politically and socially aware plays and adaptations, which include *The Jail Diary of Albie Sachs* (1978), *Nicholas Nickleby* (1981) and *Citizen Locke* (1994).

EDRIDGE Edwin
late 19th/early 20th C poet. He lived in Birmingham. His first volume, simply entitled *Poem*, was published in 1897. In 1904 appeared *New Rhymes on Old Lines*. Some of these

poems celebrate aspects and events of Birmingham; and one, 'Musings in Sutton Park parts 1 & 2', endeavours 'to explain some of the reasons for many of my shortcomings'.

EDRIDGE Emily
late 19th C poet and essayist. The younger sister of Julia Berrington*, she was born in Bilston and lived in Wolverhampton. Her work, which includes 'The Old Homestead' and 'A Lay of Wulfrune's Ham-Tun', and which is noted for its devotional calm, was published in several periodicals.

EDWARDS Michael
b.1938 poet and critic. From 1965 to 1973 he was lecturer in French at the University of Warwick. *Commonplace Poetry* appeared in 1971; *To Kindle a Starling* in 1972. His poetry, which tends to be spare and nervy, has been published in a number of periodicals including *Adam*, the *Critical Quarterly* and *The Listener*.

EDWARDS Thomas
b.1851 poet. He was born and lived in Wolverhampton. Not until he was nearly seventy, as 'Owd Tom', did he begin to contribute verses to the *Express and Star*.

EGLIONBIE Edward
1520–87 poet and translator. A magistrate in Warwick and MP for the county in 1571, he lived in Temple Balsall. His Latin verses on the deaths of the dukes of Suffolk appeared in the *University Collection* of 1551.

ELIOT George
1819–1890 (pseudonym of Mary Ann Evans) novelist, short story writer and translator. She was born at South Farm in Arbury, two miles south-west of Nuneaton, and baptised at Chilvers Coton. Her father was agent for the Newdigate family at

Arbury Hall. From 1820 to 1841 she lived in the nearby Griff House. The first school she attended was a dame school in the house opposite her own in Avenue Road. Arbury Mill was the inspiration for *The Mill on the Floss* (1860) and Nuneaton the model for Milby in *Janet's Repentance* (1857). (The town has a George Eliot Memorial Garden.) She attended boarding school at 29 Warwick Row in Coventry and, on her father's retirement, returned to the city to live at Bird Grove, Foleshill Road from 1841 to 1849. On one of her frequent visits to Rosehill in Radford Road, the home of Charles Bray, she met Rufa Brabant who, unable to finish a translation of Strauss's, *Life of Jesus*, asked her to complete it. Coventry is reputed to be the model for the town in *Middlemarch* (1871–2) and Ellastone the inspiration for the Hayslope of *Adam Bede* (1859) (see DELANEY, Mrs Mary). All her English novels are rooted in her experience of the midlands and many critics, with some justification, would claim her to be the greatest nineteenth-century English novelist.

George Eliot

ELSTOB Elizabeth

1683–1756 essayist and linguist. Born at Newcastle-under-Lyme, she later went to live in Evesham where her reputation as an Anglo-Saxon scholar grew rapidly although she often endured great poverty. Among her published works are *English-Saxon Homily of the Nativity of St Gregory*, *Aelfric's Homilies* and an Anglo-Saxon grammar.

ELTON Robert

See MEYNELL, Lawrence

EMERSON Ralph Waldo

1803–82 poet and philosopher. An American, he stayed with the Charles Brays in Coventry in 1848 when on his way from London to Liverpool to return to America. There he met George Eliot* and was much impressed by her erudition and scholarship. *English Traits* (1856) details his observations of the English character.

EMMONS Elise

early 20th C poet. She lived in Leamington Spa. Her work includes *Summer Songs Among the Birds* (1918), *Winter Songs Among the Snows* (1919), *Spring Songs Among the Flowers* (1920) and *Autumn Songs Among the Leaves* (1921). There is also a volume entitled *Songs for All Seasons* (1922)

EMSLEY Clare

mid-20th C novelist. She lived in Coventry. Her work, most of it in romantic vein, includes *The Fatal Gift* (1951), *The True Physician* (1954) and *Flame of Youth* (1957). In the novel, *Lonely Pinnacle* (1952), she uses the thinly disguised cities of Coventry and Birmingham and the town of Leamington Spa as settings for her story.

ENOCH Frederick

mid-19th C poet. He lived in Leamington Spa. *Poems* (1849) is a volume of rather charming verse, much of it to do with Warwickshire and its people.

ENRIGHT Dennis Joseph

b.1920 poet, essayist, children's writer, traveller, editor and academic. Born in Leamington Spa, he was educated at Leamington College and later taught at the Universities of Birmingham and Warwick. His wry sympathy for the human predicament extends to the Midlanders of his youth and the Orientals of his working life. A Movement poet (see FISHER, Roy), he is perhaps best known, for all his multiplicity of talents, for his poetry – beginning with *The Laughing Hyena* (1953). The delightful book, *The Joke Shop* (1976), was his first novel for young readers. *Memoirs of a Mendicant Professor* (1969) is his autobiography. He continues to write and to edit poetry anthologies.

EVANS George

1809–81 poet. Born in Woonton in Herefordshire, he lived there until he was eight when the family moved to Walsall. He was apprenticed to a chainmaker at the age of fourteen, later becoming a smith by trade. *Smithy Meditations* appeared in 1847. His work, which includes poems on local places and events as well as on his own trade, was collected and published as *Echoes from Nature* in 1875. He is well represented in Alfred Moss's*, *Songs from the Heart of England* (1920).

EVANS Simon

1895–1940 short story writer, novelist, journalist and broadcaster. From 1926 until his death in Selly

Oak Hospital from the after-effects of poison gas in the First World War, he was postman in Cleobury Mortimer. His published books include the collections of short stories, *Round About the Crooked Steeple* (1931), *At Abdon Burf* (1932), and the autobiographical novel, *Applegarth* (1936).

EVERTON William
early/mid-20th C short story writer. He was born and lived in Walsall. *Rambling Remarks* is dedicated to Jerome K Jerome* – 'for his inspiration'. *There's Nothing Like Leather*, a second volume of short stories, many of them to do with local life and industry, appeared in 1931.

EYLES Margaret Leonora
1889–1960 novelist. Born in Staffordshire, she wrote only one known novel, *Strength of the Spirit* (1930), which describes with much compassion, and no sentiment, the everyday working and domestic lives of women. Her other books are mainly to do with advice to housewives on such things as diet, sex and thrift.

F

FABER Frederick William
1814–63 hymn writer and essayist. He was educated at Shrewsbury School. 'My God, how wonderful thou art' and 'Pilgrims of the night' are perhaps his best-known hymns. He also wrote devotional books.

FARLEY Hugh
early 20th C poet. He lived in Much Wenlock. The collection, *The Singers and Other Poems*, appeared in 1920.

FARMER B J
mid-20th C short story writer. He is believed to have lived for a time in Birmingham. *Advice from Anne* (1931) is a story relating to Handsworth Public Library.

FARMER Edward
1809–76 poet and playwright. Born in Tamworth, he became an inspector on the London and Birmingham Railway when it first opened in 1837. The collection of his poems, *Ned Farmer's Scrapbook*, appeared in 1846 and ran to at least seven editions. He also wrote a farce, *Uncle Gregory*

(1849), and two pantomimes, *Don Quixote de la Mancha* (1852) and *Robin Hood* (1853), all of which were produced at the Birmingham Theatre Royal.

FARNOL Jeffrey
1878–1952 novelist and playwright. Born at 43 Wheeler Street, Lozells in Birmingham, the son of a brass founder, he was educated privately. On returning to the city from London, he worked in his father's foundry, but was not a success in the manufacturing world. A prolific and popular writer of historical thrillers, he is now best known for *The Broad Highway* (1910) and *The Amateur Gentleman* (1913).

FARQUHAR George
1678–1707 playwright. While staying at the Raven Hotel in Castle Street, Shrewsbury, in 1705, he wrote *The Recruiting Officer*. Dedicated to 'all friends round the Wrekin', the play presents a picture of Restoration Shrewsbury. In the same year he stayed at the George Inn in Bird

Street, Lichfield (commemorated by a plaque), while recruiting troops in the city. The inn is the setting in *The Beaux' Stratagem* (1707) for Aimwell and Archer to plot the revival of their fortunes.

FARR S
mid-20th C novelist. He is believed to have lived for some years in Birmingham. *Death on the Downbeat: an Orchestral Fantasy of Detection* (1941) is based on life in the city.

FEARN Susan
late 20th C poet. She was born in Wolverhampton, and worked for a time in an arts studio as an IBM composer operator. No collection of her poems appeared before the end of 1974, but much of her verse, often to do with emotion recollected in tranquillity, had previously been published in magazines including *Midland Read*. Her later work frequently draws on prehistory for inspiration.

FEARNSIDE Ian
b.1948 poet and painter. The owner of an art shop, he lives in Malvern. Many of the poems in the collection, *Scene From the Hills, Poems 1968–74* (1974), were inspired by the locality and vividly describe time and place. His work continues to appear in magazines and has been broadcast on BBC radio. Recent work combines his two interests of poetry and painting.

FEILDING Charles John
1761–88 poet. He was born at Newnham Paddox in the village of Monks Kirby in Warwickshire. *The Brothers, an Eclogue* (1782), dedicated to his brother, William, is celebrated more for its expression of fraternity than for its poetic felicity.

FELL Bernard
late 20th C poet. A missionary for thirty-four years, he has lived in Sutton Coldfield since his return to England. *Verities in Verse* was published in 1972 – in the hope that 'the scattered thoughts in ordered lines will be used by God to His glory'.

FELLOWS Anne
See MANTLE, Winifred

FELLOWS Catherine
late 20th C novelist and poet. She was born in Hereford and educated in Walsall, where she now lives. Her novel, *Leonora*, which was published in 1972, won the Netta Muskett Award from the Romantic Novelists' Association. She continues to write in romantic vein.

FELLOWS Frank Perks
1827–97 poet. Born at Wolverhampton, the son of a schoolmaster, he was educated at his father's school. His only published work, *Poems In Memoriam & The Knights Hospitalers of Saint John of Jerusalem* (1877), is an eccentric collection of pieces which include a poem on the theory and spirit of poetry and an elaborate index.

FELLOWS John
late 18th C poet. Born in Bromsgrove, he lived in the town all his life. His first work was a sacred poem in nine dialogues entitled *Grace Triumphant*. *The Bromsgrove Elegy*, a poem written in blank verse on the death of George Whitefield in 1770, appeared in 1771.

FELLOWS Malcolm Stuart
b.1924 playwright. He was born in Bilston. In 1961 he won the Play of the Year Award for his Armchair Theatre production and in 1966 his

modern morality play, *Come Fly With Me*, was first performed on the steps of Coventry Cathedral.

FELTHAM A E
1870–1943 poet. He lived in Coventry. Many of the poems in *A Few Leaves From the Tree of Everyday Experience* (1920) first appeared in the *Coventry Standard*. The vernacular verses in this collection are his most successful.

FENTON Elijah
1683–1730 poet and playwright. Born at Shelton Old Hall in Hanley and educated at Newcastle-under-Lyme Grammar School, he is best remembered for his translation of *The Odyssey* (1725–6) in collaboration with Alexander Pope*. He also published a volume of poems, *Oxford and Cambridge Miscellany Poems* (1707); and his tragedy, *Marianne*, made a profit of nearly £1,000 when it was performed in 1723.

FENTON Robert
1777–1838 poet. Born at Newcastle-under-Lyme, he was educated in the town and, having been articled to a local firm in 1799, became an attorney. Most of his poems, published in 1800 and 1809, are translations of the classics. The Fenton family produced several other, occasional, poets who contributed to various periodicals.

FERNYHOUGH William
1754–1814 poet. He was born at Great Fenton, the son of a clergyman. The collections, *Trentham Park* (1789) and *Poems on Various Occasions* (1814), are his best-known work. His voice is urbane, kindly and 'true-hearted' – often concerned with the Staffordshire he left in 1771.

FIELD Michael
(the collaborative pseudonym of aunt and niece, Katherine Bradley, 1848–1914, and Edith Cooper, 1862–1913) poet and playwright. Bradley was born in Birmingham, Cooper in Kenilworth. Though well received in contemporary literary circles, their painstaking work, which includes the collection of verse, *Wild Honey* (1908), and the tragedy, *Borgia* (1905), is now almost forgotten.

FIELD William
1768–1851 letter writer and essayist. In 1789 he settled at Warwick as pastor of the Unitarian congregation. A friend of Dr Priestley*, he published *Letters to the Inhabitants of Warwick* to explain and deplore the Birmingham Riots of 1791. An *Historical Account of the Town and Castle of Warwick* appeared in 1815. Samuel Parr said of him, he was 'a dwarf in stature, but a giant in literature'.

FIENNES Celia
1662–1741 diarist and traveller. In her journal, *The Journeys of Celia Fiennes* (1947), edited by C Morris, she described her visit to Worcester on the day William Walsh* was elected to parliament. In 1696 and in 1698 she spent some time in Stretton Grandison in Hereford – at the house of her cousin, John, and at the Foleys' new house in Stoke Edith. Also in 1698 she passed through Shropshire, on her journey from Newcastle-under-Lyme to Cornwall, and visited gardens in Whitchurch and Shrewsbury before making her way through the coalmining area and into Staffordshire. Her work has all the fascination engendered by an enthusiast for the minutiae of life.

FINDLANDER David
mid-20th C poet. He lived in Coventry. His work includes the collections, *Mirrors and Reflections* (1934) and *Without and Within* (1936).

FINNEMORE Emily P
early 20th C novelist. She is believed to have lived for a time in Birmingham. Her novel, *A Brummagem Button* (1907), is set in the city.

FINTAN-JOYCE E
?1900–? poet. He was born and brought up in Birmingham. A collection of his poetry, *Hither and Thither*, in which the verses 'vividly depict the Continental scene', was published in 1968.

FISHER Roy
b.1930 poet. He was born in Birmingham and now lives in Derbyshire. A one-time lecturer at Bordesley College of Education, he later became professor of American Literature at the University of Keele. He can loosely be classified as belonging to the Movement poets, a 1950s' group of writers who determined to re-establish 'the values of rational intelligence and skilful craftsmanship in English poetry'. His published work includes *The Memorial Fountain* (1966), *Ten Interiors with Various Figures* (1966), *Collected Poems* (1969) and *Three Early Pieces* (1971). Considered to be a particularly visual poet, he uses imagery to explore ideas and attitudes as much as to conjure feelings. He continues to write – *Poems 1955–80* being published in 1981 and the long poem, *Furnace*, in 1986.

FISK Rev George
d.1872 poet. From 1835 to 1837 he was rector at Darlaston before becoming vicar of Walsall. From 1843 he was a prebendary of Lichfield Cathedral. Most of his work, including *A Pastor's Memorial of the Holy Land* (1843), is of a religious nature and written in blank verse or prose. But the very moral and moving story, *An Orphan Tale* (1852), is 'told in rhyme'.

FLORENCE OF WORCESTER
d.1118 chronicler. He was a Benedictine monk at Worcester Priory. The claim that he was the author of *Chronicon ex Chronicis* was based on the subject matter, rather than on the style of writing, and is now disputed. With Florence, Layamon* and William Langland*, Worcestershire played no small part in the birth of a specifically English literature.

FOGERTY J
late 19th C novelist. The River Lauter in his three-decker novel, *Lauterdale: a Story of Two Generations* (1873), is a tributary of the River Severn in Shropshire.

FOOTE Samuel
1720–77 playwright and actor. He was educated at King's School in Worcester. Known as 'the English Aristophanes' for his witty, but often savage, caricatures of contemporary figures, he built the new Haymarket in London in 1767. His plays, which include *The Devil Upon Two Sticks* (1768), *The Lame Lover* (1770) and *Piety in Pattens* (1773), are now seldom performed, being of topical rather than dramatic interest.

FORD Norrey
See DILCOCK, Noreen

FORSHAW Charles Frederick
1863–1917 poet, biographer and essayist. Born in Bilston, he studied to

become a dentist. Though widely known as the 'Poets' Biographer', he also published his own work. The first collection, *Wanderings of Imagery*, appeared in 1886; his last, *Poetical Tributes to the Late Lord Kitchener*, in 1916. Much of his work is concerned with the creative process of trying to express thoughts and feelings through the medium of verse.

FORSTER E M
1879–1970 novelist. The Shropshire settings in *Howards End* (1910) were inspired by his visits to Shrewsbury and Clun. His work, which includes *Where Angels Fear to Tread* (1905), *The Longest Journey* (1907), *A Room with a View* (1908) and *A Passage to India* (1924), is enjoying a respectful revival via the media of film and television.

FOSBROKE Thomas Dudley
1770–1842 poet and antiquarian. His family came from Staffordshire. In 1810 he went as curate to Walford in Herefordshire, became vicar there in 1830 and stayed for the rest of his life. His literary interests were catholic, ranging from Anglo-Saxon poetry to the 'manufactures' of the Romans. His poem, *The Economy of Monastic Life*, was published in 1795.

FOSTER Nancy
1913–33 poet. She was born and brought up in Hednesford in Staffordshire. A memorial collection of her poems was published in 1934 following her early death.

FOURDRINIER Harriet E
mid-19th C novelist. She lived in Northwood in Shropshire. *Our New Parish*, which tells a story of homely struggles and triumphs, appeared in 1852.

FOWLER Ellen Thorneycroft
1860–1929 poet and novelist. She was born at Summerfield, a house near the West Park in Wolverhampton, the daughter of the one-time mayor of, and MP for, the town. He became a Cabinet minister and was later knighted. Her novels, often with clearly identifiable midland settings, tended to the melodramatic and are now almost entirely forgotten – though her first, *Concerning Isabel Carnaby* (1890), sold 250,000 copies.

FOWLER Sydney
1874–1965 (pseudonym of Sydney Fowler Wright) poet, novelist, short story writer and editor. Born in Smethwick and educated at King Edward's School in Birmingham, he was an accountant in the city for twenty-five years before becoming a writer. Many of his novels, among them *The Bell Street Murders* (1931) and *Who Killed Reynard?* (1947), belong to the crime fiction genre. Though primarily a poetry editor, he also produced original work including a subtle and imaginative version of *The Songs of Bilitis* (1922). *The Throne of Saturn* (1952) is a collection of short stories.

FOX-DAVIES Arthur Charles
1871–1928 novelist. In the 1880s his family moved to Coalbrookdale where he remained all his life and is buried in the churchyard. Though most of his books are concerned with heraldry, he also wrote detective novels which include *The Dangerous Inheritance* (1907) and *The Duplicate Death* (1910).

FRAUNCE Abraham
1558–95 poet. He was born in Shropshire and educated at Shrewsbury School. He probably settled in Ludlow in 1588, after he had been

called to the Bar. His early Latin comedy, *Victoria*, was written about 1583. Later works include *The Shepheardes Logike* (1586) and *The Lawiers Logike* (1588).

FREE John
See FREETH, John

FREEMAN Edward Augustus
1823–92 historian, essayist and poet. He was born at Mitchley Abbey near Harborne. Most of his work, including the four volumes of *Historical Essays* (1871, 1873, 1879 and 1892), is concerned with history and commentary, but he contributed several poems to the collection, *Original Ballads By Living Authors*, which appeared in 1850.

FREEMAN Gage Earle
1820–1903 poet. Born in Tamworth, the son of an army captain, he was a frequent visitor to the estate of his friend, Sir Philip Brockenhirst, at Swythamley Park. While here he enjoyed the falconry, especially the hawking, and wrote many poems and dramatic verse on this, his favourite sport. Five poems from his collection, *Christmas Poems*, appeared in *The Field* in 1860.

FREEMAN Hollis
late 19th C poet. He is believed to have lived in Shropshire. The collection, *An Illusive Quest and Other Poems* (1893), reveals his interest in many subjects.

FREEMAN John
1853–1944 short story writer. Born in Bilston, he lived there all his life – attending St Luke's School, working as a railway clerk and later employed at Joseph Sankey and Sons where he remained for over fifty years. Under the pseudonym of John Dangerfield, he contributed stories and articles to

the *Methodist Recorder*. In 1931 these stories were collected and published under his own name as *Black Country Stories and Sketches*.

FREETH John
1731–1808 poet and songwriter. Born in Birmingham, the son of a coffee house owner, he was apprenticed to a brass founder, but soon returned, as host, to the more convivial atmosphere of his father's business. His first published work, inspired by the Birmingham canal, appeared in 1769. His second, printed by John Baskerville, appeared in 1771 under the name of John Free. It was entitled *The Political Songster* and was addressed to the 'Sons of Freedom and Lovers of Liberty'. Many more volumes of songs, especially of the topical variety, were to follow.

FROST Arthur Broadfield
late 19th C novelist and doctor. He practised medicine in both Walsall and Rugby. *Nightlights* (1895), subtitled *Shadows from a Doctor's Reading Lamp*, a delightfully irreverent account of several incidents, medical and otherwise, ran to several editions.

FROST Robert
1874–1963 poet. An American, he lived and farmed just outside Ledbury in Herefordshire from 1912 to 1915, after which he returned to the States. His first collections of poems, *A Boy's Will* (1913) and *North of Boston* (1914), were first published in England. *Collected Poems* (1930) won him the Pulitzer Prize. His reputation continues to grow.

FULLER Thomas
1608–61 essayist and moralist. He travelled extensively in the west

midland counties researching for his *History of the Worthies of England* (1662). This decidedly moralising directory to famous places and people was dedicated to Charles II. His other work includes a book of 'characters' entitled *The Holy State and the Profane State*.

FULLERTON Lady Georgiana
1812–85 novelist and poet. Born at Tixall Hall in Staffordshire, the youngest daughter of Lord Granville, she published three novels, *Ellen*

Middleton (1844), *Grantley Manor* (1847) and *Lady Bird* (1852), and a collection of sixty short poems entitled *The Gold-digger and Other Verses* (1872).

FURLONG Agnes
mid-20th C children's writer. She lived in Coventry where she taught at the City of Coventry Training College. Her work includes *Sword of State* (1952), which is set in Coventry, and *Elizabeth Leaves School* (1956).

G

GALLETLEY Leonard
b.1872 poet. Born at Cannock, he was a student at the University of Birmingham and lived most of his life in Shropshire. He wrote several volumes of poetry, among them *The Call of the Miles* (1916), *Inishtor and Other Poems* (1925), *Evening on the Morddach Estuary* (1929) and *An English Village* (1933).

GARFITT Roger
b.1944 poet. He lives in Hereford. His first collection of poetry, *Caught in Blue* (1971), was followed by *Selected Poems* (1974). He has contributed to *Ambit*, *Encounter*, *Isis* and the *Poetry Review* among other periodicals.

GARNER Robert
1809–90 poet. Born in Longton, the son of a potter, he was educated at Aston Hall and Sedgley Park. A doctor of considerable reputation in Stoke-on-Trent, he also wrote several poems which appeared in the *Potteries' Mechanics' Magazine*.

GARNETT Henry
mid-20th C novelist. He has lived in Kidderminster and in Malvern where he wrote *Rough Water Brown* (1952) and *Secret of the Rocks* (1958), both to do with the history of the River Severn and the Worcestershire countryside, and the historical novel, *Gamble for a Throne* (1960).

GARNETT Richard
1835–1906 poet and short story writer. Born in Lichfield, the son of a clergyman, he became Keeper of Printed Books at the British Museum. He is now remembered chiefly for *The Twilight of the Gods* (1888), a reworking of eastern and classic fables.

GARRICK David
1717–79 actor and playwright. By chance – his father, a major in the army, accompanied by his wife, was at the time recruiting in the district – he was born in Hereford; and was baptised at the Church of All Saints. The family then made its way to Lichfield where his mother had lived as a girl. Here he was both a school-fellow, at the grammar school, and a

pupil, at Edial School, of Dr Johnson*. Though best known for the quality of his acting, he wrote several witty and amusing plays and sketches, amongst them *The Lying Valet* (1741), *Miss in her Teens* (1774) and *The Irish Widow* (1772).

David Garrick

GASCOIGNE George
1525–77 poet, playwright and story writer. In *The Princely Pleasures of the Court of Kenilworthe* he describes Elizabeth I's last stay in the castle in 1575. Though one of many published stories, *The Adventures of Master F.J.* (1573), a story of sexual intrigue, is the only work to have lasted into the twentieth century.

GASKELL Catherine Milnes
1857–1935 novelist. In 1876, after her marriage to Gerald Milnes Gaskell, she came to live in Wenlock Abbey where she regularly entertained literary visitors, including Henry James* and Thomas Hardy and his wife, Emma. Her own work consisted of books on Shropshire, such as *Spring in a Shropshire Abbey* (1905), and light fiction, such as *Episodes in the Lives of a Shropshire Lass and Lad* (1908).

GASKELL Mrs Elizabeth
1810–65 novelist and biographer. She attended Avonbank School in Stratford-upon-Avon. Her first published work was the chapter on Stratford in William Howitt's, *Visits to Remarkable Places* (1840). To what extent her brief stay in the town influenced her work would be difficult to gauge, but her evocation of place, whether urban or provincial – in *Mary Barton* (1848) and *North and South* (1855), for example – is always exact and unsentimental.

GATER Paul
b.1938 poet and playwright. Born in Stoke-on-Trent, he is foreman at Trentham Gardens near the city. His play, *Biddy and Perry*, was performed at the city's Victoria Theatre in 1969. His work accurately reflects life in the Potteries in that 'he does not ignore deformity of landscape or minds, but when he comes across beauty ... he offers it to the reader with child-like enjoyment'.

GEE A L
late 19th C poet. He is believed to have lived in Leek. His poem, *The Record of the Hills*, is about the town and its surroundings.

GIBBINGS Robert John
1889–1958 essayist and traveller. His book, *Coming Down the Wye* (1942), is a delightfully acerbic account of the virtues and shortcomings of Herefordshire and its inhabitants.

GIBBONS Gavin
1922–78 linguist and novelist. Born in Shropshire, he was educated at Shrewsbury School, and returned to live in the county in the 1950s – latterly at Meole Brace. Most of his work is concerned with the world of facts rather than that of the imagina-

tion; but he also wrote a science fiction novel, *By Space Ship to the Moon* (1958), subtitled *A Tale of Adventure in Outer Space for Boys*.

GIFFORD Richard
1725–1807 poet. He was born at Bishop's Castle in Shropshire and later became curate at Richard's Castle in Herefordshire. His poetry can still be found in the more traditional anthologies. 'Contemplations: a poem' (1753) is quoted by Dr Johnson* in his *Dictionary*.

GILL Thomas Hornblower
1819–1906 poet and hymn writer. Born in Birmingham, he was educated at the grammar school. Though he published several volumes of poetry, including *The Fortunes of Faith* (1841) and *Anniversaries* (1857), he is best known for his hymns. They were collected and published as *The Golden Chain of Praise* in 1868.

GILLAM J G
mid-20th C novelist. He is believed to have lived, or stayed extensively, in Birmingham. *The Crucible* (1954) relates the story of Joseph Priestley*, including his persecution at the hands of the Birmingham mob in 1791.

GILLINGHAM George W
mid-20th C novelist. He lived in Ombersley rectory in Worcestershire. His only known fictional work, *The Cardinal's Treasure, a Romance of Elizabethan Days*, was published in 1951. He also wrote *Ombersley: Historical and Sporting Guide*.

GILMORE Alfred J
early 20th C poet. He lived in Birmingham. The collection, *Patriotic Poems of the Great War 1914–15–16*, described as 'a poetical history of the many thrilling events of the war', appeared in 1916.

GISBORNE Thomas
1758–1846 poet. Curate of Barton-under-Needwood near Burton-on-Trent, he inherited Yoxall Lodge from his father. His long poem, *Walks in the Forest* (1794), was very popular in its time.

GISSING George
1857–1903 novelist. He is believed to have been educated at a Quaker boarding school in Worcester, though some commentators mention a school at Alderley Edge in Cheshire. His story, *In the Year of the Jubilee* (1895), relates to Birmingham. A writer of genius condemned by his circumstances to a much resented, and possibly exaggerated, drudgery, he is now best remembered for the two autobiographical novels, *New Grub Street* (1891) and *The Private Papers of Henry Ryecroft (1903)*.

GITTINGS Christine
mid-20th C poet and short story writer. She has lived all her life in Birmingham. Her poems, short stories and articles have appeared in several of the Birmingham newspapers as well as in the *Farmers' Weekly*, *Good Housekeeping* and *The Lady*. Much of her work is to do with the fantastic and the occult.

GLYN Herbert
mid-19th C (pseudonym of Edwin Pettitt) novelist. Father of Henry Pettitt* and a civil engineer, he published only two known works of fiction, *The Cotton Lord* (1862), in two volumes, and *Uncle Crotty's Relations* (1863), also in two volumes.

GODDARD John
b.1845 poet and playwright. The author of *Jack and the Beanstalk* (1869), *Old King Cole* and several

other pantomime pieces, he was born at Wednesbury.

GODWIN Bishop Francis

1562–1633 novelist. Appointed Bishop of Hereford in 1617, he died at his palace in Whitbourne. His novel, *The Man in the Moone* (published posthumously in 1638), must be one of the earliest examples of science fiction. It is decidedly prophetic in its descriptions of men flying 'from place to place in the ayre' and of their sending 'messages in an instant many Miles off'.

GOODALL C

mid-20th C novelist. He is believed to have lived in Birmingham. *Without Trace* (1938) relates to the city.

GOODALL Nan

mid-20th C children's writer. The daughter of a master at Bablake School in Coventry, she was born in the city and educated at Barr's Hill School. *Donkeys' Glory* appeared in 1959.

GOODERE Sir Henry

1571–1627 poet. He was born in Monks Kirby in Warwickshire and in 1595, on the death of his uncle, he inherited the title and estates of Polesworth. An amateur poet of court-liness and some vivacity, he is probably best remembered for his friendship with John Donne* who, while staying at Polesworth in 1613, collaborated with his host in a poem addressed to their respective wives. Sir Henry's name is severally spelled Goodere, Goodyer, Goodier or Goodyere. The choice is yours it seems.

GOODWIN Geraint

1903–41 novelist and short story writer. He is believed to have lived in west Shropshire. *The White Farm*

(1937), *Watch for the Morning* (1938) and *Come Michaelmas* (1939) are set in the Shropshire border country.

GORDON Adam Lindsay

1833–70 poet. A pupil at Worcester Royal Grammar School, he was brought up in the city by an uncle. His poems, published posthumously in three volumes in 1880, were obviously much influenced by the sporting company he kept in the inns and on the racecourses throughout Worcestershire.

GORDON Rev Alexander

b.1809 poet. He was minister at Bridge Street Congregational Chapel in Walsall from 1847 to 1872. *Heart-Effusions, being Original Hymns and Other Pieces* appeared in 1857. He is represented in Alfred Moss's*, *Songs from the Heart of England* (1920), by a somewhat sardonic piece entitled 'Sense and Sound'.

GOUGH George W

1869–1948 novelist. Born in Stafford, he was educated there at the King Edward VI Grammar School. His most famous novel, *The Yeoman Adventurer* (1916), is set in the town.

GOUGH T

1863–1943 short story writer. In 1886 he set up an accountancy practice in Dudley. His dialect stories originally appeared in the *County Advertiser* which he owned for ten years. In 1942 they were published in an omnibus edition by the Black Country Society.

GRAVES Charles

b.1892 poet. For a time he was on the staff of the *Leamington Spa Courier*. *The Bamboo Grove and Other Poems* (1925), *The Wood of Time and Other Poems* (1938), *Votive Sonnets* (1964) and *Emblems of Love and War* (1970) are among his published slim volumes. *Collected Poems* appeared in 1972.

GRAZEBROOK Francis
1884–1974 poet and novelist. He was born in Dudley. Having become an ironmaster and a co-director of Stourton Castle, he was later appointed a magistrate. His best-known works are a volume of poems, *Pilgrimage of a Thousand Years* (1920), and a novel, *Nicanor of Athens (1946)*.

GREATHEED Bertie Bertie
d.1826 playwright. He lived at Guy's Cliffe in Warwickshire (reputed to be the last house and burial place of Guy of Warwick, the legendary ancestor of the earls of Warwick). His tragedy, *The Regent*, which was founded on a Spanish story and dedicated to Sarah Siddons, proved to be a great success when it was produced at Drury Lane in 1788.

GREEN Bassett
1869–1962 poet and children's writer. He lived in Coventry. His work includes the collections of poems, *The Dawn and Other Poems* (1918) and *Storm and Other Poems* (1936), and two children's stories, both published in 1949, *A Cotswold Tragedy* and *The Fairies' Wedding*. In the same year, he presented the city with a statue of Lady Godiva which stands in Broadgate.

GREEN Gray
b.1952 (pseudonym of Graham Martin Green) poet. Born and brought up in Birmingham, he has recently returned to the city to live in Hall Green. His work includes *Wordwood* (1970), *Jokes by the Poet* (1971), *Spoke* (1972), *Dearth* (1972) and *Unmoons* (1974). He continues to write – with a sharp ear for the images and absurdities of everyday speech.

GREEN Henry
1905–73 (pseudonym of Henry Vincent Yorke) novelist. Although he worked in the London office of the family engineering business, he frequently visited the works in Birmingham. His novels, in which character and atmosphere emerge through dialogue, are enjoying a revival. Probably the best-known, and the best, are *Living* (1929), *Party Going* (1939) and *Loving* (1945). *Pack My Bag* (1930) is autobiographical.

GREEN J C R
b.1949 poet. He has lived in Warwickshire, during which time he organised the first Birmingham Poetry Festival in 1971. *By Weight of Reason*, a collection of original verse and translations, many of them to do with love and death, was published in 1974.

GREEN Marjorie
late 20th C novelist, playwright and short story writer. She lives in Walsall. *Heads You Win*, a one-act comedy for eight women, and *The Peaceful Days*, a comedy for seven women, both appeared in 1972. More recently, she has tended to concentrate on the writing of novels – mainly of the romantic kind.

GREEN Russell
mid-20th C novelist. He lived in Birmingham. His novel, *Prophet Without Honour* (1934), relates to the counties of the west midlands.

GRESLEY Rev William
1801–76 novelist. He lived in Kenilworth. His novel about the English Reformation, *The Forest of Arden* (1841), is set in Warwickshire.

GREVILLE Sir Fulke
1554–1628 poet, playwright and biographer. He was educated at Shrewsbury School, an exact contemporary of Sir Philip Sidney*, whose friend and biographer he was to become. In 1619 James I gave him Warwick Castle, in recognition of his services as Chancellor of the Exchequer, and in 1621 created him Baron Brooke. He was assassinated by a servant, resentful of being excluded from his will, and is buried in St Mary's Church. His poems, collected in *Caelica* and published posthumously in 1633, were greatly influenced by Sidney's preoccupation with secular love. Both his tragedies, *Alaham* and *Mustapha*, are concerned with political science in the Machiavellian sense. His *Life of the Renowned Sir Philip Sidney* (begun in 1610, but not published until 1652) is as much about his own ideas and ideals as about those of his friend and mentor.

GRICE Deryck
b.1948 poet. A founder of the drama group Pleck, he trained at Walsall Teachers Training College and now lives in Pedmore near Stourbridge. His verse has appeared in various periodicals including the *Radio Times*. *Child*, a dialogue between a child and a number of different adults, was published in 1973. He continues to write verse and verse drama.

GRICE Frederick
1910–83 children's writer and poet. Until 1971 he was head of the English department at Worcester College of Higher Education and lived in the city. Most of his many books, including *The Bonny Pit Laddy* (1960), *The Oak and the Ash* (1968), *The Black Hand Gang* (1971) and

Young Tome Sawbones (1974), relate to Durham; but *A Severnside Story* (1964), set in the fictional town of Severnbury, belongs to the west midland counties, as does the children's book, *Jimmy Lane and his Boat* (1963), which is about the River Severn. He compiled ten collections of local stories, the first being *Folk Tales of the West Midlands* (1952). In 1977 he won the 'Other Award' for children's writing.

GRIFFITHS George
1812–83 essayist, poet and playwright. Born in Birmingham, he was later a corn merchant in Bewdley. His writings were of the 'history, history-romance, drama, satire, and a miscellaneous worship of the muse' type; and include *The Life and Adventures of George Wilson, a Foundation Scholar* (1854), the tragedy, *The Two Houses* (1866), *Ribbesford and Other Poems* (1868) and the social commentary, *Going to Markets and Grammar Schools* (1870).

GRIGSON Geoffrey
b.1905 poet and novelist. His novel, *A Skull in Salop* (1967), is set in the county of Shropshire where he is believed to have lived for a time. Other work includes *Under the Cliff* (1943), *The Isles of Scilly* (1946) and the splendid love poems, *Legenda Suecana* (1953)

GRINDROD Charles F
late 19th C novelist and poet. A local historian, he lived in Birtsmorton near Malvern. *The Stranger's Story* and his poem, 'The Lament of Love' (1883), are both set in the Malvern Hills. *The Shadow of the Raggedstone* (1889), a novel set in Little Malvern at the southern end of the Malvern range, retells the legend of the weird shadow

which is reputed to be a harbinger of death and disaster when it is seen above the hills.

GRUBB David H W
b.1941 poet. He lived for a time in Malvern where he was deputy head of a comprehensive school. *And Suddenly This* (1972), *From the White Room* (1974) and *Somewhere There Are Trains* (1974) are among his books of poetry which accurately identifies and celebrates those small moments that, for most of us, manage

to compensate for the more stressful aspects of life. As far as is known, he continues to write.

GUEDALLA Philip
1889–1944 novelist, parodist and biographer. He was educated at Rugby School. Irreverent and witty, he is now remembered chiefly for his political biographies – especially those of Gladstone and Palmerston (1928). His fictional work includes *Ignes Fatui: A Book of Parodies* (1911).

H

HABINGTON William
1605–64 poet and playwright. He was born at Hindlip in Worcestershire, the son of Thomas Habington, the historian. *Castara*, a collection of love poems dedicated to his wife, Lucy, was published in 1635. A tragi-comic play, *Queene of Arragon*, appeared in 1640. He is buried in the family vault at Hindlip.

HACKETT W W
1874–1964 poet. He was born in Birmingham and educated at Dudley Road School. Later he lived in West Bromwich and worked for the engineering firm of Accles and Pollock, famous from a literary point of view for their Spooneristic advertisements in tube trains. *Poems for My Friends Mainly about My Friends* appeared in 1948.

HADDON Christopher
See PALMER, John Leslie

HALL Brian R
mid-20th C children's writer. He has lived in Kidderminster. The adventure story, *Abdul the Grey*, appeared in

1964.

HALL (or HALLE) Edward
1499–1547 chronicler. His father came from Shropshire and he himself represented Bridgnorth in the parliament of 1542. *Hall's Chronicle* (a study of the York and Lancaster dynasties, which was published posthumously and banned by Mary Tudor in 1555) was almost certainly used by William Shakespeare* as a source for some of his history plays.

HALL Patrick
b.1934 novelist. Born in Aston and educated at Moseley Grammar School, he has worked in the town clerk's office, at Cadburys in Bournville and at Kalamazoo in Longbridge. His novel, *The Harp that Once* (1967), which is set in Birmingham, was later filmed as *The Reckoning* (starring Nicol Williamson and Rachel Roberts, its setting being transferred to Liverpool in obedience, presumably, to the demands of sixties' Beatlemania). The greater part of *The India Man* (1968) is also set in Birmingham.

HALL Radclyffe
1886–1943 poet and novelist. She lived for a time in Malvern. Although her novel, *Adam's Breed* (1926), was awarded prizes in both England and France, she is now remembered chiefly for *The Well of Loneliness* (1928) which, until 1949, was banned in this country for its theme of lesbianism. Poetic works include *'Twixt Earth and Stars* (1906), *Poems of the Past and Present* (1910) and *Songs of Three Counties* (1913).

HALL Ronald
b.1929 novelist. He was born in Coventry. His only known work, *The Open Cage*, appeared in 1970.

HALWARD Leslie
1906–76 novelist. Born in Birmingham, the son of a butcher, he was a plasterer by trade before joining the RAF at the start of the Second World War. He was a member of the 1930s Birmingham Group which included Walter E Allen*, Walter Brierley*, Peter Chamberlain* and John Hampson* (see HAMPSON, John). Among his work are two collections of short stories, *To Tea on Sunday* (1936) and *The Money's All Right* (1938), a novella, *Gus and Ida* (1938), and the autobiographical, *Let Me Tell You* (1938). He later lived near Malvern.

HAMMOND Emillie
mid-20th C poet. She was born in Wednesbury, but lived most of her life in Wolverhampton. Her best-known work is almost certainly 'The Women's Institute Song' (to be sung to the tune of 'Bonny Dundee'), which begins 'Come, matrons and maidens, from far and from nigh'.

HAMPER William
1776–1831 poet and antiquarian.

Born in Birmingham, the son of a brass founder, he went into his father's business which he greatly improved and enlarged. Most of his verse has a historical or mythical background, the best known being *The Devil's Dike, a Sussex Legend* which appeared in the *Gentleman's Magazine* in 1810.

HAMPSON John
1900–55 novelist and short story writer. The grandson of the manager of Birmingham's Theatre Royal, he was born and lived in the city. All his work, which includes *Saturday Night at the Greyhound* (1931) and *Family Curse* (1936), has a west midland setting. He was radio critic for the *Birmingham Evening Dispatch* from 1946. In the same year a radio play, *You Can Keep Your Christmas Pudding*, was broadcast. His early experiences as an hotel waiter and kitchen boy were recorded in *Care of the Grand*. With Walter E Allen*, Walter Brierley*, Peter Chamberlain* and Leslie Halward* he formed the Birmingham Group of writers much concerned with exposing contemporary life – warts and all.

HANKEY Donald
1884–1916 essayist, short story writer and letter writer. Educated at Rugby School, he wrote about army life, travel and living rough – but all his work had an underlying religious purpose. *Letters of Donald Hankey* (1919), introduced by Edward Miller, does not, unfortunately for this guide, refer to his schooldays. A collection of essays, *A Student in Arms* (1916), made his name widely known.

HARDING Sylvester
1745–1809 poet and painter. Born at Newcastle-under-Lyme, he was an apprentice in his father's coach-

building business before joining a band of 'strolling players'. His poem, 'The Disaster, Strawberry Hill', has as its subject the engraver, William Banastree.

HARE Cyril
1900–58 (pseudonym of Alfred Alexander Gordon Clark) novelist. He was educated at Rugby School. Most of his novels, which are rather superior examples of the crime fiction genre, draw on his experiences as barrister and judge. His best-known is *Tragedy at Law* (1942).

HARINGTON Lucy, Countess of Bedford
d. 1627 poet and patroness. The daughter of John, 1st Lord Harington, she was brought up at Combe Abbey in Warwickshire. Though none of her own work survives, she is remembered for her patronage of John Donne*, Dr Johnson* and Michael Drayton*.

HARPER Frederick
b.1901 novelist. Born in Gordon Street, Burslem, he later lived in several different houses in Stoke-on-Trent. In 1928 he was elected to the city council. *Tilewright's Acre* (1959), a story about the potters of Staffordshire, is the first volume of a planned trilogy which was never, so far as is known, completed. The novel, *Joseph Capper* (1962), which deals sympathetically but unsentimentally with an industrial society, is also set in the Potteries.

HARRADEN Beatrice
1864–1963 novelist and short story writer. Her story, *At the Green Dragon* (1894), was inspired by her frequent visits to Little Stretton as a young woman. While lodging at the Green Dragon in the village, she spent her time in writing and walking on the

Long Mynd. Of her many novels, *Ships That Pass in the Night* (1893) was a bestseller.

HARRIS Derek
b.1945 novelist and critic. He was born and brought up in Wolverhampton where his first novel, *And Then Came Summer* (1961), is set. *Luis Cernuda*, a study of that poet's work, appeared in 1977.

HARRIS John
early 20th C poet. He is believed to have lived in Norbury in Shropshire. His only known collection, *Poems of Idle Hours*, appeared in 1903.

HARRISON Mrs Anna
1797–1881 poet and diarist. The elder sister of Mary Howitt*, she was born at Uttoxeter. Apparently there is no copy still in existence of her one work – published posthumously in 1893 and entitled *Poems, Reprinted With Life, Letters, and Journal, With Illustrations by her Daughter A.M.Harrison.*

HARRISON Arthur Cyril
b.1893 poet. Born in Walsall, he was educated at Butts Council School and Queen Mary's Grammar School. Some of his verses appear in Alfred Moss's*, *Songs from the Heart of England* (1920).

HARRISON F Bayford
late 19th C novelist. The author of several moral tales, he is believed to have lived in Shropshire. *Battlefield Treasure* (1889), a story of self-interest ultimately governed and denied, is set in and near Shrewsbury.

HARRISON Harry
late 20th C poet. He was born in Tipton in Staffordshire and educated at Princes End Primary School and Dudley Grammar School. When he left school he worked successively in

a shop, a foundry, a factory and as a pipe layer. He still lives in Tipton. Although the collection of his Black Country dialect poems, *Off the Cuff*, did not appear until 1975, he was already an established published, presented and broadcast poet. The characters of Enoch and Eli, who figure largely in his work, are fictional – though 'their kith and kin still walk the pavements of the Black Country streets'.

HARRISON Hubert Deacon
b.1898 poet. He was born in Walsall and, like Arthur Cyril Harrison*, who was possibly a brother or cousin, was educated at Butts Council School and Queen Mary's Grammar School. A sample of his work also appears in Alfred Moss's*, *Songs from the Heart of England* (1920).

HARRISON John
late 19th C poet. He lived in Birmingham. The collection, *Imaginary Loves and Other Poems*, of which several are addressed to members of the 'fair sex', appeared in 1880.

HART J Laurence
1850–1907 poet and artist. He was born at Harborne. After being articled to a firm of designers in Birmingham, he enrolled as a student at Birmingham School of Art. He lived in several parts of the west midland area, including Northfield, Stratford-upon-Avon, Leamington Spa and Birdingbury. Though he was known chiefly as an artist, a collection of his poems was published in 1912, five years after his death.

HARVEY Christopher
1597–1663 poet. He became vicar at Clifton-upon-Dunsmoor in Warwickshire in 1639; and a trustee of Rugby

School in 1653. His most important work, *The Synagogue*, a series of verses on the Book of Common Prayer, appeared in 1640.

HARVEY John Augustus
b.1908 songwriter and composer. Born in Lonsdale Street in Stoke-on-Trent, he became musical adviser to Staffordshire County Council Special Training Centres and speech adviser to Stallington Hall Hospital School. Publications include *Articulation and Activity Songs* (1955), *Mouth Percussing Songs* (1956), *Four Simple Songs for Young People* (1956) and *Sense, Speech and Concentration Training* (1959).

HATHAWAY Richard
late 16th/early 17th C poet and playwright. He is presumed to belong to the Hathaway family of Shottery in Warwickshire, which included William Shakespeare's* wife, Anne. As was common at that time, he collaborated with several other playwrights, including Thomas Dekker*. It was with Michael Drayton*, Anthony Munday and Robert Wilson that he wrote *The First Part of the True and Honourable History of the Life of Sir John Oldcastle, the Good Lord Cobham* which was successfully produced in 1599.

HATTON Charles
1905–77 novelist, journalist and media writer. Born at Kingswinford, Wordsley, he attended the Glynne Church of England School where he won a scholarship to King Edward VI Grammar School in Stourbridge. From 1923, while writing stage and radio plays, he spent nine years, six of them in Brierley Hill, working in local branches of the Midland Bank. He moved to Worcester in 1942 and in 1949 left the district to go to

Orpington in Kent where he began writing for television. Of his published novels, *No Trees in the Street* (1959) was the most successful.

HAVERGAL Frances Ridley
1836–79 poet, essayist and hymn writer. She was born in Astley near Stourport, the youngest child of the rector, W H Havergal*, and is buried there. Thirty books of her devotional writings have been published, the latest in 1962. They were extremely popular – especially *The Ministry of Song* (1870), *Under the Surface* (1874) and *Loyal Responses* (1878). Her sister collected her poems and published them in two volumes in 1884.

HAVERGAL Rev William Henry
1793–1870 hymn writer. From 1822 he was successively curate of Astley near Stourport, rector of Astley, rector of St Nicholas in Worcester and rector of Snareshill. Having been thrown from his carriage in 1829, he used the enforced rest to compose sacred music and, perhaps not quite so successfully, to write sacred songs and carols. Somewhat confusingly he named one of his sons Francis and one of his daughters Frances. Life is really difficult enough.

HAVINS Peter J Neville
late 20th C poet. He was born in Birmingham. His poems were broadcast and published in *New Writing* and in other periodicals, though *Matchbox*, the first collection of his work, did not appear until 1975. He continues to write, *Notes from Empty Churches* appearing in 1981.

HAWKES Jacquetta
b.1910 poet and short story writer. With her husband, J B Priestley*, she lived in Alveston near Stratford-upon-Avon. Though best known for her work on anthropology and archaeology, she also published a collection of poems, *Symbols and Speculations* (1948), and a collection of short stories, *Fables* (1953).

HAWLEY John Hugh
mid/late 19th C poet and linguist. He lived in Leamington Spa. His work includes two slim volumes of verse, *Ode to Her Majesty Queen Victoria on her sixtieth birthday, etc* (1879) and *In Memoriam, Louis Eugène Napoleon ... The Return ... The Greetings, etc* (1880), and several books on English grammar.

HAWTHORNE Nathaniel
1804–64 novelist and short story writer. While travelling in the west midland counties in the 1850s on a pilgrimage to see Dr Johnson's* homeland, he stayed at the Lion Hotel in Shrewsbury, visited Lichfield, dined sumptuously at the Nag's Head in Uttoxeter for only 18d and stayed at 10 Lansdowne Crescent in Leamington Spa writing much of *Our Old Home* (1863), an account of these midland wanderings. Perhaps best known in this country for *The Scarlet Letter* (1850), he is now universally acknowledged as one of America's finest writers.

HAY Mary Cecil
1840–80 novelist. Her work is almost exclusively to do with the rewards meted out to the virtuous in an idealised world. *Old Myddleton's Money* (1875) is set in Shropshire.

HAYDEN Rosa Ayscoughe
1855–1922 poet. Born and brought up in Handsworth in Birmingham, she published several volumes of poetry which included *In Sunlight and Shadow* (1912) and *This for Remem-*

brance (1917). Though perhaps too persistently optimistic, her work is pleasingly lyrical.

HAYES Alfred
1857–1936 poet. Born at Chapel Ash, he was educated at Wolverhampton Grammar School and at King Edward's School in Birmingham. After teaching at Brewood Grammar School he moved to Edgbaston and taught at King Edward's School in Birmingham. He published several volumes of poetry, much of it of an unrelievedly sombre tone and including *The Last Crusade and Other Poems* (1885), contributions to *A Fellowship of Song* (1893), *The Vale of Arden* (1895) and *The Cup of Quietness* (1911).

HAYLES Brian
b.1931 playwright and children's writer. A schoolmaster, he lived for a while in Moseley in Birmingham. His work includes stage, radio and television plays, among them episodes of *Z-Cars*, *Dr Who*, *Crossroads* and *Dixon of Dock Green*, and the serial, *Legend of Death* (1965).

HAYNES H L
mid-20th C poet. Many of the poems in *A Ballad of Evesham and Other Verses* (1933), which first appeared in print in the *Saturday Review*, are set in Worcestershire.

HAZELDEAN Jock o'
late 19th C poet. Born in Longton in Staffordshire, he was the author of *Miscellaneous Rhymes* (1878). His work is mostly concerned with local matters and interests.

HAZLITT William
1778–1830 essayist and critic. He was brought to live in Noble Street in Wem at the age of eight when his father was appointed Unitarian minister in the town. His first published work was a letter to the *Shrewsbury Chronicle* in 1791, protesting at Joseph Priestley's* treatment in Birmingham. In 1808 he went to hear Samuel Taylor Coleridge* preach in Shrewsbury Unitarian Chapel – an occasion recorded in *Conversations with Poets* (1823). His youthful years in Shropshire are detailed in *Life of William Hazlitt* (1922) by P P Howe. He is best known for *Characters from Shakespeare* (1817–18) and *Lectures on the English Poets* (1818–19).

HEATH George
1844–69 poet. Born at Gratton in Staffordshire, he went to school in the neighbouring village of Horton and later worked on his father's farm before being apprenticed to a joiner and builder in Gratton. His work, which is often sad and sometimes morbid, was admired by R W Buchanan*. *Simple Poems* appeared in 1865; *Heartstrings* in 1866; and *Tired Out* in 1869. His collected poems, many of them about the district around Rudyard, were published posthumously in 1870 as *The Poems of George Heath – Moorland Poet*.

HEATH Noah
b.?1780 potter and poet. Born at Sneyd Green in Staffordshire, the son of a potter, he attended a free school at Far Green – though it was at the Methodist Sunday School in Burslem that his taste for poetry was encouraged. He became first a potter, then later a modeller and mould-maker. Broad of humour, he wrote vividly of what he saw in the ordinary life of the Potteries. His collection, *Miscellaneous Poems*, which includes the much anthologised 'Lines Wrote

Upon Mow Cop', was published in two volumes in 1823.

HEBER Reginald
1783–1826 hymn writer and poet. Educated at Whitchurch Grammar School, he was vicar at Hodnet from 1807 until 1823 (commemorated by a tile in the chancel and a lamppost at the town's crossroads). In 1812 he published *Poems and Translations* but is best known for his hymns which include 'Holy, holy, holy' and 'From Greenland's icy mountains'.

HENNIKER Florence
late 19th C novelist. Her only known work, *Sir George* (1891), is set partly in Morton in Shropshire.

HENRIQUES R D
1905–67 novelist. He was educated at Rugby School. A writer of popular adventure stories such as *Death By Moonlight* (1938) and *Red Over Green* (1955), he also wrote factual books including *From a Biography of Myself* (published posthumously in 1969).

HENTY G A
1832–1902 novelist. One of his many and popular historical novels, *Facing Death, or the Hero of Vaughan Pit* (1882) – a tale of the coalmines – relates to Cannock Chase and Birmingham. *Both Sides of the Border*, a novel about Glendower and Hotspur, is set partly in Shropshire.

HERBERT Edward
1583–1648 philosopher and poet. He was born at Eyton-on-Severn, the home of his maternal grandmother, Lady Newport, and lived there until the age of nine. He returned to Shropshire for two years, from 1591 to 1596, to receive special tuition in Latin and Greek from Thomas Newton who lived in Diddlebury.

Less well known than his younger brother, George, he was nevertheless an accomplished poet of lyrical verse which was admired by Ben Jonson* for its 'obscureness'. A collection published by his brother, Henry, in 1665 shows the influence of John Donne*. His autobiography was published by Horace Walpole in 1764.

HERBERT George
1593–1633 poet. Until his mother's death in 1627, he spent much of his time at the maternal home in Eyton-on-Severn in Shropshire. Most of his work refers to the spiritual life and was published in 1633 as *The Temple: Sacred Poems and Private Ejaculations*.

HERBERT Mary, Countess of Pembroke
1561–1621 poet, translator and patron of literature. She was born at Tickenhill near Bewdley, the younger sister of Sir Philip Sidney*, and is known to have visited Kenilworth Castle when the Earl of Leicester was in residence there. Her work includes a *Version of the Psalms*, the poem, *Antonius*, and *A Discourse of Life and Death*.

HERITAGE Margaret
mid-20th C poet. She was born in Coventry. Her work, much of it celebrating the natural world, includes *Poems* (1938) and *Autumn Leaves* (1938).

HEWINS Mrs Elsie
d.1978 poet. Born in a house in the Bristol Road in Birmingham, now the administrative offices of the Royal Orthopaedic Hospital, she spent most of her life and died in Silvington, a small village near Cleobury Mortimer where her husband was vicar. Two collections of her poetry were

published – *Cleeton Carol* and *Silvington Songs* (1963). *Through the Years* (1971) describes her life as a parson's wife.

HEWITT John
1719–1802 criminologist. The son of a Coventry draper, he took over his father's business and later became mayor of the city in 1755, 1758 and 1760. His work includes a fictionalised account of one of the great impostresses of the age, *Memoirs of Lady Wilbrihammon*, and the non-fiction, *Journal of Magisterial Proceedings* (1779) and *A Guide to Constables* (1779).

HEWITT John
1907–87 poet. From 1957 to 1972 he was director of Coventry's Herbert Art Gallery and Museum. He described his coming to live in the city as 'one of the best things that happened to me'. His work includes *Collected Poems 1932–67* (1968), *The Day of the Corncrake* (1969) and *Out of My Time* (1974).

HEYNES Amy Elizabeth
early 20th C poet. She lived in Leamington Spa. In her only known work, *Stray Rhymes* (1911), sentiment tends to prevail, though there are some sharp insights into 'the woman's lot'.

HEYS Margaret
1912–87 novelist. She was born and educated in Coventry where she lived for most of her life. The historical novel, *In the Shadow of Elizabeth* (1970), has a Coventry setting.

HIDDEN Norman Frederick
b.1913 novelist and poet. He was educated at Hereford Cathedral School. His collections of verse include *These Images Claw* (1966), *Say It Aloud* (1971) and *Dr Kink and*

his *Old Time Boarding School, Fragments of Autobiography* (1973). He has continued to contribute to various periodicals and radio programmes. An anthology of his verse, *Over To You*, appeared in 1975.

HIGSON Philip
b.1933 (pseudonym of Philip John Willoughby-Higson) poet. Born at Newcastle-under-Lyme, he was educated in the town's high school and at Keele. His published work, which includes *The Riposte and Other Poems* (1971) and *Burlando's Mistress and Other Poems* (1974), is often to be heard on BBC Radio Stoke. His verse has been described as having 'bite and clarity and something to say'.

HILL Archie
late 20th C novelist, radio playwright and broadcaster. He was born in Brierley Hill. None of his novels, which include *A Corridor of Mirrors* (1975), *Sergeant Sahib* (1979) and *Prison Bars* (1980), was published before the end of 1974; but his autobiography, *A Cage of Shadows*, telling of his upbringing in the slums of the Black Country and of his fight against alcoholism, appeared in 1973. He is now regarded as a writer of some reputation for the raw sensitivity of his work.

HILL E S
late 19th C poet. His only known work, *A Tale of Ancient Times and Miscellaneous Poems* (1881), was published by a firm of printers in Burton-on-Trent where he is believed to have lived.

HILL Geoffrey
b.1932 poet. He was born and educated in Bromsgrove. *Mercian Hymns* (1971), made up of a series of

prose poems, celebrates the exploits of the Mercian hero, Offa. Much of his work, which includes *For the Unfallen* (1959) and *King Log* (1968), has a historical or religious theme and tends to dwell on the violent. His reputation as an austere, serious poetic voice continues to grow. *Collected Poems* was reissued in 1986.

Susan Hill

HILL Susan
b.1942 novelist, short story writer and autobiographer. She was literary critic for the *Coventry Evening Telegraph* for five years. In her early work – *I'm the King of the Castle* (1970) and *The Albatross and other stories* (1971), for example – her insight into the minds of the despairing or the disturbed was phenomenal. Since marriage and motherhood, she has written mainly non-fiction and children's books, including *One Night at a Time* and *Mother's Magic*, though a novel, *Air and Angels*, appeared in 1991. A sequel to Daphne du Maurier's novel, *Rebecca*, entitled *Mrs de Winter*, has recently been published.

HILTON Jeremy
b.1945 poet. A social worker, in 1972 he lived near Pershore and now lives in Malvern in Worcestershire. His work includes several volumes of verse, amongst them *Ornithology and Ferry* (1973) and *Fox Houses* (1974). It is through repetition and image that his work reaches its subtleties of feeling. He continues to write, *Shadow Engineering* being published in 1991.

HIND John
late 20th C poet. He was born in Stoke-on-Trent. His first collection of verse, *Personal Song*, was published in 1973. His work tends to rely on telling word and portmanteau phrase for its effects.

HINDSLEY Madeline
early 20th C poet. Born at Walsall and educated at the town's grammar school, she graduated from Birmingham University and became the principal of a college in Ceylon. She was a contributor to Alfred Moss's* anthology of Walsall poetry, *Songs from the Heart of England* (1920).

HINE Alfred
late 19th C poet. He lived in Leekfrith in Staffordshire. Many of his poems, which are mainly about the Moorlands and local and national events, were published in various periodicals. There are also two collections of poetry, *Things Old and New* (1898) and *Home Minstrelsy* (1906).

HINSULL Pattie
b.1947 poet. Educated at Dudley Technical College and now a secretary, she lives in Edgmond in Shropshire. *Prairies, Panniers and Petticoats* is her only known work.

HOBDAY Charles
late 20th C poet. A member of the

Avon Poets, he is a journalist by profession. Among the poems in the collection, *The Return of Cain* (1974), is one entitled 'The Long Mynd'. Much of his later work, which includes *Titterstone Clee* (1975), *A Wreath for Inez* (1976) and *Talking of Michelangelo* (1978), is inspired by legend and literature.

HODGKINSON W P

mid-20th C essayist. He lived at Shrawley in Worcestershire. Both of his collections of essays, *The Eloquent Silence* (1946) and *The Kingdom is a Garden* (1948), describe under other names places in the Shrawley area such as Abberley, Areley Kings, Lenchford and Holt Fleet.

HODGSON Pamela J

late 20th C poet. She lives in Wolverhampton. The poems in the collection, *A Sense of Grace* (1970), are concerned with the loss of open spaces to the technological demands of the modern world. It is believed she continues to write.

Molly Holden

HOLDEN Molly

1927–81 poet and children's writer. She lived in Bromsgrove from 1957

until her death. Her work for children includes *A Tenancy of Flint* (1969) and *White Rose and Wanderer* (1972). Two volumes of poetry, *To Make Me Grieve* (1968) and *Air and Chill Earth* (1971), were published before 1974. Her poetry, clear, sharp and uncomfortable, has a growing reputation. *Selected Poems*, edited by her husband, Alan, appeared in 1987.

HOLE William G

d.1941 poet. He lived in Selly Oak Road, Bournville in Birmingham. Only two collections of his work are known, *Procris* and *Amoris Imago* (1891).

HOLLAND Roy

late 20th C poet and short story writer. Born in Birmingham, he left school at fourteen and went to work in various midland factories, as a farmworker in Herefordshire and then as a teacher. After a year at Fircroft College in Edgbaston, he read English at Cambridge. A collection of his verse, *Poems*, was published in 1973. Later work includes the collections of short stories, *Supernatural Clwyd* (1992) and *Haunted Clwyd* (1992).

HOLLOWOOD A Bernard

b.1910 novelist and cartoonist. He was born in Burslem and educated at Hanley High School. Between 1932 and 1943 he lectured in economics at Stoke College. His work includes *Hawksmoor Scandals* (1951) and *Story of Morrho Velho* (1954).

HOLLOWOOD Jane Marian

mid-20th C children's writer. Creator of the 'Maggie' books – which include *Maggie and the Chickens* (1967) and *Maggie in the Snow* (1969) – she was born in Stoke-on-Trent.

HOLTHAM G
mid-20th C novelist. With Roger Busby*, he wrote a novel set in Birmingham, *Main Line Kill* (1968), which was published in the Cassell Crime Series.

HOMER Philip Bracebridge
1765–1838 poet. Born in Birdingbury in Warwickshire, the tenth son of the rector, he was educated at Rugby School. In 1785 he returned to the school and taught there for the next thirty-seven years. A voluminous poet, who is now entirely forgotten, he contributed frequently to the *Gentleman's Magazine. The Garland*, a collection of his verse, appeared in 1788.

HOPKINS Gerard Manley
1844–89 poet. A pupil of Richard Watson Dixon* in 1861 in Highgate, from 1866 to 1868 he taught under Cardinal Newman* at the Oratory School in Edgbaston, Birmingham. A collected edition of his work was eventually published in 1918. Though much of his poetry is obscure in meaning and difficult to read aloud, owing to its counterpointed metrical systems, his moments of brilliance are unsurpassed.

HOROVITZ Frances
1938–83 poet, actress and broadcaster. She is buried in the churchyard at Orcop in Herefordshire. Her work includes *Poems* (1967), *The High Tower* (1970) and contributions to *Children of Albion: Poetry of the 'Underground' in Britain* (1969) which was edited by her husband, Michael.

HORTON Harry Howells
mid-19th C poet. He lived in Birmingham. His work includes *Sutton Park and Other Poems* (1844), a collection which ran to four editions, and the slim volume, *Birmingham, a poem in two parts* (1853). His complaint in respect of the public being barred from Aston Hall was quoted in an article in the *Birmingham Post* on the architect, Thomas Rickman.

HORTON Samuel
mid-20th C novelist. The 'Rainbow Books', which include *Rainbow Farm* (1937) and *The Chapel on the Hill* (1938), are set in what he describes as the Shropshire Highlands. Most of his work has to do with living and working in the country.

HOSKINS John Senior
1566–1638 poet. He was MP for Hereford in 1603, 1614 and 1628. None of his work has survived to the present day, although he is known to have been much admired by his contemporaries for his 'ingeniousness'.

HOUGHAM Arthur
early 20th C novelist. A journeyman printer, he lived in Olton in Birmingham. His only known books, *Hammer Marks* (1925) and *The Street of Velvet* (1925), relate to the city.

HOUSMAN Alfred Edward
1859–1936 poet and classical scholar. He was born in Valley House in Fockbury. The family moved to Perry Hall in Bromsgrove in 1860 and stayed until 1873 when they returned to Fockbury to live in the Clock House. He was educated at Bromsgrove School. A commemorative statue of him has recently been erected in Bromsgove High Street. Many Shropshire places, including Clun, Much Wenlock, Hughley and Ludlow, are mentioned in his most celebrated poem, *A Shropshire Lad* (1896), though the Bredon Hill of the poem has been transplanted from

Worcestershire and several of the places described are not quite as they are in the real world. His ashes are buried outside the north door of Ludlow's St Laurence Church. For its vivid and moving evocation of an ideal and idealised England, *A Shropshire Lad* was the book most likely to be carried to the front by the ordinary soldiery during the Great War.

A E Housman

HOUSMAN Clemence Annie
1861–1955 novelist. The sister of Alfred Edward* and Laurence Housman*, she was born in Bromsgrove. Her only known work consists of the three novels, *Were-Wolf* (1896), *The Unknown Sea* (1898) and *Sir Aglovale de Galis* (1905). Her brother Laurence considered this last, based on the Arthurian legend, to be her best. But disappointed by its commercial failure, she wrote nothing more.

HOUSMAN Mrs Hannah
early 18th C diarist. She was born in Kidderminster. Her diaries, which are much occupied with the humdrum details of daily life, were edited and published by her brother, Richard Pearsall (1698–1762).

HOUSMAN Laurence
1865–1959 novelist and playwright. He was born in Bromsgrove and, like his older brother, Alfred Edward*, was educated at Bromsgrove School. The playlets collected together in *Victoria Regina* (1934) are his most successful work.

HOW William Walsham
1823–97 hymn writer. Born at College Hill, Shrewsbury, he was educated at Shrewsbury School. In 1846 he became a curate in Kidderminster. From 1848 to 1851 he held a similar post at Shrewsbury Abbey, before becoming rector of Whittington for the next twenty-eight years. He died in Wakefield and was buried in Whittington. Of his many hymns, 'For All the Saints' is probably the best known.

HOWITT Mary
1799–1888 poet and short story writer. From 1800 she lived in Uttoxeter and was educated there. Her best-known poem, 'Fairies of the Caldon Low', which was included in the collection, *Ballads and Other Poems* (1847), draws for its inspiration on the Staffordshire countryside. *Tales for All Seasons* appeared in 1881. With her husband, William Howitt (1792–1879), she wrote several non-fiction works of travel, history and contemporary ideas (see GASKELL, Mrs Elizabeth).

HUCKELL John
1729–71 poet. Born in Stratford-upon-Avon, the son of a burgess, he attended the local grammar school. His best-known work, *Avon, A Poem in Three Parts* (1758), which was printed by John Baskerville and published in Birmingham, describes the river and its many famous sons and daughters.

HUDDESFORD George
1749–1809 poet. He was the vicar at Loxley in Warwickshire. His work includes *Topsy Turvey; Anecdotes and Observations of the Leading Characters of the Present Government of France* (1790), *Salmagundi; Original Poems* (1793) and *The Wiccamical Chaplet, a Selection of Original Poetry, Comprising Smaller Poems, Serious and Comic* (1805).

HUDSON William Henry
1841–1922 novelist and naturalist. Of American and Argentinian origin, in 1899 he published *Wild Humphrey Kynaston*, subtitled *A Romance of the Robin Hood of Shropshire in the Reign of Henry the Seventh*. *Green Mansions* (1904) and *A Shepherd's Life* (1910) are perhaps his best-known work in this country.

HUGHES Isaac
1809–1881 poet. He lived in Oswestry where he worked as a shoemaker. Two collections of his poetry appeared, *Poems on Various Subjects* (1838) and *Home and Other Poems* (1871).

HUGHES Thomas
1822–96 novelist and biographer. Educated at Rugby School during the headmastership of Thomas Arnold, he is best known for his novel, *Tom Brown's Schooldays* (1857), which draws heavily on his own schoolboy experiences and on his deep respect for his headmaster. His later work is mostly biographical.

HULBERT Charles
1778–1857 journalist and short story writer. In 1803 he became co-owner of a cotton factory in Coleham in Shrewsbury. He lived for a while in the town before moving to Hadnall.

Having acquired a printing press from an auction in Birmingham, he founded the *Salopian Magazine* in 1814. Most of his short literary pieces, which included articles as well as fiction, were published in this magazine. He also wrote on the history and famous people of his adopted county. His autobiography, *Memoirs of Seventy Years of an Eventful Life*, was published in 1852. He is buried in the family grave at Hadnall.

HULBERT C A
1804–88 poet. The eldest son of Charles Hulbert*, he was born in Shrewsbury and educated at Shrewsbury School. His work includes *Poetical Recreations* (1828) and *Theotokos or the Song of the Virgin* (1842).

HULL Richard
b.1896 (pseudonym of Richard Henry Sampson) novelist. He was educated at Rugby School. His novels, the first being *The Murder of My Aunt* (1935), belong to the detective fiction genre.

HULME T E
1883–1917 poet and essayist. Born at Gratton Hall in Horton, Staffordshire, he was educated at the school in Endon after the family moved to the village and later attended Newcastle-under-Lyme High School. Described by T S Eliot in 1924 as 'classical, reactionary and revolutionary', he was one of the chief instigators of the twentieth century's philosophical preoccupation with language. His small output of verse, imagist and spare, appeared in the magazine, *New Age*, and in a collected edition, *Complete Poetical Works of T.E.Hulme*, in 1912.

HUMBERSTONE E H
1846–1923 poet and playwright. He was appointed headmaster of Bablake School in Coventry in 1870. The poems in the two volumes, *Lyrical Scrapbook* and *Poems Playful and Serious* (published posthumously in 1938), first appeared in the *Warwickshire Spectator* and the *Coventry Standard*.

HUMPHRIES Paul
late 20th C editor and poet. In 1973 he edited the Birmingham-based literary magazine, *Midland Read*. His own work tends to be topical and uncompromising.

HUNT Joseph
b.1913 poet. Born at Romsley and educated at Romsley's St Kenelm's School and at Halesowen Grammar School, he is administrator and librarian of the Birmingham and Midland Institute. He is a founding member of the John Betjeman Society, the George Eliot Fellowship, the Housman Society and the Francis Brett Young Society and has done a great deal to promote and foster appreciation of these writers' work. His own work includes the poetry collections, *Worcestershire Lad* (1977), *Winter Words* (1981) and *A Garland for Kenelm* (1986). He has also written about local places and people, many of them to do with Romsley and the church of St Kenelm.

HUNTER Jim
b.1939 poet, novelist, critic and short story writer. He was born in Stafford. The collection of poetry, *Introduction*, appeared in 1960, but he is best known for his novels which include *The Sun in the Morning* (1961), *The Flame* (1966) and *Walking in the Painted Sunshine* (1970). His work is mainly concerned with unsophisticated people leading ordinary lives. Among his works of criticism are *The Metaphysical Poets (1965)* and *Tom Stoppard's Plays* (1982).

HUTTON Catherine
1756–1846 novelist. The daughter of William Hutton*, she was born in Birmingham and lived there all her life. Perhaps best known as her father's biographer, she also published between 1815 and 1819 three three-decker novels, *The Miser Married*, *Oakwood Hall* and *The Welch Mountaineers*.

HUTTON William
1723–1814 bookseller, poet, stationer, traveller and commentator. He lived in Birmingham from 1750 until his death. He is now best known for his *Autobiography* (published posthumously by his daughter Catherine in 1816 – the original manuscript having been burnt in the riots of 1791) and for his *History of Birmingham* (1781). A poem, *The Barkers, or Road to Riches*, appeared in 1793.

I

INCLEDON Philip
See WORNER, Philip

INGLEBY Clement Mansfield
1823–86 poet and academic. Born in Edgbaston, the son of a lawyer, he was a solicitor in Birmingham from 1849 to 1859 and one of the original trustees of Shakespeare's Birthplace. He is best known for his researches into Shakespeare's* life and work –

notorious, even, for suggesting the disinterment of the poet's bones in order to examine the skull and resolve the vexed question of portraiture. A collection of his poems, *Poems and Epigrams*, appeared posthumously in 1887.

INGOLDSBY Thomas
1788–1845 (occasional pseudonym of R H Barham) poet. He added to the reputation of the already famous Shrewsbury cakes by referring to them enthusiastically in *The Ingoldsby Legends* (1840) – a miscellany of prose and poetry characterised by punning rhymes and slang.

INGRAM Arthur H Winnington
1818–87 poet. He was educated at Rugby. After ordination he became rector of Clifton-on-Teme and from 1845 to 1887 was rector of Harvington in Worcestershire. In 1854 he was made an honorary canon of Worcester Cathedral. For several years he worked as a schools inspector and became chairman of the Evesham bench of magistrates. He wrote two volumes of poetry, *The Doom of the Gods of Hellas* (1867) and *The Brides of Dinan: a Tale of the Barons' War* (published by his widow in 1888).

IRONSIDE John
early 20th C (pseudonym of Miss E M Tait) novelist. She is believed to have stayed frequently in Birmingham. Her book, *Jack of Clubs* (1931), relates to the city.

IRVING Washington
1783–1859 short story writer, essayist and historian. An American, he stayed at the Red House, Bridge Street in Stratford-upon-Avon in 1818 and wrote about the town in *The Sketch-Book* (1819–20) under the pseudonym of Geoffrey Crayon, Gent. This collection of stories contains the reinterpreted German folk tale, *Rip Van Winkle*, probably his most famous work. In the same year he visited his brother-in-law in Birmingham. In 1819 he went to live in Calthorpe Road in Edgbaston, staying there until 1824. Aston Hall, now owned by the city of Birmingham, is accepted as the original of his *Bracebridge Hall* (1822), the title of a collection of his essays.

IRVING-JAMES Thomas
b.1914 novelist. He lives in Bridgnorth. Amongst other works, he has published *Tomorrow is Mine* (1947), *Dinner After Death* (1964), *A Glimpse of Evil* (1967) and *Deserted by the Devil* (1971). All his work is to do with crime and its detection. More recently *A Rag-bag of Dreams* (1984) has appeared.

ISACKE Peter Patrick
late 20th C poet. An audit clerk, educated at Sutton Coldfield College of Further Education and Birmingham College of Dramatic Art, he now lives in Edgbaston in Birmingham. Most of his collections of poems have a west midland theme and include *Poems from Sutton Coldfield* (1972) and *More Poems from Sutton Coldfield* (1973). He continues to write poetry and promote the work of local poets.

J

JACK Sheila
b.1918 poet. A Wolverhampton teacher of English as a second language, she has lived in Wrockwardine in Shropshire. Her work, which is frequently very personal, includes *Thirty-Two Poems* (1962) and *Another Thirty-Two Poems* (1974).

JACKS L P
1860–1955 novelist. He was for several years a Unitarian minister in Birmingham. The city of Smokeover in his collections of stories, *The Legends of Smokeover* (1921), *The Heroes of Smokeover* (1926) and *The Last Legend of Smokeover* (1939), represents Birmingham. All his work shows a deep sympathy for men and women trapped in the inhumanities of an industrialised society.

JACKSON Georgina Frederica
1824–95 linguist and folklorist. She was born at Pulverbatch in Shropshire. With the assistance of Charlotte Burne*, she published her investigations into the Shropshire dialect in *The Shropshire Word Book* (1879–81). In 1880 she was granted a civil list pension.

JACKSON T E
early 20th C novelist. He lived in Stafford. His only known novel, *The Voice in the Wilderness*, appeared in 1914.

JACOT B L
mid-20th C novelist, short story writer, scriptwriter and editor. Born in Birmingham, he was educated at King Edward VI Grammar School in Aston. He abandoned the legal profession in order to become subeditor of *The Times* and to have sufficient time to produce his annual

volume of short stories. His novels, *Just Wesley* (1929) and *Crying for the Moon* (1968), have a Birmingham setting. In 1931 he was contracted by British International Pictures to write eight film scripts in two years.

JAGO Richard
1715–81 poet. Born at Beaudesert in Warwickshire, the son of the rector, he was educated at Solihull School at the same time as William Shenstone*, who was to become a lifelong friend. In 1738 he became the curate at Snitterfield. After appointments as rector in Harbury and Chesterton Green, he returned to Snitterfield in 1754 (see COVENTRY, Lady Anne). His collected poems – the best being *Edge Hill, or the Rural Prospect Delineated and Moralised*, a topographical poem in four books – were published posthumously in 1884.

JAMES Alice
1848–92 diarist. The younger sister of Henry James*, she lived in Leamington Spa from 1886 to 1890. Her diaries, which were eventually edited and published in 1934 as *Alice James: Her Brothers – Her Journal*, describe many incidents from her stay in the west midland area.

JAMES Henry
1843–1916 novelist. An American, he stayed with the Gaskell* family at Wenlock Abbey in 1877, 1878 and 1882, and visited Stokesay, Ludlow and Much Wenlock which are mentioned in *English Hours* (1875), the record of his travels in this country. Though the detailed subtleties of his work may not be altogether to modern taste, he retains an enthusiastic following for such

novels as *What Maisie Knew* (1897), *The Spoils of Poynton* (1897) and *The Ambassadors* (1903).

JAMES James Henry
b.1813 poet. He lived in Hereford. The collection, *The Banks of the Wye*, was published in 1857; his long poem 'Herefordia' in 1861. All his work reflects his interest in and love of local places.

JAMES M R
1862–1936 short story writer and antiquarian. A frequent visitor to Worcestershire, in 1910 he instigated the restoration of the window-glass in Great Malvern Priory. Though much of his writing is concerned with religious themes, he is now chiefly remembered for his ghost stories – of which the first volume, *Ghost Stories of an Antiquary*, appeared in 1905. A collected edition was published in 1931.

JAMES Thomas Irving
mid-20th C poet. He is believed to have lived in industrial Staffordshire. His work includes the collection, *Stammering*. A second collection, *Tomorrow is Mine* (1947), is dedicated to 'my workmates for their interest, courtesy and inspiration'. Without sentiment, he details the harshness and struggle of working life.

JARMAN Rosemary Hawley
b.1935 novelist. Born in Worcester and educated at Alice Ottley School, she has worked as a civil servant in Worcester and lives at Colwall near Malvern. Most of her novels, such as *We Speak No Treason* (1972) and *The King's Grey Mare* (1973), belong to the historical genre and demonstrate her unfailingly exact eye and ear for the past.

JEFFERIES Joyce
d.1649? diarist. She was the daughter of Henry Jefferies of Homme (or Ham) Castle at Clifton-on-Teme in Worcestershire. Her diary, which gives a vivid and detailed description of a Royalist gentlewoman's existence during the Civil War, was published in part in the periodical, *Archaeologia*.

JEFFERY G E
mid/late 19th C novelist. He is believed to have lived in Birmingham. *The Avenging Hand, A Story of Old Brum* (1868) relates to the city. *Mr Birch's Magnet – a Tale of Love and Law* (1875) also relates to Birmingham, especially to the county court.

JENKINS Elizabeth
late 20th C novelist and short story writer. She is believed to have lived for a time in Malvern. Her work includes the novel, *Dr Gully* (1973), and *Lady Caroline Lamb: A Biography* (1972). *Silent Jay* appeared in 1992.

'Saint' Montmorency

JEROME Jerome K
1859–1927 novelist, essayist, actor and playwright. He was born in Bradford Street, Walsall, the son of an

ironmonger/vicar. His reputation now rests on the novel, *Three Men in a Boat* (1889), and the modern morality play, *The Passing of the Third Floor Back* (1908). His autobiography, *My Life and Times* (1926), reveals his good-natured humanitarianism.

JOHNSON Aleck

b.1900   poet. He lived in Coventry for many years. His only known collection, *The Pond and Other Poems*, appeared in 1973.

JOHNSON David

b.1927 novelist. He was born at Meir in Stoke-on-Trent and educated at Newcastle-under-Lyme Grammar School. His books include *Sabre General* and *Promenade in Champagne*.

JOHNSON Dr Samuel

1709–84 lexicographer, critic and poet. The son of a bookseller, he was born in Lichfield and baptised at St Mary's Church. (The house is now the Samuel Johnson Birthplace Museum.) In 1714 he went to Dame Oliver's School in Dam Street and later attended the grammar school. Throughout his life he kept close contact with the city, staying on his frequent visits at the Three Crowns Inn or with his stepdaughter at Redcourt House. From 1726 to 1727 he spent six months as a pupil usher at King Edward VI Grammar School in Stourbridge; returning there in 1731 to apply unsuccessfully for the post of usher. At Edmund Hector's house in Old Square, Birmingham, he met his future wife, Mrs Porter. While living in the city he contributed essays to the *Birmingham Journal*. In 1735, the year after his marriage, he and his wife went to live in Edial House in Edial. There they opened a school which numbered David Garrick*

among its pupils. When this school failed, he was given work in London by Edward Cave*. In 1749 *The Vanity of Human Wishes*, his most memorable poem, appeared. After nine years of labour, his *Dictionary* was finally published in 1755. In 1774, in the company of Mr and Mrs Thrale*, he visited Hagley Hall, the home of the Lyttelton family, and Ilam Hall in north-east Staffordshire. Neither visit seems to have been altogether satisfactory. More successful was his visit in the same year to Hawkstone in Shropshire, the gothic splendours of whose grotto he compared favourably to those of Derbyshire. There is a bas-relief in Uttoxeter commemorating the 'penance' he imposed on himself for refusing, fifty years earlier, to look after his father's bookstall in the market there. Nathaniel Hawthorne* made a sentimental journey to view the scene. *Lives of the English Poets* appeared in 1779–81. A statue of his biographer, James Boswell (1740–95), stands in Lichfield.

Dr Samuel Johnson

JONES Dylis Henrik

mid/late 20th C poet. She was born in Coventry. Her work, often claustrophobic and melancholy, includes *Each Lighted Place* (1961) and *Tourist in Time* (1970).

JONES Elijah
early/mid-19th C poet and editor. Born in Hanley, he was the author of several poems which were inspired by his surroundings and which appeared in various magazines between 1819 and 1821. In 1859 he also edited *The Beacon*, a temperance journal.

JONES Jim William
1923–93 poet. Born and educated in Coseley in Staffordshire, he worked in industry and local government before becoming a speech and drama lecturer at the Adult College in Wolverhampton. Later he lived in Sedgley. His work, which is mainly made up of poems and dialect ballads, includes *From Under the Smoke* (1972) and *Factory and Fireside* (1974). The *Black Countryman* regularly published his verse.

JONES John Idris
b.1938 poet and short story writer. He took his degree at the University of Keele. The collection of short stories, *Way Back to Ruthin*, appeared in 1966; to be followed by *Barry Island and Other Poems* in 1971.

JONES Margaret A B
b.1906 poet. She lives in Shrewsbury. The collection, *Lake Vyrnwy*, many of which poems are to do with specific places in Shropshire such as Telford New Town, was published in 1974. Other collections have since appeared. Most of her work first came out in periodicals.

JONES Peter
b.1929 poet. He was born in Walsall. *The Peace and the Hook*, his first full-length collection of poetry, was published in 1972. Earlier slim

volumes include *Rain* (1969) and *Seagarden for Julius* (1970). He continues to write with 'a feeling for language [that] is delicate and subtle'.

JONES Richard
1779–1851 playwright, actor and elocutionist. Born in Birmingham, the son of a builder and surveyor, he was generally known in the theatrical world as 'Gentleman Jones'. His acting career began with appearances in Lichfield, Newcastle-under-Lyme and Birmingham. On his retirement from the stage, he gave lessons in elocution. His four known plays, *The Green Man*, a comedy in three acts, *Too Late for Dinner*, a farce in two acts, *The School for Gallantry*, another comedy, and *Peter Fin's Trip to Brighton*, a farce, were all well received.

JONSON Ben
1572–1637 playwright. He visited Sir Henry Goodere at Polesworth, commenting in his verses on his host's 'well-made choice of books and friends'. He was also an occasional guest of Sir Henry's daughter, Anne, at her home in Clifford Chambers. *Everyman in his Humour* (1598), *Volpone* (1605) and *The Alchemist* (1610) are perhaps his best-known plays.

JORDAN John
1746–1809 poet. He was born in Tiddington in the parish of Alveston, which is two miles from Stratford-upon-Avon. The family soon moved into the town – where he was apprenticed as a wheelwright in his father's business and lived for the rest of his life. His first published verse, in celebration of Shakespeare's jubilee in 1769, was addressed to David Garrick*, the steward of the festival. Other contributors included Richard

Jago* and John Huckell*. The poems, 'Welcombe Hill, near Stratford-upon-Avon', which tells of the struggle between Saxon and Briton for dominance in the area, and 'The

Charnel House at Stratford', both appeared in the *Gentleman's Magazine* in 1777. He was well known in the town as 'the poet Jordan'.

K

KARK Leslie
b.1910 poet and short story writer. He lived in Shropshire. The autobiographical novel, *Red Rain* (1945), details a rural childhood in his native county and life as a young man in Bomber Command during the Second World War.

KAULFUSS Edward
b.1904 poet. The son of a midlands railway worker, he has lived in Hereford. He became blind in 1932. His second collection of verse, *In Square Orbit*, was published in 1971. Much of his work debates unemotionally the curious absurdities of existence.

KEARY C F
d.1917 novelist. He is believed to have lived in or near Walsall. His only available work, *The Mount* (1909), which is set in Hartlebury, a fictionalised version of Hartwell in Staffordshire, dwells on the fortunes and misfortunes of families involved in the brewing industry.

KEELING Isaac
1789–1869 poet and religious writer. Born at Newcastle-under-Lyme and educated at Mr Thomas Kemp's school, he was for some time a designer and engraver at the Wedgwood Pottery Works in Etruria. In 1811 he became a Wesleyan minister. Two years after his death a volume of his sermons, which included several

poems on sacred themes, was published.

KEELING Nancy Cosette
mid-20th C novelist. She lives in Coventry, a member of the family which directs the Keelavita Company. Her work, which belongs in the main to the romantic genre, includes *Gaunt Hand* (1952) and *One Master Passion* (1955).

KELLY Edward
1555–95 poet and medium. Born in Worcester, he was educated at the King's School. In 1582 he met Dr Dee, one-time rector of Upton-upon-Severn, and travelled abroad with him as his 'interpreter' of the spirits. He left various writings and poems which were to do with, and inspired by, his supernatural experiences.

KEMBLE George Stephen
1758–1822 actor, playwright and poet. He was born in Kington in Herefordshire, the son and grandson of actors and the brother of John Philip Kemble, Sarah Siddons and Charles Kemble. The family made Hereford their headquarters for a time. Apprenticed to Mr Gibbs, a surgeon in Coventry, he could not resist the call of the stage. In 1809 he published *Odes, Lyrical Ballads and Poems*.

KEMP Gene
b.1926 children's writer. Born at Wigginton near Tamworth, she now

lives in Exeter. Her first books included *The Smuggling Ship* (1950) and stories about the famous Tamworth pig. School stories, such as the 1978 Carnegie Medal winner, *Turbulent Term of Tyke Tiler*, and stories for teenagers, such as *The Room with No Windows* (1989), are among her later work. *The Clock Tower Ghost* (1981) was prompted by the tower at Abberley in Worcestershire.

KENNEDY Benjamin Hall
1804–89 poet and translator. Born at Summer Hill in Birmingham, the son of a master at King Edward's School, he was educated there and at Shrewsbury School where he became head boy. In 1827 he went back to Shrewsbury School to teach; and after a short period away, he returned in 1836 to become headmaster of the school for the next thirty years. From 1843 to 1867 he was a prebendary at Lichfield Cathedral. In 1866 he accepted the living at West Felton near Oswestry. Most of his original verse is included in *Between Whiles, or Wayside Amusements of a Working Life* (1877) – a curiously bitter-sweet collection.

KENNEDY Charles Rann
1808–69 poet and solicitor. Like his elder brother, Benjamin (see above), he was born at Summer Hill and educated at King Edward's School and Shrewsbury School. Qualified as a barrister in 1835, he was Professor of Law at Owen's College in Birmingham from 1849 to 1856. Though best known for his litigatory activities – especially his action in 1862 against a previous client, Mrs Swinifen, for non-payment of fees – he also had time to publish *Poems: Original and Translated* in 1843.

KENNEDY Charles Rann
1871–1950 actor and playwright. He was educated in Birmingham and worked as a clerk in the city before going on the stage. His play, *The Servant in the House*, is similar in theme and style to Jerome K Jerome's*, *The Passing of the Third Floor Back*, in that it explores the effect on ordinary people of a Christ-like stranger in their midst. It is not known whether he is related to the above.

KENNEDY Geoffrey A Studdert
1883–1929 poet and religious writer. He is buried in Worcester cemetery. Nicknamed Woodbine Willie, he came to prominence during the First World War when he was chaplain to the armed forces. His books, which were written primarily to promote practical Christianity for the ordinary man, are now out of print; though *Rough Rhymes of a Padre* (1918) can still be found in the more explorable secondhand bookshops.

KENNEDY George John
mid-19th C poet. Brother of Benjamin and Charles, he became a master at Rugby School where he occasionally indulged in writing poetry which was published in various periodicals.

KENNEDY Rann
1772–1851 poet and playwright. He lived at Withington near Shrewsbury from 1784 to 1791. A friend of Samuel Coleridge*, a master at King Edward's School in Birmingham and father of Benjamin, Charles and George (see above), he also was of a literary turn of mind. His work includes *Poem on the Death of Princess Charlotte* (1817), *A Tribute in Verse to the Character of George Canning* (1827) and *Britain's Genius, a masque on the occasion of the marriage of Victoria, Queen of Great Britain* (1840).

KETTLE Rosa Mackensie
d.1895 novelist. Her novel, *Under the Grand Old Hills*, is set in Malvern where she was born and brought up. She visited Shropshire frequently, to stay with her brother at Dallicott Hall, and affectionately dedicated to him the novel, *The Carding-Mill Valley, a Romance of the Shropshire Highlands* (1882), which is set in the county's Long Mynd. Other works include *The Falls of Loder* and *My Home in the Shires*.

KILBOURN John
1838–98 poet and essayist. Born at Walsall, the son of a basket maker, he was educated locally in private schools. On the death of his father, he took over the business; but at the age of forty he decided to devote himself entirely to literature. Some of his work appears in Alfred Moss's*, *Songs from the Heart of England* (1920). Only one collection of his poetry, Wordsworthian in its tendency to derive philosophical ideas from natural phenomena, ever appeared. A collection of his essays and poetry was published by public subscription in 1907 by W H Duignan

KILLMINSTER Abraham K
1807–58 poet and playwright. Born in Leek in Staffordshire, he lived there all his life. Best known for *The Dalesman*, a play in five acts, he also contributed prose and verse pieces to *The Mirror* and other newspapers and periodicals (sometimes under the name of Cymbeline). As Tom Oakleigh, he wrote articles on sport and other topics.

KILVERT Francis
1840–79 diarist and notebook-keeper extraordinaire. He was vicar of Bredwardine in Herefordshire from 1877 until his death. A white cross marks his grave in the churchyard. In 1879 he visited Brinsop Court and in his notebooks, begun in 1870, he mentions the house, the swans on the moat, and the cedar planted on the lawn by William Wordsworth* in 1843. *The Diaries* were eventually edited and published by William Plomer in 1938.

KIMBELL William Henry
mid/late 19th C poet and short story writer. He lived in Coventry. His collection of poetry and prose, *The Gift of Leisure Hours*, appeared in 1848. The sketch in verse, *The History of a Shilling* (1879), describes how a coin began its life in Roman Britain and after journeying worldwide returned to 'old England's shore'.

KING Edward
mid-19th C poet. He lived all his life in Coventry. Some of the verses in his only known collection, *Poems of Liberty* (1864), relate to his home city.

KINGSFORD Anna Bonus
1846–88 poet, essayist, editor and religious writer. In 1867 she married Algernon Godfrey Kingsford who was then vicar of Atcham near Shrewsbury. Much of her writing was to do with the early feminist movement and for a while, in 1872, she owned and edited *The Lady's Own Paper*. *River Reeds*, a volume of verse, appeared in 1866.

KINGSLEY Henry
1830–76 novelist and journalist. A visitor to the west midlands, he was the younger brother of the novelist, Charles Kingsley. One of his own novels, *Stretton* (published posthumously in 1895), is set in Shropshire. Other work includes *Leighton Court*

(1866) and *The Boy in Grey* (1871).

KIRKHAM Nellie
1897–1979 novelist and historian. She was the daughter of a Stoke-on-Trent pottery manufacturer and lived for most of her life in Newcastle-under-Lyme. As well as a book about Sudan (1892), four local history books and an account of the lead mines in the north midlands, she published a novel, *Unrest of Their Time* (1935).

KNIGHT Edward
1774–1826 actor and playwright. A well-known comedian, commonly called 'Little Knight', he was born and brought up in Birmingham. His first stage appearance was in Newcastle-under-Lyme as Hob in the sketch, *Hob in the Well.* Unfortunately his performance received scant applause. Later, as a member of the Stafford Company, he had more success. *The Sailor and Soldier; or, Fashionable Amusement*, his dramatic piece in two acts, was first performed in 1805.

KNIGHT Eric
mid-20th C poet. He was born and brought up in Birmingham where he attended the university and trod the boards of the Rep. He later worked for Cadbury Brothers in Bournville, managed the Crescent Theatre and was secretary of the Birmingham and Midland Institute. His collection, *Beyond Words*, in which 'lovers of poetry will find ... solace and satisfaction', was published in 1957.

KNIGHT Henrietta (Lady Luxborough)
d.1756 poet and letter writer. She lived all her married life in a house called Barrels in the parish of Wootton Wawen in Warwickshire. Her correspondence with her friend and neighbour, William Shenstone*,

includes several appreciative references to the poetry of William Somervile*. The lines of hers written to describe a *ferme ornee* near Birmingham and addressed to Shenstone* were published in a volume of his poetry.

KNIGHT M Forster
mid-20th C children's writer and illustrator. She lived in Leamington Spa. Her work includes *Uncle Blunder's Studio* (1942) and *Aldous Greenwing's Fortune* (1945).

KNIGHT Richard Payne
1751–1824 poet and horticulturalist. Born at Wormsley Grange, north west of Hereford, he did not attend school until the age of fourteen because of delicate health. Of the Whig persuasion, he was MP for Leominster in 1780 and Ludlow in 1784. He inherited the estate of Downton from his grandfather who had been an ironmaster in Coalbrookdale. Here he built a mansion and laid out the famous gardens. His poetry includes *The Landscape; a Didactic Poem* (1794) and *A Monody on the Death of Charles James Fox* (1806). (see PRICE, Sir Uvedale)

KNOWLES Mary
1733–1807 poet and religious writer. She was born at Rugely. A Quaker and friend of Dr Johnson*, she published her *Poetical Correspondence* (with Captain Morris) in the *Gentleman's Magazine* in 1791.

KNOX E V
1881–1971 poet and parodist. He was educated at Rugby School. Most of his humorous articles, poems and parodies appeared first in *Punch.*

KYNASTON Francis
1587–1642 poet. He was born at Oteley, near Ellesmere. His sonnets

are regularly anthologised and admired. The verse romance, *Leoline and Sydonis*, appeared in 1642.

KYNASTON Herbert
1809–78 poet. Born in Warwick, he lived there until 1821. A lyrical poet

inspired mainly by the glories of the past, he published *Miscellaneous Poetry* in 1841; *Lays of the Seven and a Half Centuries* in 1859; and *The Number of the Fish, a Poem* in 1864. Much of his work was written first in Latin.

L

LAMBOT Isobel
b.1926 novelist. She lives in Kington in Herefordshire and from 1973 to 1979 was a tutor at Lichfield Evening Institute. Her work, usually of the detective fiction variety, includes *Taste of Murder* (1966), *Shroud of Canvas* (1967) and *Let the Witness Die* (1969). *Still Waters Run Deadly* appeared in 1986.

LANDOR Robert Eyres
1781–1869 poet and playwright. The brother of W S Landor*, he was born in Warwick and educated at Broms-grove School. His first curacy was at Colton in Staffordshire and in 1829 he became rector of Birlingham in Worcestershire where he stayed for forty years. His work includes the tragedy, *Count Arezzi* (so good, some critics thought it to have been written by Lord Byron), a poem, 'The Impious Feast' (1828), two other tragedies, *The Earl of Brecon* (1841) and *Faith's Fraud* (1841), and a drama, *The Ferryman* (1841). *The Fawn of Sertorious* (1846) and *The Fountain of Arethusa* (1848) – for several years mistakenly ascribed to his brother – are considered to be his best work.

LANDOR Walter Savage
1775–1864 poet and essayist. The son of a physician, he was born at Warwick, spent time at Ipsley Court

near Redditch and was educated at Rugby School. (He is commemorated by a bust below the east gate in St Mary's Church, Warwick.) A collection of poems, *Simonidea*, which contains the famous 'Rose Aylmer', appeared in 1806. The legend of Coventry's Lady Godiva is the subject of one of his essays in *Imaginary Conversations of Literary Men and Statesman* (1824–29). A tablet in the church at Bishop's Tachbrook near Leamington Spa, the village where his family lived, was erected at the time of his death in Italy. He is generally presumed to be the inspiration for the character of Boythorn in Charles Dickens's* *Bleak House* (1852).

LANG Frances
See MANTLE, Winifred

LANG JONES H
early 20th C poet. The verse in his only known collection, *Songs of a Buried City* (1913), refers to Wroxeter in Shropshire where he is believed to have lived.

LANGBRIDGE Frederick
b.1849 poet. Born in Birmingham, at the age of thirteen he sent a poem to the *Birmingham Gazette* which was duly published. Thus encouraged, he spent most of his time, when free from his parish duties in Limerick, composing verse.

LANGFORD Jane
See MANTLE, Winifred

LANGFORD John
1823–1903 poet. Born in Deritend, one of the oldest quarters of Birmingham, he received scant education locally and was early apprenticed as chair maker to his father. Later he became a printer and then a journalist on the *Birmingham Daily Gazette* and the *Birmingham Morning News*. Much of his work, which includes *The Lamp of Life* (1856) and *Poems of the Field and of the Town* (1859), is concerned with love and its ability to place us only 'a little lower than the angels'.

LANGLAND William
?1332–?1400 poet. His history is somewhat obscure – Great Malvern, Cleobury Mortimer, Colwall and Ledbury all claiming to be his birthplace – though scholars are now almost sure he was born at Cleobury Mortimer. More certainly, he was educated at Cleobury Mortimer and at the monastery in Great Malvern. The only work now confidently attributed to him is *Piers Plowman* (1367–70), a long allegorical poem written in what is now generally described as Middle English. (see FLORENCE OF WORCESTER)

LAPWORTH Edward
1574–1636 poet and physician. He was born in Warwickshire, possibly at Lapworth. His poems, written in both English and Latin, are to be found scattered through various contemporary collections – such as Joshua Sylvester's, *Du Bartas*, and editions of the *Oxford Poets* (see ABERCROMBIE, Lascelles).

LARKIN Philip
1922–85 poet, critic and novelist. Born in Coventry, he was educated at the city's King Henry VIII School. From 1943 to 1946 he was librarian at Wellington Public Library and his first novel, *Jill*, was published in his last year there. He returned to the town briefly in 1962 to attend the opening of the new and enlarged library premises. His experiences at Wellington are recorded in an article in the *Library Association Record* (October 1977). Though often the subject for his derision and contempt, his provincial 'mid-land' upbringing provided a rich source of inspiration for his work – especially demonstrated in the poems of *The Less Deceived* (1955) and *The Whitsun Weddings* (1964) and in his second novel, *A Girl in Winter* (1947). His later work, in the collection, *High Windows* (1974), tends to be even more bleak. Considered by some to be a Movement poet (see FISHER, Roy), he is perhaps not so easily categorised.

Philip Larkin

LAWLEY George Thomas
1845–1920 poet. He was born in Bilston and educated at St Leonard's School and Rev Samuel Cozen's school. A prolific writer, he contri-

Malvern Ridge (looking north)

buted hundreds of poems and articles to the *Midlands Counties Express*, the *Birmingham Post* and the *Bilston Mercury*. Most of his work is concerned with his much loved native county – its past and its present.

LAWRENCE Margery
d.1969 poet, short story writer and novelist. She was born at Wolverhampton. Though her first work was the book of poems, *Songs of Childhood*, published when she was only sixteen, she is perhaps best known for her novels which include *Red Heels* and *Nights of the Round Table*. *Snapdragon* and *Bohemian Glass* (which became a great hit after it was banned) are collections of short stories.

LAYAMON
early 13th C chronicler. He was the son of Leovenath. In *The Brut* (c.1200), written in a language transitional between Early English and Middle English, he mentions he was a priest at Areley Kings (or Areley Regis) near Redstone. This work, which tells the history of England following the arrival of the legendary Brutus, is the earliest version of the Arthurian story to be written in English. (see FLORENCE OF WORCESTER)

LAYTON Frank G
b.1872 novelist, poet and playwright. He lived in Walsall. *The Old Doctor* (1923) and *Behind the Night Bell* (1938) derive from his experiences as a general practitioner in the Black Country. *Dr Grey* (1911) and *Sable and Motley* (1912) were written under the pseudonym of Stephen Andrew. His plays include *The Prophet* (1922) and *The Feryport Election*. *The Land of Make Believe* (1929) is a play for children. He is well represented in Alfred Moss's*, *Songs from the Heart of England* (1920).

LEA Alec
b.1907 novelist and children's writer. The children's story, *A Whiff of Boarhound* (1974), tells of the adventures of four Birmingham children who, led by the 'Shropshire Lad'- quoting Roger, go on a camping holiday in Much Wenlock.

LEA Kennett
mid-19th C poet. He lived in Worcester. His only known collection, *Poemata Melica, Original Odes*, appeared in 1863.

LEA Margery
mid-20th C poet. She has lived in Attingham near Shrewsbury. The collection, *These Days*, was published in 1969.

LEACH Robert
b.1942 poet and playwright. He lives in Walsall and has worked at the Midlands Arts Centre in Birmingham. *A Tinker's Curse*, in which most of the verse is concerned with local legends and tales, was published in 1971. *Cats Free and Familiar* appeared in 1974. He has since extended his creative range to include drama and musical drama.

LEE Rev A Hampden
early 20th C poet and hymn writer. He was pastor of Vicarage Walk Church in Walsall for forty years. 'War-time Hymn', which has a distinctly 'Newboltian' ring about it, appeared in Alfred Moss's*, *Songs from the Heart of England* (1920).

LEE Ernest George
1896–1985 novelist, short story writer and religious writer. He was minister at the High Street Unitarian Church in Shrewsbury in the 1930s. While there he wrote several religious pamphlets and short stories and, under the pseudonym of Edward Dodge, published his first novel, *The Fleshly Screen* (1937).

LEECH Arthur
late 19th C poet and essayist. Born in Newcastle-under-Lyme, he became councillor, alderman and twice mayor of his native town. His three slim volumes of verse are *The Arlington Lays*, *The Vision of Lord Littleton, a Poem* and *The Braggart, a Poem* (1870).

LEES-MILNE James
b.1908 diarist and novelist. He was born at Wickhamford Manor in Worcestershire. During and after the Second World War he toured the country visiting properties, including Charlecote Park, that had been offered to the National Trust. His autobiography describing these visits, and published in four volumes, takes the form of diaries. As well as many historical books, he wrote the 1964 *Shell Guide to Worcestershire* and the novel, *Heretics in Love* (1973) – and he continues to contribute to the letter page of *The Guardian*.

LEIGH Chandos, 1st Baron Leigh of Stoneleigh
1791–1850 poet. Though born in Middlesex, he always claimed to be a Warwickshire man. His poem, *Warwickshire*, is much decorated with notes, allusions and references – a practice not unknown in the twentieth century. Both the books by the Cubbington farmer, Joseph Russell (1760-1846) – *A Treatise on Agriculture* (1830) and *A New System of Agriculture* (1840) – were dedicated to him for being 'the ardent and steady friend of the British Farmer'. He is described in Debrett as having 'gained favourable reputation as a poet'.

LEIGH Cordelia M
early 20th C poet and children's writer. The granddaughter of Chandos, Baron Leigh*, she was born at the family home, Stoneleigh Abbey, and lived in Leamington Spa all her life. Most of her work, which includes *The Call of the Children*, first published in the *Pall Mall Magazine*, reveals her ample philanthropy and love of nature. *Our School Out of Doors* (1906) and *Christmas in the Woods* (1919) are nature books for very young children.

LEIGHTON William
early 17th C poet and composer. He lived at the family home of Plaish Hall near Longville in Shropshire. Little is known of his creative life, except that he published *Vertue Triumphant, or a Lively Description of the Foure Vertues Cardinall* in 1603 and *The Teares or Lamentations of a Sorrowfull Soule* in 1613.

LELAND John
1503–52 topographical writer and antiquarian. On the orders of Henry VIII, he travelled throughout England and Wales collecting information about castles, bridges, roads and religious establishments. As well as many other places in the area, he is known to have visited Dinmore, Hampton Court (on the River Lug), Hereford, Kenchester and Leominster. His observations were collected in *Itineraries*, a book not published until 1710.

LEON Val
b.1940 poet and short story writer. The secretary of the Birmingham Poetry Centre, she lives in Northfield in Birmingham. Many of the poems in the collection, *Scab* (1974), contrast the natural world with the horrors of an industrialised environment.

LESTER Paul
b.1949 poet and short story writer. Born and brought up in Birmingham, where he read for his doctorate at the university, he lives in Edgbaston. Although his work was already well known in the city's poetry circles, his first collection, *A Funny Brand of Freedom*, did not appear until 1975. He continues to write very slim volumes of topical prose and verse.

LEWIS Cecil J
mid-20th C poet. He lives in Solihull.

All his known work, which includes *Poems Please, Pokes*, and *Before the Birds Take Wing*, has been published in aid of different charities.

LEWIS C S
1898–1963 novelist, critic and children's writer. Though sent to Malvern School, he disliked it so much, he stayed for less than a year. He is perhaps now best known for his children's books, which include *The Lion, The Witch and The Wardrobe* (1950) and *The Last Battle* (1956), and for his popular religious and moral writings, of which *The Screwtape Letters* (1940), under the auspices of Donald Wolfit, transferred successfully to the stage in 1964.

LINDOP Audrey Erskine
mid 20th C novelist and playwright. When she was sixteen, she and her mother went to live in Codsall while her father was stationed at Cosford. At the beginning of the Second World War, she wrote children's articles for the *Wolverhampton Express and Star*. The counties of Shropshire and Staffordshire sometimes provide the settings for her novels which include *In Me My Enemy* (1948), *The Tall Headlines* (1950) and *The Singer not the Song* (1953).

LINWOOD Mary
1755–1845 poet and needlewoman. She was born in Birmingham. Though *The Anglo-Cambrian*, a poem in four cantos, appeared in 1818, she is probably best known for her needle-point picture, The Judgement of Cain, which she completed at the age of seventy after ten years work.

LISTER Thomas Henry
1800–41 novelist. He was born in Lichfield. His work includes the novel, *Granby*, which appeared in 1826.

LIVELY Penelope
b.1933 children's writer and novelist. Born in Egypt, she has lived for a while in Warwick. Though now best known for her adult fiction, in 1973 she won the Carnegie Medal for her childen's story, *The Ghost of Thomas Kempe*. Her reputation continues to grow following her triumph in the Whitbread Award, won with *A Stitch in Time* (1976). *Moon Tiger* (1987), winner of the Booker Prize, is her best-known, and perhaps her best, novel.

LIVINGSTONE Thomas L Fenton
1829–91 poet and playwright. Born at Longton Hall and educated at Lichfield Grammar School, he succeeded his great uncle, Sir Thomas Livingstone, to the estate. *Mammon, a Play; and Other Poems and Translations* appeared in 1893.

LLOYD Charles
1775–1839 poet and novelist. A member of the well-known banking family, he was born in Edgbaston Street in Birmingham. In 1796, urged by his friends, Samuel Taylor Coleridge* and Charles Lamb, he published *Poems on Various Subjects*. All three poets contributed to the anthology, *Blank Verse* (1798). His novel in two volumes, *Edmund Oliver*, appeared in 1823.

LOCKWOOD David
mid/late 20th C poet. He lives in Worcester. Of his published works, *Private View* appeared in 1968 and *There Is a Gate* in 1973. Though frequently concerned with love, his poetic voice is often sardonic and always unsentimental.

LODGE David
b.1935 novelist, academic and critic. A student at the University of Birmingham, he joined the staff in 1969 and became Professor of Modern English Literature in 1976. Early fiction includes *Ginger, You're Barmy* (1962) and *The British Museum is Falling Down* (1965). Originally better known for his critical works, especially *Language of Fiction* (1966), he is now a leading exponent of the campus novel (see BEDE, Cuthbert). Later novels include *Changing Places* (1975), *Small World* (1984), *Nice Work* (1988) and *Paradise News* (1991).

LODGE Oliver William Foster
1878–1955 poet and playwright. He was born at Brampton House in Newcastle-under-Lyme. Among his published works are a tragedy, *The Labyrinth* (1911), the tragi-comedy, *The School of Trimalchio* (1920), a comedy, *The Arbitration Case* (1921), and two volumes of verse, *Poems* (1915) and *Love in the Mist* (1921).

LOMAX Montagu
early 20th C poet. He lived in Leamington Spa. Several of the poems in the collection, *Frondes Caducae*, first appeared in local magazines and newspapers.

LONGBOW Laurence
late 19th C novelist. He is believed to have lived in or near Birmingham. *The Fate of the Fair Fifteen* (1874) relates to old Harborne.

LONGVILLE Tim
b.1940 poet. Born in Staffordshire, he now lives in Brierley Hill. His first collection, *Familiarities*, was published in 1967. Other work includes *Pigs With Wings* (1970) and *Spectacles, Testicles, Wallet and Watch* (1974). His work is very much concerned with language – how it not only conveys meaning, but also elicits

and encourages emotion, through the unlikely juxtaposition of ideas or images. He continues to write. An anthology of his work appeared in 1987.

LOOKER Samuel Joseph
early/mid-20th C poet. He lived in Cheadle in Staffordshire. Many of the poems in *Between the Churnet and the Dove – Poems of North Staffordshire* (written between 1910 and 1950) are about local places, especially those near Oakamoor.

LOVELACE-STREET John
b.1921 poet. He was born and brought up in Shrewsbury, the son of a master at Shrewsbury School. John Betjeman* described him as 'a real poet [who] expresses himself clearly and forcibly'. The collection, *Jungle Paths*, appeared in 1968.

LOVELOCK Yann
b.1939 poet and Buddhist chaplain. Resident for a while in Birmingham, he has helped with the meditation programme at the West Midland Buddhist Centre and has been Visiting Buddhist Chaplain to several of Her Majesty's prisons. Among his earlier collections of poems are *Strange Habitation* (1960) and *Not Unto Them* (1961). His later work, which is also often to do with the lonely and the disappointed, includes *Colour of Weather* (1981).

LOWBURY Edward
b.1913 poet and physician. He lives in Birmingham and was at one time visiting professor at Aston University. He has published several volumes of poetry including *Fire: A Symphonic Ode* (1934), *Time for Sale* (1961), *New Poems* (1965), *Daylight Astronomy* (1968) and *Nightwatchman* (1974). He describes poetry as 'an exploration through words of various experiences

and in particular of painfully exciting or disturbing or conflicting experiences'. *Green Magic* (1972) is a collection for children. *Collected Poems* appeared in his eightieth year.

Edward Lowbury

LOWE Thomas
mid/late 19th C poet. Born in Staffordshire, he became a Methodist preacher and contributed various writings to magazines during the years 1860 to 1887 including 'A Poem on Stratford-on-Avon Shakespeare Memorial Fountain' (1887).

LOWE Thomas Hill Peregrine Furye
1781–1861 poet. Born in Bromsgrove, he became curate at Shelsley Beauchamp in Worcestershire in 1809. The collection, *Poems, Chiefly Dramatic*, appeared in 1840.

LOWNDES Mrs Belloc
1868–1947 novelist. A descendant of Joseph Priestley* of Birmingham, and sister of Hilaire Belloc*, she wrote many novels, including *The End of her Honeymoon* (1914) and *The House By the Sea* (1937). Her work often reflects the cultured, well-heeled society in which she lived, though her best, *The Lodger* (1913), describes the seamier side of life.

Hagley Hall

LOWRIE Stuart
mid-20th C children's writer. He lived in Coventry. *The Secret of Rock Cottage*, which is set in the Warwickshire countryside, appeared in 1950.

LUCAS F L
1894–1967 novelist, poet, literary historian and critic. Educated at Rugby School, a classicist, he generally writes in the traditional mode, impatient and suspicious of modern experimentation with language and form. His work includes the novels, *The River Flows* (1926) and *The Wild Tulip* (1932), and *Poems* (1935). His literary studies, among them *Authors Dead and Living* (1926) and *The Search for Good Sense* (1958), combine erudition with entertainment.

LUDLOW Geoffrey
See MEYNELL, Lawrence

LYALL Edna
1857–1903 (pseudonym of Ada Ellen Bayly) novelist. Her ashes are buried in Bosbury in Herefordshire where she often stayed with her brother who was vicar there. Her novels, including *Donovan* (1882) and its sequel, *We Two* (1884), favoured religious and socially aware sentiments. *Doreen* (1894) was praised by William Ewart Gladstone for its support of 'Home Rule for Ireland'. Bosbury churchyard is featured in *In Spite of All* (1901).

LYALL Gavin
b.1932 novelist. Born in Birmingham, he has written very many novels in the mystery/crime/suspense genre, including *Shooting Script* (1960), *The Wrong Side of the Sky* (1961) and *Venus With Pistol* (1969). He continues to write, *Spy's Honour* appearing in 1993.

LYON Elinor
b.1921 children's writer. She lived for a time in Rugby. Her first book, *Hilary's Island*, appeared in 1948. Other work includes *The Day That Got Lost* (1968) and *The Wishing Pool* (1970).

LYTTELTON George, Lord
1709–73 poet, editor, biographer and patron of literature. He was born and lived at Hagley Hall, the family home in Worcestershire where he entertained, among other west midland authors, Joseph Addison*, Alexander Pope*, James Thomson* and William Shenstone*. Had he still been alive

when Dr Johnson* and Mr and Mrs Thrale* visited the house in 1774, they might have received a less cool reception. Horace Walpole* (1717 to 1797), a frequent visitor, praised the gardens at the hall fulsomely. The volume, *Collected Poems*, was published posthumously in 1801. His chief prose writings are *Dialogues of the Dead* (1760) and *Life of Henry II* (1767). Variations in the spelling of the family name seem to have originated at source – each generation signing itself as the whim took it.

LYTTLETON Thomas, Lord
1744–79 poet. He was known as the 'wicked lord', in contradistinction to his father, the good Lord Lyttelton (see above). A small volume of his poems was published soon after his death at the age of thirty-five – an event reputed to have been prophesied by an apparition half bird, half woman.

LYTTON Edward Robert Bulwer, 1st earl of Lytton
1803–73 novelist, playwright and poet. A frequent visitor to Great Malvern for the curative waters, he published several volumes of poetry, two dozen novels and ten plays – all of which, though tremendously popular during his lifetime, are now all but forgotten. They include the novels, *The Last Days of Pompeii* (1834) and *Rienzi* (1935), and the plays, *Richelieu* (1839) and *Money* (1840).

M

MCCORQUODALE Barbara
See CARTLAND, Barbara

MCEVOY B
1842–1932 novelist and journalist. Born in Birmingham, he wrote a story about life in the city entitled *A Matter of Business* (1882). In 1891 he went to Canada where he became literary editor of a Vancouver newspaper and a member of the expatriate Old Brums.

MACHEN Arthur
1863–1947 novelist. He attended Hereford Cathedral School from 1874 to 1880 when his impoverished father could no longer afford the fees. He is considered now to be the master craftsman of Victorian gothic horror tales – of which *The Great God Pan* (1894) is the best. *The Hill of Dreams* (1907) and *The Secret Glory* (1922) are poetic novels of unusual vision.

MACLAREN Ian
1850–1907 (pseudonym of J Watson) short story writer. The collection, *Beside the Bonny Brier Bush* (1894), was written while the author was living at The Tan House in Little Stretton.

MCLACHLAN Dame Laurentia
early 20th C letter writer. She was Abbess of Stanbrook Abbey near Worcester. Her correspondence of many years with George Bernard Shaw* has recently been published.

MCLEOD John Malcolm G
mid-20th C poet. He is believed to have lived in Stourbridge. A volume of poetry, *Poetical Expressions*, was published in 1963.

MACMILLAN John
1819–91 poet. He was born in Walsall. Examples of his work appear in

Alfred Moss's*, *Songs from the Heart of England* (1920).

MCNEICE Louis
1907–63 poet and radio playwright. From 1930 to 1935 he lectured in classics at the University of Birmingham. His poetry, which includes *Poems* (1935), *Letter From Iceland* (1937, with W H Auden*) and *Autumn Journal* (1939), is accessible, good-humoured and humanitarian. A radio play, *The Dark Tower*, broadcast in 1947, remains one of the major achievements of that underrated art form.

MCQUEEN James Milroy
early/mid-20th C playwright and doctor. He lived and worked in Halesowen. His plays include *The Marrying of John Marston, The New Locarno, or the Peace of Thompson's Inn* (1929), *Old Ebenezer's Charlie* (1929), which is dedicated to his wife, and *Stranger Macs* (1933).

MAINWARING Arthur
1668–1712 poet and critic. Born at Ightfield in the north of Shropshire, he was educated at Shrewsbury School. His best-known work is *The King of Hearts* (1690) and he was also founder of the satirical periodical, *The Medley*.

MAJOR Alfred Bernard
mid-19th C novelist. He lived in Leamington Spa. *Jottings From My Notebook*, a lighthearted attempt to launch himself on 'the broad sea of literature', appeared in 1859.

MALLIN Tom
b.1927 novelist and radio playwright. He was born in the Black Country. His novels, which reveal a remarkable imagination, include *Dodecahedron* (1970), *Curtains* (1971), *Knut* (1971) and *Erowena* (1972). He continues to write with vision and intensity. Radio plays include *Spanish Fly* (1978) and *Halt, Who Goes There?* (1980).

MANFORD Alan and Frank
late 20th C poets. Born and brought up in Cold Hatton near the Wrekin in Shropshire, they are believed to live now in Birmingham. As their titles indicate, both their collaborative collections, *Out of Shropshire* (1974) and *About Shropshire* (1979), relate to that county.

MANNING Frederic
1882–1935 novelist. An Australian by birth, in 1914 he joined the King's Shropshire Light Infantry. His novel, *Her Privates We* (1930), is based on his experiences of being an ordinary soldier in the Great War.

MANNING Hugo
mid/late 20th C poet. He is believed to have lived for a time in Shropshire. His work includes *Beyond the Terminus of Stars* (1949), *The Room Before Sunrise* (1952), *Encounter in Crete* (1971) and *Woman at the Window* (1974). Of the volume, *Madame Lola*, Kathleen Raine wrote: '... this finely sustained poem may be his masterpiece'.

MANTLE Winifred
1911–83 novelist and children's writer. She also used the pseudonyms Frances Lang, Jane Langford and Anne Fellows and has been a winner of the Romantic Novelists' Historical Novel Award. Educated at Wolverhampton High School, she lived with her two sisters in Finchfield. Her first book, a romance entitled *Happy in the House*, was published in 1951.

MAP (or MAPES)
1140–1209 chronicler and poet. Probably born at Wormsley, where his family were lords of the manor, he

later became a canon at Hereford Cathedral. As well as his most famous work, *De Nugis Curialium* – a mixture of legends, anecdotes and gossip, devised for the entertainment of Henry II – he seems to have produced several disreputable poems.

MARASH Jessie Grace

b.1906 playwright. She lived in Coventry and was principal of Bremond College from 1938. Though remembered mainly for her textbooks – on French, acting lessons and elocution – she also wrote several plays including *Godiva of Coventry* (1946), *Thou Bethlehem* (1949), *Henry Mounier* (1951) and the collection of mime plays based on Old Testament stories entitled *And It Came to Pass ...* (1950).

MARSDEN Rev Thomas

mid-19th C poet and hymn writer. A native of Leek in Staffordshire, he published a collection of his poems, *The Poets' Orchard – or Miscellaneous Poems, Psalms and Hymns*, in 1848.

MARSH Jean

b.1897 (pseudonym of Evelyn Marshall) novelist. A teacher in Halesowen until 1919, she later lived in Kidderminster and Bewdley. Most of her work, published during more than fifty years, belongs to the crime or the historical/romantic format and includes *The Shore House Mystery* (1931) and perhaps her most popular, *Death Among the Stars* (1955). She continued to publish into the 1980s.

MARSH-CALDWELL Mrs Anne

1791–1874 poet and novelist. Born at Linley Wood near Talke-o'-the-Hill in Staffordshire, she published a prose-poem translation of *The Song of Roland*.

MARSTON John

1575–1634 poet and playwright. He was born in Coventry, the son of an attorney. Much given to feuding with his fellow playwrights, he is now best remembered for *The Malcontent* (1604) which is dedicated to Ben Jonson*. Swinburne, in his *Sonnets on English Dramatic Poets*, addressed him as 'this noble heart of hatred'.

MARSTON John Westland

1819–90 playwright and reviewer. Born in Coventry, he is best known for the verse tragedy, *The Patrician's Daughter* (1842), though it was *Hard Struggles* (1858) which Charles Dickens* most admired. His other work includes theatrical reviews for *The Athenaeum* and *Our Recent Actors* which has proved a valuable source of theatrical history.

MARTIN F Easthorpe

1882–1925 songwriter. He was born in Stourport-on-Severn. His work includes *Evensong, Songs for the Fair* and *The Mountebanks*.

MARTINEAU Harriet

1802–76 novelist, journalist, essayist and short story writer. She is buried in the cemetery on Key Hill in Birmingham. Though chiefly remembered now for her essays and articles on social reform, her own favourite work was her novel, *Deerbrook* (1839). *Devotional Exercises for the Use of Young Persons* appeared in 1823.

MASCHWITZ Eric

1901–69 novelist and playwright. He was born in Birmingham. Most of his professional life was spent working for the BBC, as editor of the *Radio Times* and in other senior positions. His musical plays include *Carissima* (1948) and *Belinda Fair* (1949). *No Chip On My Shoulder* (1957) is his autobiography.

MASEFIELD Charles John Beech
1882–1917 poet and novelist. He was born at Abbots Haye in the Staffordshire Cheadle. A collected edition of his poems was published in 1919. He is now best known for his *Little Guide to Staffordshire* in which, in celebration of his native county, he re-treads the steps of Michael Drayton* – a journey the earlier writer described in his *Poly-Olbion*.

MASEFIELD John
1878–1967 poet, playwright and novelist. The son of a solicitor, he was born at Knapp House at Ledbury in Herefordshire. After his mother died in 1884, he went to live with relatives and attended King's School in Warwick. At the age of thirteen he joined the Merchant Navy. Both Ledbury church and Bredon church are mentioned in his poetry which often recalls the countryside of his youth. In the volume, *In Glad Thanksgiving* (1966), there are several poems about Shropshire – perhaps inspired by his visits to relatives at Buttery Farm near Kinnersley. In 1930 he became poet laureate and received the freedom of the city of Hereford. His reputation as a poet tends to fluctuate; but a handful of his poems – such as 'Sea Fever' (1902) and 'Cargoes' (1910) – undeniably have their place in our sense of national identity. Other work includes the novels, *Sand Harker* (1924) and *Dead Ned* (1938), and the enduring children's books, *The Midnight Folk* (1927) and the superb *The Box of Delights* (1933).

MASON Geoffrey
mid/late 20th C poet. He lives in Much Marcle in Herefordshire. Though none of his work was published in book form before 1974, the poem, 'Littoral', was broadcast on the radio in 1969 and 'Geriatric Ward' and 'Caption' appeared in the *Birmingham Post*. Later work includes the collection of parodies, *Newer Numbers* (1988), and contributions to *One for Jimmy* (1992), an anthology of Herefordshire and Worcestershire poets. An anthology devoted entirely to his own work has recently appeared.

MASON Kathleen H
mid-20th C poet. She lived in Walsall. The only known collection of her verse, *First Flight*, was published in 1935.

MASON Stanley
b.1917 poet. Born of English parents in a mining village in the Rocky Mountains of the USA, he was brought to England at the age of four and lived near Wolverhampton. A collection of his work, *Best Poems*, appeared in 1964.

MASSINGHAM Harold John
1888–1952 essayist, naturalist and agriculturalist. Although he never lived in the west midland area, he was an enthusiastic and persistent visitor. His descriptions of many places – especially of parts of Herefordshire – in the collection, *Southern Marches* (1952), are a mixture of the poetic and the prosaic.

MAYO Margaret
b.1936 novelist. Born in Birmingham, she now lives in Acton Trussell near Stafford. Though many of her romantic novels, including *Destiny Paradise*, were written before the end of 1974, none was published until 1976. Her work is very popular with the borrowing public.

MERCHANT Paul
late 20th C poet. He studied at the University of Warwick. His sequence

of poems, *Robinson Crusoe in Florida*, was read on Radio 3 in 1973. Much of his work is characterised by vivid detail. He continues to write and later work includes *Bone from a Stag's Heart*.

METEYARD Eliza
See SILVERPEN

MEYNELL Lawrence
1899–1989 novelist and short story writer. A prolific writer, he was born in Wolverhampton into a family connected with the industry of the town. Most of his work, which includes *One Step from Murder* and *The Curious Crime of Julia Blossom*, belongs to the mystery genre. He also wrote under the names of Robert Elton and Geoffrey Ludlow.

MILBOURNE Luke
1649–1720 poet and critic. He was born in Wroxall in Warwickshire, the son of a Nonconformist minister. Regarded by Alexander Pope* as a 'cut-throat bandit type of critic', he is best remembered from a literary point of view for *The Christian Pattern Paraphrased* (1697), a poetical version of Thomas à Kempis's *Imitation of Christ*.

MILES Keith
b.1941 playwright, novelist and children's writer. The husband of Rosalind Miles*, he lectured at a college of further education in Wolverhampton from 1963 to 1966. His work includes versions of the Coventry Mystery Plays, novels and children's books.

MILES Rosalind
late 20th C critic, broadcaster and novelist. Born and educated in Sutton Coldfield, she lives at Corley Hall in Warwickshire. After taking her first degree at Oxford, she returned to the county to study for her MA and PhD at the Shakespeare Institute, University of Birmingham. For some time she was head of the Centre for Women's Studies at the Lanchester Polytechnic, Coventry. Her first book, *The Fiction of Sex*, published in 1974, discusses the themes and functions of the sex difference in the novel. Later work includes books on Elizabethan and Jacobean drama and on women's studies. *The Women's History of the World* appeared in 1988. She has written three novels, the latest being *I Elizabeth* (1993).

MILLS Nora
mid-20th C children's writer. She has Coventry connections. Her only known book, *Bobby's Adventures*, appeared in 1969.

MILLS Paul
b.1948 poet. He has taught at Highgate School in Birmingham. His poems have been widely published and broadcast, though his first collection, *North Carriageway*, did not appear until 1976. Most of his later work, which includes *Half Moon Bay* (1993), is characterised by plain speaking and an air of disillusionment.

MILLS Thomas
mid-19th C poet and religious writer. Born at Hanley, he is the author of many poems and articles on religious subjects, including 'The Death of Christ', which were published in various periodicals.

MILNE Les
b.1930 poet. He came to Coventry in 1968 and began writing poetry which he published in the magazines, *Pause*, *New Poetry* and *Street Poems* – and sang 'wherever anyone would let him'. Much of his verse creates a

collage effect of image, idea and colloquialism.

MILNER Ashley
b.1881 short story writer extraordinaire. He lived in Oxley near Wolverhampton. The number of his short stories published in magazines and newspapers totalled more than eight thousand. His formula, used throughout a career that spanned over fifty years, was to sympathise with his characters and to provide them with a happy ending.

MILTON John
1608–74 poet and theologian. In 1634, while staying in Ludlow, he wrote the masque, *Comus*, which in the same year was performed in the Great Hall of the castle – in celebration of the Earl of Bridgewater's appointment to the presidency of Wales and the Marches. There is a bench seat, placed near Hagley church so as to overlook the grounds of Hagley Hall, on which is written the description of Eden to be found in Book V of his *Paradise Lost* (1657). Horace Walpole believed this description of Eden to be the inspiration for the design of the gardens. The reading of Milton these days is perhaps not the most popular of literary pursuits; but he continues to command respect as the author of *Paradise Lost* (1667) and the verse drama, *Samson Agonistes* (1671).

MONTAGU Lady Mary Wortley
1689–1762 poet and letter writer. There is a memorial to her in Lichfield Cathedral – which Nathaniel Hawthorne*, during his west midland pilgrimage in 1856, was delighted to discover. She is now best known for her letters, written mostly when she was abroad in Turkey (1716–18) and in France and Italy (1739–62). Other

work includes the two collections, *Town Eclogues* and *Court Poems*. With her husband she wrote an anonymous periodical, *The Nonsense of Common-Sense*. Letters and Works eventually appeared in 1837 edited by Lord Wharncliffe.

MONTGOMERY-CAMPBELL M
late 20th C novelist. He is believed to have lived in Shrewsbury. The novel, *Uncle Ben's Whims, or Friends All Round the Wrekin*, was published in 1899 by the Society for Promoting Christian Knowledge. (See FARQUHAR, George for the possible source of this title.) His other work reveals a similarly moral flavour.

MOORE Francis
1657–1715 astrologer. Born at Bridgnorth in the cave dwellings at St Mary's Steps, he is the originator of *Old Moore's Almanac* – a publication considered by some to belong to the world of fiction.

MOORE John
1907–67 novelist. Educated at Malvern School, he lived in the south of Worcestershire for many years. Bredon is the inspiration for *Brensham Village* (1946), a story set between the two world wars which 'breathes the very spirit of our native land, England'. A gentle compassion and love of the countryside informs all his work.

MOORE Thomas
1779–1852 poet. From 1813 to 1817 he lived in Mayfield Cottage (now Standcliffe Farm) just off Gallowstree Lane in Upper Mayfield, Staffordshire. Here *Twopenny Postbag* (1813) and the very successful, *Lalla Rookh* (1817), were written. His daughter, Olivia Byron (named after his friend, Lord Byron), is buried in the

churchyard. In 1827 he went to see her grave, and while staying as Lady Shrewsbury's guest at Alton Towers in 1835 once more visited Mayfield. He is perhaps best remembered now for his songs – such as 'The Minstrel Boy' and 'The Last Rose of Summer'.

MOORHOUSE William Vincent
early 20th C poet. He lived in Wellington. His only known collection, *The Thresher and Other Poems*, appeared in 1828.

MORGAN Walter J
d.1924 short story writer. He lived in Handsworth. *Our Anuk, and Other Black Country Stories* (1909) is written in a dialect which must be read aloud to achieve its full flavour.

MORLEY George
1852–1918 rural writer. He lived in Leamington Spa. All his books, which include *In Russet Mantle Clad* (1857), *The Language of Sweet Arden* (1906) and *The Love-lore of Sweet Arden* (1906), relate to Warwickshire and its legends, songs and poems.

MORRIS Edith
late 19th C poet. She was born at Dresden near Stoke-on-Trent. The collection, *Hours of Meditation*, which contains a poem on the Tay Bridge Disaster to rival William McGonagall's, was published in 1890. Her work is generally concerned with the beauties of 'dear old country lanes'.

MORRIS Stephen
b.1937 poet. Born in Birmingham, he was educated at Moseley Art College and Fircroft College in Edgbaston. For a while he taught creative writing at Wolverhampton Polytechnic and has published several volumes of poems including *Alien Poets* (1965), *Wanted for Writing Poetry* (1968),

Born Under Leo (1972) and *Penny Farthing Machines* (1973). He continues to write his vivid and poignantly telegrammatic poems.

MORRISON John
b.1773 poet. Born at Wednesfield, he was educated at Wolverhampton Grammar School and seems to have been something of an infant prodigy as his verse translation of the *Aeneid* (Books II and IV) is recorded as being published in 1787.

MORSE Brian
b.1948 poet and children's writer. Born in Birmingham, he has taught in the west midland area. In 1970 his poetry collection won him the Eric Gregory Award. He is now known chiefly for his children's books which number ten titles, the latest being *Plenty of Time* (1994).

MORTIMER Mrs Favell Lee
1802–78 children's writer. In the 1850s she lived for a while at Brosely Hall in Shropshire. Her best known book, *Peep of the Day* (1836), is a reworking of 'the Christian message for infant minds'.

MOSS Alfred
b.1859 poet and editor. He was born at Longwood near Walsall and educated at Aldridge. Editor of an anthology of Walsall poetry entitled *Songs from the Heart of England* (1920) and founder of the South Staffordshire Music Festival (1921), he also wrote several short poems, many of them to do with music and composers, and a memorial to Sister Dora*. His other work includes a biography of Jerome K Jerome* (1929).

MOSS Thomas
?1740–1808 poet. Almost certainly Bilston was his birthplace and he was

educated at Wolverhampton Grammar School. He worked as a clergyman in parishes in both Worcestershire and Staffordshire, amongst them Brierley Hill, Trentham, Kingswinford and Stourbridge. He is best known for the poem, 'The Beggar's Petition' (1769), which begins 'Pity the sorrows of a poor old man'. His hope – recorded in *The Imperfections of Human Enjoyment* (1783) – that 'his work, on examination, is found to have more in it to praise than to condemn' is also mine.

MOULTRIE Gerard
1829–85 poet and hymn writer. Born in Rugby, the son of the rector, he was educated at Rugby School and later became an assistant master at Shrewsbury School. In 1867 he published *Hymns and Lyrics for the Seasons and the Saints Days of the Church*; in 1870 *The Espousals of St Dorothea and Other Verses*; and in 1880 appeared *Cantica Sanctorum, or Hymns for the Black-Letter Saints' Days in the English and Scottish Calendars*.

MOULTRIE John
1799–1874 poet and hymn writer. The father of Gerard and Mary, he was rector at Rugby from 1828 and, having rebuilt the rectory, lived there for the rest of his life. The collection, *Poems*, appeared in 1838, to be followed by *The Dream of Life* (1843), *The Black Fence* (1850) and *Altars, Hearths and Graves* (1854). Most of his hymns were published in B H Kennedy's, *Hymnologia Christiana* (1863).

MOULTRIE Mary Dunlop
1837–66 poet. Born in Rugby, she collaborated with her elder brother, Gerard*, in many of the poems in *Hymns and Lyrics for the Seasons and the Saints Days of the Church (1867)*.

MOUNTFORD William
1664?–92 poet, playwright and actor. He was born in Staffordshire, possibly as early as 1659. Chiefly known for his acting skill, he wrote several verse prologues and epilogues and a number of full-length plays, including *The Injured Lovers* (1688) and *Greenwich Park* (1691), which were collected and published in two volumes in 1720.

MUNDY F N C
b.1739 poet. He wrote about the Staffordshire district of Needwood, where he is believed to have lived. The collection, *Fall of Needwood*, was published in 1808.

MUNTHE Major Malcolm
b.1912 novelist and enthusiast. He lived in Hellens, the manor house at Much Marcle. *Hellens: a Herefordshire Manor* (1957) is a delightful description of its history and its people. The semi-autobiographical novel, *Sweet is War*, is based on his experiences in the Second World War.

MURPHY Arthur
1727–1805 playwright, journalist, barrister and actor. A friend of David Garrick* and Dr Johnson*, to whom he introduced the Thrales*, he was present at the jubilee in Stratford-upon-Avon in 1769 which was organised by Garrick to open the Shakespeare Hall. His work includes the farce dramas, *The Apprentice* (1756), *The Citizen* (1761) and *Three Weeks After Marriage* (1776).

MURRAY David Christie
1847–1907 novelist. Born in a house in West Bromwich High Street, he began his career as a journalist by working without payment for the *Wednesbury Advertiser*. Later he

became borough librarian at West Bromwich Library. His best novel, *A Capful O'Nails* (1896), set in the Black Country, has recently been reprinted. Of his other work, *Joseph's Coat* (1892) is set in Birmingham and West Bromwich, *A Rising Sun* (1895) relates to Birmingham's theatrical life, and *The Church of Humanity* (1902) has a Black Country setting. *The Making of a Novelist* (1894) and *Recollections* (1908) are autobiographical.

MUSTO Barry
b.1930 novelist. He lived for a while in Solihull. His published work includes *Storm Centre* (1970), *Codename Bastille* (1972), *No Way Out* (1973) and *The Weighted Scales* (1973). Most of his later work also belongs to the thriller genre.

MYRK (or MYRKES) John
mid-15th C poet and essayist. He was an abbot at Lilleshall Abbey in Shropshire. Although his collection of essays, *Liber Festialis*, dealing with the ordinary things of life, was one of the earliest English books to be published, his work is now almost forgotten.

N

NABBES Thomas
1605–45 playwright. Of obscure Worcestershire origins, in 1625 he returned to the county from Oxford, having failed to obtain his degree, and entered the service of a nobleman. His first comedy, *Covent Garden*, which made fun of the new and growing middle classes, was performed by the Queen's Servants Company in 1632. He has been described as the writer of 'fair comedies, unattractive tragedies and ingenious masques'.

NADEN Constance C W
1855–89 poet. Born in Edgbaston, the daughter of an architect, she was brought up by her maternal grandmother. One of the most brilliant students at Mason College – the nucleus from which the University of Birmingham grew – she lectured there briefly in 1889. Only two volumes of her poetry were published, *Songs and Sonnets of Spring-time* (1881) and *A Modern Apostle, the Elixir of Life and Other Poems* (1887).

NEEDHAM Elizabeth A
b.1868 poet. Born in Kidsgrove, in 1889 she published a slim volume entitled *Leisure Moments; or, The Breathings of a Poetic Spirit*.

NEVILLE George T
late 19th C poet. Born in Lichfield, in 1878 he published the collection, *Youthful Musings; Being Original Miscellaneous Poems*.

NEWBOLT Sir Henry
1862–1938 poet, short story writer, novelist and barrister. The elder son of the vicar of St Mary's, he was born in Baldwin Street, Bradley, a district of Bilston, and was baptised in his father's church. The family soon moved into St Mary's vicarage, staying there until his father died in 1866. They then moved to a house in Bilston which is now the premises of Barclays Bank, before settling on the outskirts of Walsall. Now best remembered for the rousing quality of such poems as 'Drake's Drum' (1892) and 'Vitae Lampada' (1897), he also

served on the committee for the Royal Literary Fund and wrote a novel based on the Grenville family, *The Book of the Grenvilles* (1921). His memoirs, *My World As In My Time*, appeared in 1932.

Cardinal Newman

NEWMAN Cardinal John Henry
1801–90 poet, novelist, essayist, theologian and man of letters. In 1847 he founded the Oratory of St Philip Neri in the Hagley Road in Edgbaston; and had put up a tablet to himself in the memorial church of the Immaculate Conception. He is buried in the graveyard of the Oratory Fathers' country house in Rednal. Of his more than seventy published works, the poem, 'The Dream of Gerontius', which appeared in *The Month* (1865) and a year later in book form – and which Sir Edward Elgar set to music – is probably his most famous literary work. He also wrote two novels, *Loss and Gain* (1848) and *Callista* (1856). (See TREVOR, Meriol.)

NEWTON Bishop Thomas
1703–82 essayist and flatterer. The son of a brandy, wine and cider merchant, he was born in Lichfield and educated at the city's Free Grammar School. His dissertation, *Prophecies*, went through twenty editions; his annotated version of John Milton's*, *Paradise Lost* and *Paradise Regained*, long enjoyed, according to Dr Johnson*, a reputation far beyond its merit. His autobiography, completed a few days before his death, reveals he thought it 'quite right and proper for a clergyman to hunt for preferment by flattery'.

NICHOLAS Clifford
b.1928 poet. A member of the Birmingham Poetry Centre, he has lived in the city. His spare abrupt poetry first appeared in the collection, *Eye of my Belly*, which was published in 1972 – to be followed by *To Walsingham at Easter* in 1973. He has been a frequent contributor to radio poetry programmes.

NICHOLLS Derek
late 20th C playwright. He has lived in Birmingham. With Raymond Speakman* he wrote the play, *The Fire King* (1972), a retelling of the story of Matthew Boulton, which was presented by the Birmingham Youth Theatre at Birmingham College of Food and Domestic Art.

NICHOLS Wallace Bertram
b.1888 poet, playwright and novelist. He was born at Handsworth. His main published works are the epic poem, *The Song of Sharruk* (1916), the narrative poems, *The Saga of Judas* (1949) and *Jericho Street, Selected Poems* (1921), a trilogy of historical plays entitled *Earl Simon* (1922), a one-act play in blank verse, *The Glory of the World* (1924), and a novel called *Secret Market* (1928).

NICHOLSON Mrs Celia

mid-20th C novelist. She is believed to have spent some time in Birmingham. *A Boswell To Her Cook: a Cautionary Tale* (1931) is a novel that relates to the city.

NICKLIN Edward

late 18th C poet. He lived in Birmingham. *Pride and Ignorance* (1770) debates in verse form the effects of succumbing to these twin temptations.

NOAKE John

1816–94 local historian, writer and journalist. He spent twenty-one years working for Worcester newspapers – seven with *Berrows Journal,* seven with *The Herald* and seven with *The News.* His best-known books are the anecdotal *The Rambler in Worcestershire, or Stray Notes on Churches and Congregations* (1848–51–54), *Guide to Worcestershire* (1868) and *Worcestershire Nuggets* (1891).

NOKE Mrs Dora

early 20th C poet and short story writer. She lived in Birmingham. The two collections of verse and prose pieces, *Ambition* (1928) and *Hope* (1929), contain in the main work of an uplifting and encouraging nature.

NOKES Harriet

1830–95 poet. Born at Bilston, the daughter of a printer, she was educated privately. Her only published volume of poems, often effusive, but always good-hearted, appeared in 1857 as *The Home Wreath and Other Poems.* She is described by Boase as spending 'all her life in the recovery of the fallen'.

NORWAY Kate

b.1913 (pseudonym of Olive Claydon) novelist. From 1954 to 1959 she worked for the *Birmingham News* and is now believed to be living in Four Oaks in Warwickshire. A prolific writer of historical and romantic fiction, much of it with a hospital setting, she published her first novel, *Sister Brookes of Bynds,* in 1957.

NOWELL Stella

late 20th C novelist. She lives in Walsall. Of her several novels, *The Waterfall,* which is dedicated to Norrey Ford (DILCOCK, Noreen*) 'who walked by my side', was published in 1972 and *The Whistling Sands* in 1973.

NOYES Alfred

1880–1958 poet and novelist. He was born in Chapelash, Wolverhampton – though he always claimed the unspecific Staffordshire as his birthplace. When he was still very young, his family moved away from the west midland area. A most prolific writer, and able to live entirely by his poetry, he is now regarded as rather trite. *The Highwayman,* perhaps his best-known poem, was made into a film. His novels, which include *Walking Shadows* (1918) and *The Hidden Player* (1924), are experiments in the literature of fantasy.

O

OAKES Philip

b.1928 poet, scriptwriter and novelist. He was born in Burslem and educated at the Royal Grammar School in Wolverhampton. From 1959 to 1960 he was a scriptwriter for Granada Television. His work includes a collection of twenty poems entitled

Unlucky Jonah (1954) and the novels, *In the Affirmative* (1969) and *Experiment at Proto* (1973). *Shopping for Women* appeared in 1994.

OAKLEIGH Tom
See KILLMINSTER, Abraham K

O'CONNOR Armel
1886–1955 poet. While living at Mary's Meadow, Ludford in Shropshire, he worked from 1909 to 1946 as a part-time music master at Ludlow Grammar School. He wrote several volumes of poetry, among them *The Happy Stillness* (1920) and *The Little Company* (1925). With his wife, Violet (see below), he wrote *Peacemakers* (1916).

O'CONNOR Violet
early 20th C poet and children's writer. She lived at Mary's Meadow, Ludford and collaborated with her husband in the writing of *Peacemakers* (1916). She also published several books for children, including *The Songs for Mary's Meadow and Other Verses* (1926) and *Romantic Ludlow* (1934). *Sweet Scented Leaves* (1913) is a volume of short stories of 'conduct and character'.

O'DONNELL Maureen
b.1934 children's writer. From 1952 she worked in Coventry City Library. *The Lorry Thieves* appeared in 1961.

OLDFIELD Jenny
b.1949 poet and children's writer. She teaches English at Edgbaston High School. The collection, *Tomorrow Shall Be My Dancing Day*, appeared in 1974. She is now known chiefly for the children's books, including *Yours Truly* and *The Terrible Pet*, which were published in the Roundabouts series. *Misfits and Rebels* appeared in 1990.

OLE-LUK-OIE
1868–1951 (pseudonym of E D Swinton) short story writer. Educated at Rugby School, he wrote the very popular book, *The Green Curve* (1909), a collection of short stories.

OLLIVANT Alfred
1874–1927 novelist. He was educated at Rugby School. As the result of a spinal injury suffered while serving in the Artillery, he turned to writing as a career. *Owd Bob* (1898) is still considered to be one of the best dog stories ever written.

ORAM Vera
mid/late 20th C poet. She lives in Birmingham. The collection, *In a Pause of the Shuttle*, was published in 1969; *A Frame to Fit* in 1974. Her later work is noted for the way it transforms the language of prose into a spare urgent poetry.

ORGILL Douglas
b.1922 novelist, journalist and military historian. Born in Walsall, he was educated at Queen Mary's Grammar School. His novels, which include *The Death Bringers* (1962) and *Ride a Tiger* (1963), belong to the thriller genre.

ORMEROD Roger
b.1920 novelist. Born in Wolverhampton and having attended a secondary school until he was sixteen, he worked for twelve years at the county courts in Queen Street before moving on to Rubery Owen's factory at Darlaston. He still lives in Wolverhampton. His first novel, *Time To Kill*, was published in 1972. All his work – up to, and including, *A Shot at Nothing* (1993), the latest in more than thirty novels – has to do with crime detection and the physical and mental thrill of the chase.

ORTON Job

1717–83 essayist and religious writer. Born in Shrewsbury, the son of a grocer, he was educated at Shrewsbury School. In 1741 he was appointed minister of the town's High Street Unitarian Church. He stayed there until his retirement in 1766, when he moved to Kidderminster. He is buried in the chancel of Old St Chad's Church, Shrewsbury. Though a prolific writer of essays, articles, sermons and lectures, he is now best remembered for his book, *Memoirs of Doddridge* (1766), in which he recalls his years spent training for the ministry in the academy in Northampton run by this Unitarian divine.

OSBORNE John

b.1929 playwright. He lives in Puddleston in Herefordshire. His play, *Look Back in Anger* (performed in 1956, published in 1957), encapsulates the mood of change – from mute acceptance of the status quo to articulate dissatisfaction – which marked fifties' society. He was the originator of the 'angry young man'. Later work, which includes *West of Suez* (1971) and *Watch It Come Down* (1976), is less fiery and more waspish.

OUSELEY Sir Frederick Arthur

1825–89 song and hymn writer. He founded the choral college at Tenbury Wells in Worcestershire in 1856. His work is made up of both sacred and secular songs.

OVERBURY Sir Thomas

1581–1613 poet. He was born in Compton Scorpion in the parish of Ilmington, Warwickshire, in the house of his maternal grandfather where he received his early education. *A Wife*, generally believed to be his masterpiece, appeared in 1614. A series of harshly delineated 'characters', included in its second edition, were later added to by Thomas Dekker*. He is best known as the victim of the Countess of Essex's hatred, which led to his murder by poison in the Tower of London.

OWD TOM

See EDWARDS, Thomas

OWEN Gareth

late 20th C poet, actor and playwright. He lives in Birmingham and has lectured at Bordesley College. For some time he has been associated with the Crescent Theatre and the Pub Theatre where several of his plays have been successfully performed. The volume of verse, *Nineteen Fragments*, was published in 1974. Later work includes the collections of poems, *Salford Road* (now a musical) and *Song of the City*, and several storybooks for children, among them *The Final Test*, *Omlette: A Chicken in Peril!* (1990) and *My Granny is a Sumo Wrestler* (1994).

OWEN Goronwy

1723–69 poet. In 1745 he became curate at Selattyn near Oswestry, where he married Ellen Hughes, daughter of an Oswestry alderman. He moved to Uppington in 1748, obtaining both the curacy there and a teaching post in nearby Donnington Grammar School. In the next five years he produced his best work. Much of his poetry was written in Welsh and is much admired by Welsh scholars for exemplifying the imagery and cadences of the language.

OWEN John

d.1622 epigrammist. He became headmaster of King Henry VIII School in Warwick in 1594. His Latin epigrams, published in twelve books (the first three in 1606) were so popular they were almost immediately translated into English.

OWEN Wilfred
1893–1918 poet. The son of a railway worker, he was born at Plas Wilmot in Oswestry, the home of his mother's parents, and stayed there for four years until the house had to be sold following the death of his grandfather. The family returned to Shropshire in 1907 and lived first in Cleveland Place and then in Monkmoor Road in Shrewsbury. He was educated at Shrewsbury Technical School. For a short while he taught in a school in Wyle Cop, before leaving to train for the ministry. The verses he wrote during the war years – *Poems* (published posthumously in 1920) – reveal an intense compassion for ordinary men caught up in the struggles of power hungry states. Some of his poems were incorporated into Benjamin Britten's *War Requiem*, composed for the dedication of the new Coventry Cathedral in 1962. His parents in Shrewsbury heard of his death on Armistice Day.

Wilfred Owen

P

PAGET Francis Edward
1806–82 children's writer. From 1835 to his death he was rector of Elford in Staffordshire. *The Hope of the Katzekoffs* (1844) has been described as the first English fairytale.

PAKINGTON Humphrey
1888–1974 novelist. He belonged to the Pakington family who lived at Westwood Park near Droitwich. Most of his novels are concerned with middle-class, often rural, families and are set in the fictional county of Severnshire. These include *Four in the Family* (1931), *The Washbournes of Otterley* (1948), *The Brothers Bellamy* (1953) and *Willoughby Carter* (1954).

PALMER Francis Paul
1808–72 poet and short story writer. For many years he was medical officer of health for Walsall. His work includes the volume, *Old Tales for the Young*, and several poems in Alfred Moss's*, *Songs from the Heart of England* (1920).

PALMER John Leslie
1885–1944 novelist and theatre writer. He was educated in Birmingham. A most prolific writer, he used several pseudonyms – Francis Beeding and David Pilgrim, when collaborating with Hilary St George Saunders, and also Christopher Haddon in his own work. Most of his novels, which include *The King's Men* (1916), *The Seven Sleepers* (1925),

Under the Long Barrow (1939) and *Eleven Were Brave* (1951), are of the thriller variety. He also produced a number of books of literary criticism.

PALMER John Richard
b.1858 poet, novelist and religious writer. Born in South Staffordshire and tutored by William Travis of Stourbridge, he returned to his native county in 1905 as vicar of Kingstone and rector of Gratwich. The collection, *Lines of Poetry*, was published in 1876 and his best-known work, a devotional piece entitled *Burden-Bearing*, appeared in 1884. *A Hero in Strife*, *Sunbeam's Influence* and *From Darkness to Light* are three of his prose fiction works.

Edith Pargeter

PARGETER Edith
b.1913 novelist. She also writes under the name of Ellis Peters. Born and brought up in Coalbrookdale, she attended the local church school and the county high school before becoming a chemist's assistant. She now lives in the Shropshire Madeley. Her first novels, beginning with *The City Lies Foursquare* (1939), were successful; though it was her creation of Brother Cadfael which made her a bestselling author and put Shrewsbury firmly on the literary tourist map. The detecting monk made his first appearance in *A Morbid Taste for Bones* (1977) and has now solved twenty medieval mysteries.

PARKES Sir Henry
1815–85 poet and politician. Born in Stoneleigh in Warwickshire where he attended a dame's school and the village school, he had completed his education by the time he was eleven and was then apprenticed to an ivory turner in Birmingham. In 1836 he married and went to live in the city. Before emigrating to Australia at the age of twenty-four, he founded a liberal newspaper, *The Empire*. As a politician in Australia, he did much to foster interest in poetry. The best of his own literary output of five volumes of verse is *Murmurs of the Stream* (1857).

PARKES William Kineton
1865–1938 novelist. He was born at Aston Manor in Warwickshire and educated at King Edward VI Grammar School in Aston and Mason College in Birmingham. From 1891 to 1911 he was librarian at the Nicholson Institute in Leek. His novels include *Potiphar's Wife* (1908), *The Altar of Moloch* (1912) and *Hardware* (1914) which is set in Birmingham.

PARISH Leonard
early 20th C poet and actor. Born and brought up at Eckington in Worcestershire, he served abroad during the Great War before becoming an actor in Stratford-upon-Avon. A collection of over fifty of his poems, *Dusk of Avon*, appeared in 1921. He later emigrated to Australia.

PARRY Harold
1896–1917 poet and letter writer. Born at Bloxwich, he was educated at Queen Mary's Grammar School in Walsall. Though wordy, his poetry is colourfully descriptive. His letters and poems were published posthumously in 1917 and his work is well represented in Alfred Moss's*, *Songs from the Heart of England* (1920).

PARRY James
b.1712 novelist and ?autobiographer. His only known work, *The True Anti-Pamela* (last printing in 1770), presents a vivid picture of eighteenth-century Ross-on-Wye. Whether the central character of this melodramatic story is fictional or a self-portrait is still unknown.

PARSONS Harold
1919–92 short story writer, editor and radio writer. The son of a shopkeeper, he was born and brought up in Dudley. He attended The Park School and was later employed in a factory in Wolverhampton, before going into the army. His first published work, *As You Were* (1948), was a short story. He moved to Kinver in 1965. His autobiography, *Substance and Shadow*, appeared in 1982 after he had had over thirty years as a published writer. For a time he was editor of the *Black Countryman*.

PATTISON Samuel
late 18th C poet. The author of *Original Poems, Moral and Satirical* (1792), he was born near Etruria in Staffordshire. At first glance his work is most correct in style and apparently sincere in its celebration of the achievements of local dignitaries – the claws are there, however.

PAUL Leslie
b.1905 poet, novelist and short story

writer. He lived for a while in Madley in Herefordshire and lectured at the University of Birmingham from 1964 to 1970. A collection of verse, *Exile and Other Poems*, appeared in 1957 and his first novel, *The Boy Down Kitchener Street*, was published in 1969.

PAX
See CHOLMONDELEY, Mary

PAYNE Charles
1888–1961 novelist. He was mayor of Coventry in 1935. His work includes the historical novels, *The Secret of Josiah Black* (1934) and *Four Men Seek God.*

PEARCE J
mid-20th C short story writer. *Cherry Tree Chapel and other stories* (1933) relates to Methodism in the city of Birmingham where he lived.

PEARCE Mary E
b.1932 novelist. Though she now lives in Gloucestershire many of her novels, amongst them *Apple Tree Lean Down* (1973) and *Jack Mercybright* (1974), are set in Worcestershire. Her later work, which includes *Old House at Railes*, continues to be concerned with rural themes.

PEARCE Noel
late 19th C novelist. He is believed to have lived in Stourbridge. *Thomas Harris's Dream – giving an account of his Wanderings Among the Stars* (1881) was published by a Stourbridge firm.

PEARSON Hesketh
1887–1964 actor, travel writer and biographer. He was born in Worcestershire. *Whispering Gallery* (1926), a fictional rendering of a diplomat's diary, became the subject of a court case; but he is now best known for his lively biographies of theatrical and

literary figures – including those of William Hazlitt* (1934) and Beerbolm Tree (1956).

PEARSON John
1772–1841 poet. Born at the manor house in Tettenhall, he was educated at Wolverhampton Royal Grammar School. A collection of his poems, *Poems on Various Occasions*, was published in 1796.

PEATE-HUGHES Thomas A
early 20th C poet. He lived in Brose-ley in Shropshire. The only known collection of his verse, *Follow Your Genius*, appeared in 1924.

PELLES Senor Erasmo
early 20th C poet. One of Cuba's national poets and Chancellor of the Consulate of Cuba, in 1926 he was consul in Birmingham. He has been described by a leading dramatic critic as the 'little Shakespeare of Cuba'.

PEMBERTON Sir Max
1863–1950 novelist. Born in Birmingham, he was educated at Merchant Taylor's School. The writer of several adventure stories, among them *The Diary of a Scoundrel* (1891) and *The House Under the Sea* (1902), from 1896 he was also editor of *Cassell's Magazine* for ten years.

PERCY Cyril Heber
mid-20th C novelist. The son of an alderman, he lived at Hodnet Hall in Shropshire. His work includes *Hym* (1959) and *Us Four* (1963).

PERCY Thomas
1729–1811 poet, antiquarian and translator. The son of a grocer, he was born in a house named Forester's Folly in Bridgnorth and was baptised at St Leonard's Church. At the age of eight he went to Bridgnorth School. In 1761 he published his translation in four volumes of the Chinese novel,

Hau Kiou Choaan. On a visit to his friend, Humphrey Pitt, at Priors Lee Hall in Shifnal, he discovered an old manuscript (being used to light the fire). The poems, songs and ballads in this manuscript, and many other ballads collected from England and abroad with the help of David Garrick* and William Shenstone*, were published in *Reliques of Ancient English Poetry* (1765), his best-known work. Of his original work, the ballad, 'Sir Cauline', is the most successful. His ballad, 'Hermit of Warkworth' (1771), prompted Dr Johnson* to a parody and to pronounce of the writer, 'He runs about with little weight upon his mind'.

PERKS Francis
mid-19th C poet. He lived in Stourbridge. A selection of his poetry was published posthumously in Birmingham in 1853.

PESCADOR Martin
mid/late 20th C children's writer. He lives in Telford. His work includes *The Balloon that Burst, Mr Bubbles' Bonfire Party* and *Three Boys and Three Wishes*.

PETCH Tony
b.1943 poet. He has lived in Rugby, a member of the Rugby Poetry Workshop. A collection of his work, *Poems*, which often draws on ordinary, everyday objects and articles for its inspiration, was published in 1973.

PETERS Ellis
See PARGETER, Edith

PETTITT Henry
1848–93 poet, short story writer and playwright. The son of Edwin Pettitt (Herbert Glyn*), he was born at Smethwick and educated at a private

school in the town. A prolific writer of light theatre pieces, he won the Best Christmas Story Award from the magazine, *Boys' Miscellany*. His play, *Golden Fruit* (1873), was produced at the Pavilion Theatre in Camden Town and his pantomime, *Harlequin King Frolic*, had the longest recorded run at the Grecian Theatre in (1880/81). Though a frequent visitor to Birmingham, he always remained proud of being a Smethwick man.

PETTY John
1919–73 novelist. A scrap-picker who always wanted to write fiction, he lived in Walsall and survived by scavenging waste metal from a local furnace tip. *Five Fags a Day* (1956) is mainly autobiographical, but he also wrote two other novels, *Flame in my Heart* (1958) and *The Last Refuge* (1966). For many years a sick man, he died in Dawley in Shropshire at the age of fifty-four.

PHILIPS Ambrose
1675–1749 poet and playwright. Born in Shrewsbury, the son of a draper, he was baptised in St Alkmund's Church and educated at Shrewsbury School. A series of *Pastorals*, the first of which was published in 1706, are his best-known work. On account of the fulsomeness of his verse, he was dubbed 'Namby-Pamby' by Jonathan Swift* and Alexander Pope*. He also wrote two tragedies, *The Briton* (1722) and *Humfrey, Duke of Gloucester* (1723).

PHILIPS John
1676–1708 poet and playwright. A member of a well-established Herefordshire family – his father was a canon at Hereford Cathedral, his grandfather a Ledbury clothier – he eventually came to live in Withington and is buried at Hereford Cathedral.

His work includes the burlesques, *The Splendid Shilling* (1701), *The Campaign* (1704) and *Blenheim* (1705). Though not altogether to Dr Johnson's* taste, his long poem, *Cyder* (1708), is a fascinating celebration of the Herefordshire apple.

PHILLIPS Mrs Elizabeth A
See NEEDHAM, Elizabeth A

PHILLIPS Stephen
1868–1915 poet and playwright. Part of his education took place in Stratford-upon-Avon. The collection, *Poems* (1898), was published while he was working as a teacher. His meteoric rise to fame with his fifth verse play, *Paola and Francesca* (1900), was not sustained and he died in poverty.

PHILP Peter
mid-20th C playwright. He lived in Kidderminster. His only known work, *The Castle of Deception*, was first performed in 1952.

PILGRIM David
See PALMER, John Leslie

PITT William
1749–1823 poet and agriculturist. Born at Tettenhall, he lived at Pendeford and later at Edgbaston. *The Bullion Debate: A Serio-Comic Satire ... in English Verse* was published in 1811.

PITTAWAY Rev T
mid-20th C poet. He was rector at St Kenelm's church in Clent. The collection, *St Kenelm and Other Poems*, appeared in 1940.

PLOMER William
1903–73 novelist, poet and librettist. He was educated at Rugby School. Many of his novels, the first being *Turbott Wolfe* (1926), are vituperative attacks on the regime in South Africa. His poetry is more urbane and

contemplative – though it can sometimes be macabre, as in 'The Dorking Thigh' (1948). He wrote several libretti for Benjamin Britten's operas. *Collected Poems* (1960) won the Queen's Gold Medal for Literature.

PLUMMER T Arthur
b.1883 novelist. The son of an obsessive anti-vaccinator, he was born and lived in Coventry. Before turning to writing as a career he was an actor for eleven years. His work, which was much admired in its day, is mainly of the thriller/mystery variety and includes *The Ace of Death* (1928), *Lonely Hollow Mystery* (1933) and *Who Fired the Factory?* (1947).

PODD
See COLE, Thomas E

POINTON Priscilla
b.1750 poet. She was born and brought up in Lichfield where, at the age of thirteen, she became blind. *Poems on Several Occasions* appeared in 1770. Her second volume was published in 1790, two years after her marriage to a Mr Pickering of Birmingham. Though generally all too predictable, some of her poetry has a surprising candour.

POPE Alexander
1688–1744 poet. He was a frequent visitor to the west midland counties. In 1723 he formed an attachment with Lady Mary Wortley Montagu* of Lichfield, but the friendship ended in unpleasantness. Elijah Fenton*, his collaborator in *Odyssey* (1725–6), lived in Stoke-on-Trent. John Kyrle, the 'Man of Ross', is the subject of his *Moral Essays, Epistle III, to Lord Bathurst* (1732). He is known to have spent time at Hagley Hall, the home of the Lyttelton* family – in his

capacity as garden enthusiast, perhaps, rather than as poet – and in 1709 William Walsh* invited him to stay at Abberley Lodge. He is now best remembered for his *Essay on Criticism* (1711) and the satirical, *The Rape of the Lock* (1712, 1714).

PORTER John
1838–1922 novelist and racehorse trainer. He was born at Rugeley in Staffordshire. His only known work, *Kingsclere* (1896), was very popular in its day.

PORTER Sheena
b.1935 children's writer. Shropshire Regional Librarian from 1961 to 1962, she lives in Ludlow. Her many novels, mostly describing the exploits of venturesome girls, include *The Bronze Chrysanthemum* (1961), *Hills and Hollows* (1962) and *Nordy Bank* (1964). *The Knockers* (1965) is set on the Long Mynd in Shropshire; *The Scapegoat* (1968) in Shrewsbury.

POSTGATE Isa
late 19th C poet. Born in Birmingham, the sister of John Postgate*, she lived all her life in the city. *Dream of the Rood* retells in verse the story of the Anglo-Saxon, Caedmon. *Song and Wings, Bird Poems for Young and Old* reveals her exceptional love of nature; *A Christmas Legend* (1888) demonstrates her faith and her charity.

POSTGATE John Percival
1853–1926 poet and academic. Like his sister Isa*, he was born in Birmingham. Much of his verse and prose was written in Latin. *"In Memoriam Condensed"*: a *Tennysonian Study* neatly encapsulates in three verses the original's melancholy expression of love bereft.

POTTER Dennis
b.1935–1994 playwright. He lived in Ross-on-Wye. Best known for his television plays, which include his first, *Where the Buffalo Roam* (1966), and *Vote, Vote, Vote for Nigel Barton* (1965), he also wrote a novel, *Hide and Seek* (1973). His work is extraordinarily varied, though it almost always relentlessly exposes that self-seeking self-delusion – the modern equivalent of Ibsen's 'life-lie' – without which very few of us could manage to function. He continued to write, often combining aspects of popular culture, such as lovesongs or detective stories, with barbed attacks on our unthinking social assumptions. *Brimstone and Treacle* and *The Singing Detective* are perhaps his best, and best known, plays – though *Blackeyes* exposes the bitterest truths of our modern culture.

POWELL Enoch
b.1912 poet and politician. Born at Stetchford in Birmingham, he was MP for Wolverhampton SW from 1950 to 1974. His literary output of poetry and biography is still overshadowed by his challenging political ideas. *First Poems* appeared in 1937 and *Dancer's End and Wedding Gift* in 1951.

POWELL William
1735–69 actor and playwright. Born in Hereford, he was educated at the Cathedral School. In 1763 he joined David Garrick's* company where he made his reputation as actor and writer.

POWER Norman
b.1916 poet and children's writer. A regular contributor to the *Birmingham Evening Mail* and the *Birmingham Post*, he became vicar at Ladywood in 1958. His work, which includes *Ends of Verse* (1971), has been described as 'the poetry of everyday life'. *The Forgotten Kingdom* (1970) and *Fear in Firland* (1974) were written for children.

PRICE Albert J J
early 20th C poet. *The Legend of the Leper of Kenelmstowe* (1927) relates to Romsley where he may have lived.

PRICE Candelent
early 20th C poet. He was born at Handsworth in Birmingham and spent much of his life in Staffordshire. The collection, *Celtic Ballads*, was greatly admired by the then poet laureate, Robert Bridges.

PRICE Frederick
1804–84 poet. Born in Bilston, he worked as a compositor for the *Staffordshire Advertiser* before becoming a printer in Birmingham. His collection, *Rustic Rhymes* (1859), has a primitive vivaciousness that is rather winning.

PRICE George
mid-19th C poet. Born at Bilston, he was first a printer and then a lock manufacturer. His only known poem, the long *The Church of Christ*, was published in 1863.

PRICE Graham
b.1949 poet. He was born in Worcester and lived for a time in Hereford. With Alan Sherratt, another 'underground poet', he wrote *Thou Art Not So Unkind as Man's Ingratitude* – a collection undoubtedly published before 1974 as the copy in Madeley Library is price-marked 2/-. He is believed to have continued to write.

PRICE Nancy
1880–1970 (pseudonym of Mrs Maude) actress and novelist. She was born at Kinver and educated at

Malvern Wells. Her novel, *Ta Mera*, was published in 1950.

PRICE Susan
b.1955 children's writer. She was born in Tividale in Warley, and still lives in the town. While working as a part-time shelf-filler in a local supermarket, she began writing and at fourteen years old won the *Daily Mail* Short Story Competition. Her first book, a fantasy called *The Devil's Piper* (1973), was published soon after she left school; *Twopence a Tub*, about mining families in the Black Country, appeared in 1974. She has worked as a guide in the Black Country Museum and has been writer in residence at Worcester Central Library. Her later books, which include *Ghost Song* (1992) and *Heads and Tales* (1993), continue to engage with, and speak directly to, the confusions of adolescence.

PRICE Sir Uvedale
1747–1829 essayist and horticulturalist. He lived in the family home at Foxley where he developed and improved the natural beauty of the estate – especially the famous Lady Lift Ride. His best-known work, *Essay on the Picturesque* (1794), which describes how the study of pictures can suggest ways of improving garden design, was extremely influential on contemporary landscape aesthetics in England. A neighbour, friend and correspondent of Richard Payne Knight*, he not only wrote *A Dialogue on the distinct characters of the Picturesque and the Beautiful, in answer to the objections of Mr Knight* (1801), but also consulted him for his *Essay on the Greek and Latin pronunciation* (1827).

PRICKETT Miss
early 19th C novelist. Her three-decker historical novel, *Warwick Castle* (1815), which refers to Warwick, Birmingham and many other places in the west midland counties, contains several poems and anecdotes about the locality.

PRIESTLEY Brian
mid-20th C novelist. Born in Birmingham, he worked first as a reporter and then as assistant editor on the *Birmingham Evening Mail*. Later he turned to thriller writing. His work includes the novel. *Marakiri Gold*. In 1968 *The Listener* printed his Third Programme talk on the replanning of Birmingham.

PRIESTLEY John Boynton
1894–1984 novelist, playwright, critic and historian. He lived with his wife, Jacquetta Hawkes*, in Alveston near Stratford-upon-Avon. His play, *Music at Night*, was commissioned and first performed at the Malvern Festival in 1938. Best known for the novels, *The Good Companions* (1929) and *Angel Pavement* (1930), for his 'time' plays, which include *Dangerous Corner* (1932) and *Time and the Conways* (1937), and for his later 'morality' plays, among them *An Inspector Calls* (1945) and *The Linden Tree* (1947), he published in total more than sixty books. His work is always accessible and at its best both poignant and perceptive.

PRIESTLEY Joseph
1733–1804 essayist. He came to live in Birmingham in 1780. On 14 July 1791 his house in the city was virtually destroyed by a mob enraged at his support for the French Revolution, an event made the subject of William Hazlitt's* first piece of published prose. His own published

work includes *The History and Present State of Electricity* (1767) and *The History of the Corruptions of Christianity* (1782) (see TOWNSEND, G A), and many other diverse subjects. Samuel Taylor Coleridge*, in *Religious Musings* (1796), called him 'Patriot and Saint and Sage'.

PRING John
1777–1853 poet. He is believed to have lived for a while in Stourbridge. His work includes *Millenium Eve, a Poem Begun in Florence* (1843) and *Seasons of Sorrow, Original Poems* (1845).

PRYCE Richard
1864–1942 novelist and adaptor. A prolific and popular novelist, he was educated at Leamington Spa. His work includes the early *An Evil Spirit* (1887) and the much later *Morgan's Yard* (1932). He also adapted novels for the stage, such as those of Arnold Bennett* and Christopher Morley.

PURSHOUSE Benjamin
mid-20th C poet. He lived in Wolverhampton. *Survival*, in which 'the author, by blending a certain amount of fact and fiction, has endeavoured to present a story which touches upon history, superstition, romance, reincarnation and witchcraft spread over some six hundred years', appeared in 1961.

PYM Barbara
1913–80 novelist. She was born in Oswestry, the daughter of a solicitor. Her reputation as a writer of quiet humour and compassionate subtlety is now established. *Excellent Women* (1952) and *A Glass of Blessings* (1958) are perhaps the best of her early novels. Her renaissance, instigated by Philip Larkin* and Lord David Cecil, began with *Quartet in Autumn* (1977). She continues to have a quietly enthusiastic following.

Q

'Q'
See QUILLER-COUCH, Sir Arthur

QUIGLEY Aileen
late 20th C novelist and short story writer. She lives in Walsall. A frequent contributor of short stories to BBC Morning Story and Woman's Hour, she published the novel, *Devil in Holy Orders* in 1973. She continues to write.

QUILLER-COUCH Sir Arthur
1863–1944 novelist, poet and critic.

(He sometimes used the pseudonym 'Q'.) A West Countryman, it is known that he visited the Worcestershire village of Eckington which inspired his writing of the poem 'Upon Eckington Bridge, River Avon'. He spoke of Worcestershire as the 'pastoral heart of England'. Perhaps he is now best remembered for his editorship of the *Oxford Book of English Verse* (1900), though his Cornish novels and his published lectures can still delight.

R

RADFORD Edwin
b.1891 journalist and novelist. He was born and brought up in West Bromwich. His work, which belongs to the thriller genre, includes *The Heel of Achilles* and *Death on the Broads*. The detective novels featuring Inspector Manson, amongst them *Inspector Manson's Success* (1944), *Who Killed Dick Whittington?* (1947), *Death at the Chateau Noir* (1960) and *Murder Magnified* (1965), were written in collaboration with his wife, Mona Augusta Radford.

RADFORD Mona Augusta
See above

RAGG Thomas
1808–81 poet. From 1839, after moving from Nottingham where he was known as the 'Nottingham Mechanic', he lived for a while in Birmingham where he was editor of the *Birmingham Advertiser* and the *Midland Monitor* and a stationer and printer from 1845–58. Following his ordination in 1858, he was appointed curate of Malin's Lee in Shropshire and perpetual curate of Lawley. Early work includes *The Deity* (1834), *Sketches from Life* (1837) and *Lays of the Prophets* (1841). The collection, *Scenes and Sketches from Life and Nature; Edgbaston and Other Poems*, appeared in 1850.

RALPH Lester
1878–1936 novelist. He was appointed to teach at the Priory School for Boys in Shrewsbury in 1914. Having stayed only a short time, he left to fight in the Great War. Returning to the town in the 1920s, he eventually became second master at the Priory School. His three novels, *Eve of*

Sheba (1922), *Geoghan's Kid* (1922) and *Hurricane* (1923), are based on his experiences of teaching abroad.

RANDALL Maud
b.1909 poet. Born in Croxton in Staffordshire, she attended the local church school. She later moved to Wolverhampton where, for eleven years, she taught at St Jude's Primary School. Four of her poems were published in the anthology, *Spring Poets* (1970). A volume of her collected poems appeared in 1971.

RANSFORD Val
late 20th C poet. She is believed to have lived in Birmingham. *Quits*, which is addressed to nagging women and has as its background the streets of the city, was published in 1970.

RANSOME Arthur
1884–1967 novelist and children's writer. He was educated at Rugby School. His best-known work is the sequence of children's books beginning with *Swallows and Amazons* (1930) and ending with *Great Northern?* (1947) which reveal his love of the countryside and his gift for understanding the child's need to dramatise life into a succession of 'adventures'.

RAVEN Jon
late 20th C playwright, broadcaster, collector and singer of folk songs. He lives in Tettenhall near Wolverhampton. His particular interest is in the songs and legends of the Black Country. With Malcolm Totten*, he wrote *Up Spaghetti Junction*, a musical review of Birmingham life and times, first performed at the Birmingham Repertory Theatre in 1973, and *The Canal Show*,

performed at the same theatre in 1974. *Black Country Canal Songs* (1974) is a collection of folk songs. He continues to write.

REA Lorna
b.1897 novelist. She was educated in Malvern. Her first novel, *Six Mrs Greenes* (1929), was her greatest success.

READE Charles
1814–84 novelist, theatre manager and playwright. Part of his reforming book, *It Is Never Too Late To Mend* (1856), is based on events which took place in Winson Green Prison in the early 1850s. His best-known work, much of it also of a reforming nature, is the historical novel, *The Cloister and the Hearth* (1861).

READING Peter
b.1946 novelist and poet. First published in 1974 with the collection, *Water and Waste*, he now lives in Little Stretton. Described by the *Poetry Review* as 'Britain's Number One Poet of the Unpleasant', he continues to write – *Last Poems* appearing in 1994.

REDFERN Francis
1823–95 poet and historian. He came to live in Uttoxeter at the age of seventeen to learn the trade of cask maker. The only known collection of his verse, *Dove Valley Rhymes*, was published in 1875.

REED Henry
1914–86 poet, translator and radio playwright. Born in Birmingham and educated at King Edward's School, he took his degree at the city's university. He is perhaps best known for his much anthologised poem, 'Naming of Parts' (first published in *A Map of Verona*, 1946) and for his radio plays, *The Streets of Pompeii*

(1971) and *Hilda Tablet and Others* (1971), in which he demonstrates the frequently underrated comic power and emotional range of radio.

REHM Roger
mid-20th C poet. He is believed to have spent some time in Shropshire. The collection, *Sonnets from Caer Caradoc* (1960), describes many of the places in the west of the county which the poet 'can see and is inspired by as he progresses from hill to vale'.

REID Captain Mayne
1818–83 novelist and short story writer. An Irish-born American, in 1875 he came to live in Herefordshire – first to a cottage called Chasewood and then, in 1877, to Frogmore, a large house in Weston-under-Penyard where he wrote *Gwen Wynn, a Romance of the Wye* (1877). Most of his extensive body of work, which includes *The Boy Hunters* (1853) and *The Castaways* (1870), is to do with adventures in all sorts of out-of-the-way places. His books are admirably researched, his characters vividly drawn.

REYNOLDS Dorothy
mid-20th C playwright and actress. Born in Handsworth, she spent eight years at the Wolverhampton Royal Grammar School after her parents died. Though she left school at sixteen, she went on later to take her degree at the University of Birmingham. She is best known as co-writer, with Julian Slade, of the musical, *Salad Days*, the longest running musical comedy in the world which was first produced in the Vaudeville Theatre in London in 1954.

REYNOLDS John
1667–1727 poet and religious writer.

Born at Wolverhampton and educated at King Edward VI Grammar School in Stourbridge, he became a dissenting minister – first at Shrewsbury and then at Walsall. *Death's Vision, a sacred and philosophical poem* was published in 1709.

REYNOLDS John Hamilton

1796–1852 poet and parodist. Born in Shrewsbury, the son of a schoolmaster, he was baptised in St Mary's Church and educated at Shrewsbury School. He was a close friend and correspondent of John Keats. His early work, *The Naiad: a Tale with Other Poems* (1816) especially, showed great promise which was not fulfilled. His best serious work is *The Garden of Florence* (1821). *Peter Bell, Peter Bell, a Lyrical Ballad* (1819) is a parody of William Wordsworth.

RICHARDS Alfred Bate

1820–76 journalist and playwright. Born at Baskerville House, in 1851 he became editor of the *Daily Telegraph*. As well as several tragedies, his fictional work includes five one-act dramas, *Croesus* (1845), *Runnymede* (1846), *Cromwell* (1847), *Isolde* (1848) and *Vandyke* (1850).

RICHARDS Richard

mid-19th C poet. He lived in Oswestry and ran schools in Croxon's Square and in Willow Street. His only known collection, *Wayside Musings: a Book of Poems*, was published in 1859.

RIDGEWAY John

1786–1860 poet. The author of *Africa: A Missionary Poem*, he was born at Hanley, the son of a potter.

RIDLER Anne

b.1912 poet and playwright. She was born in Rugby. Her work includes several volumes of poetry, the first being *Poems* (1939), and some verse drama, of which *Cairn* (1943) is the best known.

RIDLER William

mid-20th C novelist. *The Knocker*, a novel set in the city of Birmingham where he is believed to have lived for a time, was published in 1966.

RIGBYE Kellet

mid-19th C poet. He lived in Leamington Spa. The only known collection of his verse, *Poetical Works*, appeared in 1874. Most of his work is to do with the relation between the natural world and man.

RILEY Madeleine

b.1933 poet, novelist and short story writer. She lives in Wolston in Warwickshire. The collection, *A Spot Bigger Than God*, was published in 1966.

RIMMER Mona

mid-20th C poet. She lived in Craven Arms in Shropshire. Most of the poems in the collection, *Links of a Chain*, originally published in the 1950s in the *Wellington Journal* and the *Ludlow Advertiser*, are to do with her home county.

ROBERT OF GLOUCESTER

early 14th C chronicler. A canon of Hereford Cathedral and chancellor of the diocese, he was the author of the *Metrical Chronicle*, an evocative description of contemporaneous events such as the battle of Evesham and the rebellions during Henry III's reign.

ROBERTS J Eric

d.1991 short story writer. He was born and brought up in Broome Hill in Staffordshire. Before becoming a trade union officer, he worked as a baker. *Bilberry Pie* (1963) and *More*

Bilberry Pie (1966), both published by the Cannock Chase Literary Society, are written in the colourful language of O'd Hedgefud who first gave voice in the *Cannock Chase Courier*.

ROBERTSON Stephen L
mid-20th C poet. His parodies of A E Housman*, *Shropshire Racket*, were published in 1937.

ROBINSON A Mary F
early 20th C poet. Born in Leamington Spa, she was the sister of the novelist, Frances Mabel Robinson*. Slight though her poetry is, much of the work in *The Collected Poems, Lyrical and Narrative* (1912) is pleasingly evocative of place and time.

ROBINSON Emma
1814–90 novelist. She was a prolific writer of romantic novels much concerned with the wronged woman. The heroine of her three-decker novel, *Dorothy Firebrace* (1865), was the daughter of the Birmingham Armourer.

ROBINSON Frances Mabel
mid-19th C novelist. Born in Leamington Spa, she was the sister of A Mary F Robinson*. Her work is now entirely forgotten – though may possibly still be found in private collections.

ROBINSON Veronica
mid-20th C novelist. She was employed for a time as a librarian in Dudley. Her work reflects her own experience of life, but is not explicitly autobiographical. *David in Silence* (1965) has a Black Country setting.

ROBINSON William Henry
1847–1926 poet, novelist, printer, journalist and astronomer. He was born at Cannock, the son of a

stationer who later founded the *Walsall Advertiser*. Educated at Mr Jackson's School in Aldridge, on the death of his father he took over the stationery business. His *Collected Poems* appeared in 1900 and several of them are published in Alfred Moss's*, *Songs from the Heart of England* (1920). His other work includes two novels, *Kathleen O'Leovan* (1896) and *Till the Sun Grows Cold* (1904), which tells the story of the Harpur family of Rushall Hall in Herefordshire.

ROBY Mary Kirton
1828–67 poet. The author of a volume of verses, *The Story of a Household and Other Poems* (1862), she was born at Tamworth. Her father and uncle compiled *A History of Tamworth*.

RODWAY A
late 19th C novelist. He is believed to have lived in Birmingham. *Dangerous Ground: a Tale of Our Time* (1876) is set in the city.

ROE A M
early 19th C poet. Born at Walsall, and deaf from birth, she suffered the most dreadful poverty throughout her lifetime. In 1807 a volume of her work entitled *Poems on Several Occasions* was published in two volumes. Most of these poems had been written when she was between fourteen and twenty years old.

ROGERS Samuel
1763–1855 poet and banker. A frequent visitor to The Hill near Stourbridge, home of his paternal grandfather, Thomas Rogers, he was also invited to the Leasowes, the Halesowen home of William Shenstone*, a friend of his father. The beauty of these two places and of the nearby villages provided inspiration for his

best known work, *The Pleasures of Memory* (1792). Offered the poet laureateship in 1850, he declined.

ROGERS Thomas
1660–94 poet. He was born in Hampton Lucy in Warwickshire, the son of the rector of Bishop's Hampton where he attended the free school. In 1693 he wrote several poems, of which 'The Commonwealth Man Unmasked' is dedicated to William III.

ROHMER Sax
1883–1959 (pseudonym of Arthur Sarsfield Ward) short story writer. As a small child, he lived for a time in Ladywood in Birmingham. He is known chiefly as the creator of the evil Fu Manchu – first introduced in *Dr Fu Manchu* (1913).

ROLFE Frederick
1860–1913 novelist, short story writer and eccentric. Confusingly, he also called himself Baron Corvo and Father Rolfe. In 1887 he briefly attended Oscott College in Erdington. He is best known for his quasi-autobiographical fantasy, *Hadrian VII* (1904), in which the central character is made pope. This work was popularised by A J A Symons's study, *The Quest for Corvo* (1934), which became cult reading in the 1960s.

ROUSSEAU Jean-Jacques
1712–78 essayist and philosopher. On being forced to leave France in 1766, he and his mistress, Thérèse le Vasseur, were lent Wootton Hall by a Mr Davenport. They stayed for two years in the house, which is near Ellastone in Staffordshire. While there, they visited Calwich Abbey, the home of Bernard Granville. Rousseau's *Discourses* and many of his other works, having been translated into English, continue to influence thought and ideas.

ROUTH Mrs Martha
1743–1817 diarist. She was born at Stourbridge. At the age of seventy she began her journal which was eventually published in 1920.

ROWE Alick
mid/late 20th C radio and television playwright. Born in Kington, he was taken to Hereford at the age of one and brought up in a pub called The Commercial. He was educated at the local primary school and at Hereford Cathedral School where he later taught for five years. Having written several radio plays, he had his first piece for television accepted in 1970. He has now returned to live in the county. *Boy at the Commercial* (1978) is autobiographical. He continues to write, mainly for the media. *Panic Wall* appeared in 1993.

ROWE Sid
b.1918 novelist. An Indian, he taught at Wolstanton Grammar School in Staffordshire and in 1966 published his only known work, *'It's a Wog's Life,' by Golly* – a novel specifically written to aim a blow at colour prejudice.

ROWLEY Dave
b.1946 poet and short story writer. He was born in Newcastle-under-Lyme. Having worked as a labourer and van driver in the North Staffordshire area, he became a student at Madeley College. His first volume, *Winter Poems*, was published in 1974. Later work includes both verse and prose pieces. *The Ebenezer* appeared in 1988.

RUDKIN David
b.1936 stage and television playwright. Educated at King Edward's

School in Birmingham, he taught at Bromsgrove High School from 1961 to 1964 and made his name with the play, *Afore Night Come* (1962), which is set in a rural part of the Black Country. Other works include *Ashes* (1974) and the television play, *Penda's Fen* (1974), described in the printed stage directions as being set 'against a backcloth of the purple Malvern Hills'. His later work, which includes *Sons of Light* (1976), tends to replace polemic with myth and allegory.

RUDLAND Ernest Marston
1875–1935 poet and playwright. He lived in Birmingham. Known as the 'Councillor Poet' and described as belonging to the 'virile school' of poetry, he published several volumes of verse and a blank verse play, *The Life and Death of Oliver Cromwell*. *Ballads of Old Birmingham* (1911) is dedicated to the 'Citizens of Greater Birmingham' and includes an introduction written by the mayor of the city. He was also famous for appending verses to the greetings cards he sent to family and friends.

RUEGG Judge
d.1941 novelist. He was a county court judge in Staffordshire from 1907 until 1939. His novels include *A Staffordshire Knot or The Two Houses* (1926) and *Flash* (1928). *John Clutterbuck* is perhaps his most well-known work.

RUSKIN John
1819–1900 essayist and man of letters. Worried about his health, his parents took him to Leamington Spa to consult a Dr Henry Jephson. He stayed first at the Bedford Hotel and then in lodgings in Russell Terrace, undergoing a strict regime of baths and exercise. While in the town, he wrote a fairy story, *The King of the Golden River*, for twelve-year-old Effie Gray who was later to become his wife. In 1887 he visited the Guild of St George, a land settlement scheme on the edge of the Wyre Forest which he had promoted. The scheme later failed. The five volumes of *Modern Painters* (published between 1843 and 1860), *The Seven Lamps of Architecture* (1849) and *The Stones of Venice* (1851–53) are his best-known work.

RUSSELL Sylvia
mid-20th C poet. She lives in Birmingham. *Worded Canvasses* was published in 1964; *The Poems of S.J.Russell* in 1973. She has been described as 'a lover of nature, [who] finely expresses with sympathy and full understanding both the commonplace and the more abstruse aspects of daily life'.

RYLAND John
1753–1825 poet and hymn writer. He was born in Warwick. Best known as an Oriental scholar, he also published *Hymns and Verses on Sacred Subjects*.

S

SADLEIR Michael
1888–1957 novelist and biographer. He was educated at Rugby School. *Fanny By Gaslight* (1940) is his best-known novel and he also published a number of books on nineteenth-century society and literature.

SADLER Campbell H
late 19th C novelist. *Gilbert Malory, A Romance of Old Shrewsbury in the Days of Charles II* (1897) was inspired by the author's frequent visits to the town.

ST GERMAIN Christopher
1460-1540 playwright. Born at Shilton near Coventry, he is best known for the dialogue, *Doctor and Student* (in Latin, 1518; in English, 1531), in which the laws of England are debated by a doctor of divinity and a student of law.

SALT Henry
1780-1827 poet and Egyptologist. Born in Lichfield, the nephew of the poet George Butt* and cousin of Martha Sherwood* and Lucy Cameron*, he attended Lichfield Grammar School. His poem, *Egypt* (1824), attempts to evoke the spirit of the land in which he spent so much of his working life investigating tombs. It also makes many references to his native town.

SALWAY T
mid-19th C poet. He was vicar of Oswestry in the 1840s and 1850s. His book of verse, *Gospel Hymns*, was published in 1847.

SANDFORD Jeremy
b.1934 television playwright. The son of the administrator of the Golden Cockerell Press, he was born at Eye Manor in Herefordshire. An early play, *Dreaming Bandsmen*, which included a 40-piece brass band, was first produced at the Belgrade Theatre in Coventry. His semi-documentary play for television, *Cathy Come Home* (1966), brought him instant recognition as a voice for the unheard – a reputation enhanced by *Edna the Inebriate Woman* (1971). He continues to write. *Virgin of the*

Clearway appeared in 1978.

SANDYS Oliver
1892-1964 (pseudonym of Mrs Carados Evans) novelist. An extraordinarily prolific writer of romantic fiction, as both Oliver Sandys and Baroness Barcyuska, in the 1950s she came to live at The Ancient House in Little Stretton. Church Stretton is used as the setting for her novel, *Quaint Place* (1952). Two other novels, *I Was Shown Heaven* (1962) and *The Poppy and the Rose* (1962), also have Shropshire as the background to their action.

SATCHWELL Benjamin
1732-1815 poet. He was born in Leamington Priors in Warwickshire. At the age of thirteen, on the death of his father, he was apprenticed to a shoemaker who also taught him a love of books. Now chiefly remembered as the founder of the Spa, he also wrote poetry. His most important pieces are 'The Rise and Fall of Troy' and 'Astronomical Characters and Their Use'.

SAVILLE Malcolm
1901-82 children's writer. Though he never lived in the county, he was a regular visitor to Shropshire and used the Long Mynd and Stiperstones areas for the settings of many of his popular children's novels, the first being *Mystery at Witchend* (1943).

SAVINE Nicholas de Toulouse
mid-20th C novelist. He was a frequent visitor to Lutwyche Hall on Wenlock Edge, the home of Stella Benson*. With her, he wrote *Pull Devil – Pull Baker* which was published in 1933. It is a series of connected stories, mostly written in broken English. His other work includes *Mehalah*.

Kenilworth Castle

SAYER J F

early 20th C poet. The collection of verse, *A Visit to Dowles – Near Bewdley* (1916), was inspired by his own experiences there.

SCOTT Barbara

See EASTVALE, Margaret

SCOTT Edith Hope

d.1939 poet, novelist and short story writer. A prolific writer and a member of the Guild of St George, she lived in one of their settlements in the Wyre Forest (see RUSKIN, John). Her work includes the collection, *Mother Holda Stories* (1901), a novel, *The New Neighbours* (1934), a Christmas play with carols and a book about the Guild.

SCOTT Geoffrey

1883–1929 poet, critic and biographer. He was educated at Rugby School. His *Portrait of Zelide* (1925), an account of the life of Madame de Charriere, was described by Edith Wharton as 'well-nigh perfect'. His poetry, which includes the collections, *Poems* (1921) and *A Little Learning* (1923), also appeared in several periodicals.

SCOTT Sir Walter

1771–1832 novelist and poet. In 1821 he stayed at the King's Arms in Kenilworth while working on the novel, published in 1821, which he named after the town. The ruined Norman castle in Clun is reputed to be the model for Garde Doloureuse in *The Betrothed* (1825), part of which he wrote while staying at the Buffalo Inn in the village. His signature is scratched on the window of the Birth Room in Shakespeare's Birthplace in Stratford-upon-Avon. He is known to have visited Anna Seward*, the 'Swan of Lichfield'. A prolific writer, he is less popular than previously at this end of the twentieth century.

SEAMAN Sir Owen

1861–1936 poet and parodist. He was educated at Shrewsbury School. In 1897 he joined the staff of *Punch*, becoming assistant editor in 1902 and editor from 1906 to 1932. Among his published volumes are *In Cap and Bells* (1899) and *Interludes of an Editor* (1929).

SEDGWICK S N

1872–1941 novelist and playwright. He was born in Birmingham and educated at King Edward's School. His novel, *The Master of the Commandery*, is set in Worcester. None of his plays seems to have survived.

SERRAILLIER Ian
b.1912 poet and children's writer. He taught at Dudley Grammar School from 1940 until 1946. A prolific and respected writer of historical and adventure books, he is most popular in my household for *The Silver Sword* (1956).

Anna Seward

SEWARD Anna
1747–1809 poet and letter writer. Generally referred to as the 'Swan of Lichfield', from 1754 to 1809 she lived in the Bishop's Palace, the residence of her father, a canon of Lichfield Cathedral. The literary group, of which she was the centre, included Erasmus Darwin*, Thomas Day* and George Butt*. Sir Walter Scott* is known to have visited her and in 1810, after her death, he published her poems with a memoir. As her grandfather, John Hunter, had taught Dr Johnson*, she was able to give James Boswell information for *The Life of Samuel Johnson* (1791).

Her letters were printed in six volumes in 1811.

SEWELL Rev Arthur
late 19th C playwright. He lived in Leamington Spa. His work includes 'the comic drama or historical travestie', *Duncan; or, the Nihilist Conspiracy*, which appeared in 1880.

SHAKESPEARE William
1564–1616 poet, playwright and actor. The son of a wool merchant and glover, he was born in Henley Street in Stratford-upon-Avon. The claim of Clifford Chambers to be his birthplace is hardly tenable, though there were Shakespeares living in the village at that time. The house where he was born, bought by the Shakespeare Birthplace Trust in 1847, is now a museum; as is also the house in the village of Wilmcote where his mother, Mary Arden, lived. He attended the grammar school, then situated in the Guildhall, from whose first-floor windows he may have seen Lord Leicester's or Lord Danby's travelling players. In 1582 he married Anne Hathaway from Shottery. (Her house is also now a museum, having been bought by the Shakespeare Birthplace Preservation Trust in 1892.) The bond naming the two men who stood surety for the marriage can be seen in the Hereford and Worcester Record Office (St Helen's branch). The story of his running away to London in 1586 after being caught poaching deer at Sir Thomas Lucy's estate of Charlecote Park is probably apocryphal – though at about this time he certainly left for the city. In 1597 he bought New Place in Stratford-upon-Avon – a house he frequently visited, and which from 1610 he lived in permanently. He died in 1616 and is buried in Stratford churchyard.

Nothing even passably adequate can be said of his work in this brief reference.

William Shakespeare

SHANE John
mid/late 20th C poet and short story writer. A caravan dweller, he has travelled with his wife extensively in the west midland area. The collection, *From a Country Cottage* (1974), was published in Hereford. Both his prose and his poetry vividly evoke the smells and sounds of the country. He went on to write novels – notably *The Last Great Pub Crawl* (1976), in which it has been said 'every line includes something with which every individual can identify'. He was described by BBC WM Radio as 'the 1970's answer to Dylan Thomas'.

SHANNON Jessie Lee
early 20th C poet. Born at Walsall, she contributed to Alfred Moss's*, *Songs of the Heart of England* (1920). Her native place is the inspiration of most of her poems.

SHANNON John C
late 19th/early 20th C short story writer. He lived in Sutton Coldfield. The stories in *Who Shall Condemn?* (1894), printed by a Walsall company,

first appeared in the *Walsall Advertiser*. *Zylgrahov and Other Stories* (1901) are much concerned with mystery and romance.

SHAW Alfred Capel
b.1847 poet and librarian. Born in Leamington Spa, he returned to work in the west midland area in 1878 when he joined the staff of Birmingham City Library and was chief librarian there from 1889 to 1912. He did much to restore the Reference Library after the fire of 1879 and to develop the Shakespeare Memorial Library. *Poems*, a collected edition of his early work, appeared in 1874. *The Vision of Erin* (1892) is dedicated to William Ewart Gladstone, in support of his Irish policies. He is now best known for his collection of verse, *Two Decades of Song* (1896), several of which poems first appeared in *Cassell's Magazine*, *Chambers' Journal*, *Good Words* and *Sunday Magazine*.

SHAW Edward J
early 20th C short story writer and photographer. He lived in Walsall. *The 'Leopard' at Redmere, a Christmas Tale* (1904?) is set in a Black Country tavern.

SHAW George Bernard
1856–1950 playwright, novelist and philosopher. He was a frequent visitor to Malvern in the 1920s and 30s. His friendship with Sir Edward Elgar contributed to the founding of the Malvern Festival of Music and Drama where nineteen of his plays have been performed, six of them being premiered there. Though his political/philosophical work is far more extensive than his other writings, he is chiefly remembered for his plays – especially *Major Barbara* (1905), *Pygmalion* (1914),

Heartbreak House (1921) and *Saint Joan* (1924). (See MCLACHLAN, Dame Laurentia and TERRY, Ellen.)

SHAYER Michael
mid-20th C poet. *Persephone* (1961), which has an introduction by Gael Turnbull*, is set in Worcestershire.

SHENSTONE William
1714–63 poet. Born at Leasowes, an estate on Mucklow Hill near Halesowen, he was educated first at Sarah Lloyd's Dame School, then at Halesowen Grammar School and later at an academy in Solihull. In 1732 on the death of his grandmother, he inherited the estate and after completing his studies at Pembroke College he returned to spend the rest of his life there. He is known often to have visited Hagley Hall, the home of Lord Lyttelton* – perhaps in order to exchange ideas on garden design, a particular interest of his which prompted him to transform the grounds of Leasowes. He worked occasionally with Thomas Percy* on editing *Reliques of Ancient English Poetry* (1765) and was adviser to the Birmingham printer, John Baskerville (1706–75). There is a memorial to him in the church. His reputation as a poet was established by *The Judgement of Hercules* (1741) and *The Schoolmistress* (1742) – a pen portrait of his first mentor, Sarah Lloyd.

SHEPHARD Fred H
early 20th C poet. He lived in Coventry. The verse in his only known collection, *Crown of Nothing* (1923), is mainly about the Warwickshire countryside.

SHEPPARD John George
1818–69 poet and historian. He was headmaster of King Charles I Grammar School in Kidderminster

from 1851 to 1869. The narrative poem, 'St Paul at Athens', won the poetry prize at Wadham College. His other work is mainly non-fiction.

SHERIDAN Richard B
1751–1816 playwright and politician. From 1780 to 1806 he was MP for Stafford. On visits to the town he stayed at Chetwynd House. He is best known for *The Rivals* (produced at Covent Garden in 1775) and for *The School for Scandal* (which ran for seventy-three performances between 1777 and 1779 and made £15,000 profit).

SHERWOOD Mrs Martha
1775–1851 novelist. She was born and brought up in Stanford-on-Teme, where her father, George Butt*, was rector. Her happy childhood is described in her *Life* (1854) – in which she mentions the occasion of her father buying for one guinea (£1.05p) a wagonload of books at the auction of William Walsh's* library from Abberley (c1790). Her first novel, *Traditions*, appeared in 1794. In 1795, on the sudden death of her father, the family moved to Bridgnorth where she and her sister, Lucy, taught in Sunday schools. In 1803 she married Henry Sherwood, on leave from the Indian army, and left the town. On returning to England from India, she went to live in Lower Wick where she wrote over seventy books in eight years and also established a school. *Little Henry and his Bearer* (1814) ran to over a hundred editions and was translated into French, German, Hindustani, Chinese and Sinhalese. The last volume of her most well-known work, *The Fairchild Family* (1818, 1842 and 1847), was written while she was living in Britannia Square, Worcester.

SHORE Henry
1911–77 poet and doctor. A refugee from Nazi Germany, he came to England in 1939 and stayed for a while in Aldridge in Staffordshire. His work includes *The Roundabout* (1972), *The Nomad and Other Poems* (1973) and *Apple Harvest* (1974).

SHORTHOUSE Joseph Henry
1834–1903 novelist. Born in Great Charles Street in Birmingham, he was educated at a Quaker school in the city. While living in Beaufort Road, he wrote his most famous novel, *John Inglesant* (1881), a work much influenced by John Ruskin* and the writers of the Oxford Movement. In 1876 he moved to Wellington Road. He died there and is buried in Old Edgbaston cemetery.

SHUTE Neville
1899–1960 (pseudonym of N S Norway) novelist. He was educated at Shrewsbury School. A popular and respected writer, especially for his skill in addressing contemporary dilemmas within the fictional framework, he is best known for the novels, *Pied Piper* (1942), *No Highway* (1948) and *A Town Like Alice* (1949).

SIBLEY John
1920–79 poet and novelist. In 1945 he married the daughter of a Hagley schoolteacher. After a period lecturing in Uganda, he taught English at Dudley Grammar School in 1953 and lived first in Cradley and later in Quinton. In 1966 he was appointed a lecturer at Birmingham Polytechnic. Books of his poetry were published in 1949, 1957 and 1965; and three novels were published in 1957, 1958 and 1960. Though he completed a novel set in the Black Country, it was never published.

SIBREE John
1795–1877 poet. From 1822 to 1859 he was minister of Vicar's Lane Church in Coventry. His work includes *Fancy and Other Rhymes* (1880), *Poems* (1884) and *Poems With Rosalie* (1890).

SIDDONS Henry
1774–1815 playwright and actor. The son of Sarah Siddons, he was born at Wolverhampton. His father was a Walsall man. *A Tale of Terror*, his best-known play, was first produced at Covent Garden while he was a member of the travelling players managed by his uncle, Stephen Kemble. *Time's a Tell-Tale* was performed in 1807. The second edition of *Illustrations of Gestures and Action* – a volume no self-respecting drama student should be without – appeared in 1822.

SIDGWICK Ethel
1877–1970 novelist. She was born in Rugby. Her novels, which include *The Accolade* (1915) and *The Bells of Shoreditch* (1928), show a fascination, somewhat in the 'Henry Jamesian' mode, with the minutiae of thought and behaviour.

SIDNEY Sir Philip
1554–86 poet. As a child he would almost certainly have visited Ludlow Castle, the seat of his father, Sir Henry Sidney, who was Lord President of the Council of the Marches from 1560 to 1586. Educated at Shrewsbury School, he was the exact contemporary of his friend and biographer, Fulke Greville* whose home, Warwick Castle, he later often visited. While a schoolboy he stayed many times with his uncle, the Earl of Leicester, at Kenilworth Castle where at the age of eleven he saw Elizabeth I on her first visit there. He was a

frequent guest at Polesworth, where lived Sir Henry Goodere*, who was with him when he died and present at his funeral. *Arcadia* (1590), *Astrophel and Stella* (1591) and the delightful *Apologie for Poetrie* (1591) are his best-known works.

SILVERPEN
1816–79 (pseudonym of Eliza Meteyard) novelist, short story writer and children's writer. She was born in Shrewsbury, the daughter of a surgeon. *Struggles for Fame* (1845) was her first novel. *The Nine Hours Movement* (1872) contains a number of tales about industrial and domestic life, including 'John Ashmore of Birmingham', 'The glass of gin' and 'Mrs Dumple's Cooking School'. Most of her work has a distinctly moral flavour.

SILVERSTON C J
early 20th C novelist. He is believed to have lived in Birmingham. His book, *The Dominion of Race* (1906), relates to the Jewish community in the city.

SILVESTER F B
early 20th C poet. He lived in Birmingham. His only known collection, *Working Class Songs and Poems*, many of them to do with the city's life and industry, appeared in 1922.

SIMCOX John Lea
1814–40 poet. The author of *The Outcast: A Poem in Six Cantos* (1837), he was born at Harborne.

SIMMONDS Charles Herbert
mid-20th C poet. He lived in Kidderminster. His work includes his first collection, *A Dream of Seasons* (1947), and the volume, *And Golden Memories* (1953), containing several 'word-pictures' of Bewdley, Upper Arley and Alum Brook, which was dedicated to his wife 'to whose nobility of character and love of truth and beauty I owe my inspiration'.

SIMONS David
mid-19th C poet and novelist. His verses, *Vision of Pengwerne and Other Poems*, were published in Shrewsbury in 1841. In 1860 a novel, *The Lady of Warkworth*, appeared. He was eventually imprisoned in the town's gaol for printing libellous attacks on local dignitaries in his weekly broadsheet, the *Salopian Budget and Border Sentinel*. (This publication he later renamed the *Salopian Telegraph and Border Review*, but it showed no noticeable change in tone.)

SLADE Joan
See WALTON, Stella V

SMART Peter
1569–1648 poet. The son of a clergyman, he was born in Warwickshire. Most famous for his sermon on Psalm xxxi. 7, preached in Durham Cathedral in 1628, he also published poems in Latin and English which were known, a little derisively, as 'Old Smart's Verses'.

SMITH Edmund
1672–1710 poet and playwright. Born at either Hanley Castle or Tenbury Wells in Worcestershire, he was left an orphan and brought up by an uncle. His tragedy in five acts, *Phaedrus and Hippolitus*, was performed at London's Haymarket Theatre in 1707. Dr Johnson* considered his elegy on John Philips* to be 'among the best elegies which our language can show'.

SMITH Elizabeth
late 18th C poet. She lived for a time in both Birmingham and Malvern.

The Brethren, a Poem: in Four Books, paraphrased from Part of the History of Israel and his Family, in Holy Writ (1787) is 'earnestly recommended to the attention of the rising generation'. The collection, *Poems on Malvern and Other Subjects* (1829), though perhaps rather sugary for modern tastes, ran for several editions.

SMITH Emma
b.1923 novelist. *Maiden's Trip*, a novel about life on the narrow boats on the canals of the west midland area, appeared in 1948. It is not known whether she continued to write.

SMITH Frank
1901–61 poet. He was born at Longton in Stoke-on-Trent and spent most of his life in Trentham. His only known collection, *Seventy and More Poems*, was published posthumously in 1971.

SMITH Gordon
mid/late 20th C poet. Some of the poems in his collection, *Imago* (1974), are described as having been written in Birmingham, though it is not known whether he ever lived for any length of time in the city. He also has connections with Walsall. His work is often concerned with revealing and regretting the lack of communication between people.

SMITH Mark
1890–1977 poet. A Coventry man, in 1974 he published *Faith in Verse*, a book of poems mainly to do with the spiritual life.

SMITH William
1711–87 poet. He was born at Worcester where his father was rector of All Saints. It was not until after his death that a collection of his work, *Poems*, appeared.

SNAITH John Collis
d.1936 novelist. He is believed to have lived in Dudley. *Love Lane* is set in the fictional midland city of Blackhampton. Other work includes *The Adventurous Lady* and *The Council of Seven*.

SNEYD Ralph de Tunstall
1863–1949 poet. He lived at Keele Hall near Newcastle-under-Lyme and was High Sheriff of Stafford in 1892. Volume I of *Poems* (1929) contains several pieces about Leek and the Moorlands.

SOMERS-COCKS Henry Lawrence
1862–1940 novelist. He is believed to have retained the family connections with west Worcestershire. *The Mystery of Malvern Mire: a Story of the Druids and Caractacus* (1925) is set in the area. It was to an ancestor of his, John Somers (1651–1716) from Claines, that Jonathan Swift dedicated his *Tale of a Tub* (1704).

SOMERVILE William
1675–1742 poet. A friend and neighbour of William Shenstone*, he is thought to have been born at Wolseley near Colwich in Staffordshire; though Dr Johnson* mentions Edstone in Warwickshire as his birthplace. He was educated in Stafford and there is a memorial to him in the church at Wootton Wawen, which is situated near his home at Edstone. His best-known work is *The Chace* (1735), a blank-verse celebration in four volumes of the pleasures of country sports, especially hunting. He is also the author of *Field Sports* (1740), *Hobbinol* (1740), a mock-heroic pastoral describing May games in the Vale of Evesham, and an ode addressed to Lady Coventry* which was written on viewing her fine chimneypiece of shellwork.

SPARROW G William S
early 20th C poet. He lived at Albrighton Hall near Shrewsbury. *His Rubaiyat of a Minor Statesman* was published in 1913.

SPEAKMAN Raymond
late 20th C playwright. He has associations with Birmingham. *The Fire King* (1972), written in collaboration with Derek Nicholls*, retells the story of Matthew Boulton, one of the city's eminent men.

SPEKE Charlotte
early 20th C poet. Some of the poems in *Night Musings* (1917) are concerned with Dudley and its surroundings; though there is some doubt as to whether or not she ever lived in the town.

SPENCE Eleanor
b.1928 children's writer. An Australian, she has lived in Coventry and was children's librarian at Coventry City Libraries from 1952 to 1954. Her work includes *The Summer In Between* (1959) and *The Green Laurel* (1963), the first of her books to be published in England

SPENCER Lady Sarah
1787–1870 letter writer. In 1813 she married William Henry Lyttelton, 3rd Baron Lyttelton, and went to live at Hagley Hall. The collection of her letters was edited by her great-granddaughter, Mrs Hugh Wyndham, and published as *The Correspondence of Sarah Spencer, Lady Lyttelton 1787–1870*.

STAFFORD John
late 19th C (pseudonym of Horace Pendred) short story writer. *A New Ophelia and other stories* (1892) relates to life in Birmingham, a city where he is believed to have spent some time.

STALLWORTHY Jon
b.1935 poet and editor. Described as 'a quiet poet, a fastidious craftsman', he was educated at Rugby School. His work includes the first collection, *The Earthly Paradise* (1958), *Astronomy of Love* (1963) and *The Apple Barrel* (1974). More recently, he has edited the *Penguin Book of Love Poetry* (1989).

STANLEY Elijah
1831–1915 poet. He was born in Walsall. Some of his work appears in Alfred Moss's*, *Songs from the Heart of England* (1920).

STAYLEY George
1727–79 poet, playwright, actor and elocutionist. Chiefly known as the author of *The Life and Opinions of an Actor* (1762) and the comedies, *The Rival Theatres* (1759) and *The Chocolate Makers*, he was born at Burton-on-Trent.

STEVENS Austin
mid-20th C novelist, editor and short story writer. He was born in Stoke-on-Trent and educated at Ellesmere College. His first novel, *Time and Money*, was published in 1959. Other work includes *The Moon Turns Green* (1961) and *The Antagonists* (1963).

STEVENS E
mid/late 20th C poet. All the poems in *Tales from the Woods* (1974) are about places and people in the Telford area. She continues to write about north-east Shropshire.

STEWART Sheila
mid/late 20th C novelist. She lives in Ascott near Coventry. Most of her work belongs to the historical genre. *Country Kate* (1971) describes life in the Warwickshire village of Long Compton before the Great War. In 1974 the radio script based on this

novel won the Writers' Guild Award for the Best Radio Feature Script. She went on to write several sequels to her first novel.

STEWART-TAYLOR Margaret
mid-20th C novelist. She also writes as Margaret Collier. Born in Coventry, the daughter of a headmaster, and educated at Nuneaton, she was a librarian in the city from 1927 to 1930. She published a number of novels, among them *Another Door Opened* (1963), *Marian's Daughter* (1967) and *Napoleon's Captor* (1971).

STOKES Cedric
See BEARDMORE, George

STONE Samuel John
1839–1900 poet and hymn writer. The son of a vicar, he was born at Whitmore rectory in Staffordshire and as a boy lived at Colwich. He later succeeded his father as vicar at St Paul's in Huggerston, moving to All Hallows in 1890. Known chiefly for his hymns, especially 'The Church's One Foundation', he also published volumes of sacred poetry, which include *The Knight of Intercession* (1872), *Sonnets of the Sacred Year* (1875), *The Idylls of Deare Childe* (1876) and *Lays of Iona and Other Poems* (1897). He was a member of the editing committee for *Hymns Ancient and Modern* (see BAKER, Sir Henry William).

STRETTON Hesba
1832–1911 (pseudonym of Sarah Smith) novelist and short story writer. She was born in Wellington, the daughter of a New Street bookseller and stationer, and educated at Mrs Cranage's School for Girls at the Old Hall in Watling Street. Much of her childhood was spent in and near All Stretton (the origin of her pen name) where her sister owned a house. The memorial to her in the church at Church Stretton is in the form of a lancet window containing a stained-glass picture of her most famous character, Jessica, who figures in *Jessica's Last Prayer* (1865). Another book, *The Children of Claverly*, is set in a nearby valley. All her novels have a religious tone.

STRONG Rev Charles
1784–1864 poet and translator. He is believed to have visited, or lived for a time in, Walsall. A volume of his sonnets, dedicated to the Earl of Harroby, appeared in 1835.

SWAINE Edward
1795–1862 poet and hymn writer. He was born at Hanley. *The Hand of God: A Fragment, and Other Poems* was published in 1839. Other work includes several hymns printed in pamphlet form.

SWANN Annie S
late 19th C novelist. She is believed to have lived in Wolverhampton. *A Bitter Debt: a tale of the Black Country* was published in 1893.

SWANN George
mid-19th C poet. He lived in Stafford. His only known work, the collection, *Autumn Wreath*, appeared in 1869.

SWIFT Theophilus
d.1815 poet and letter writer. He is known to have been born at Goodrich in Herefordshire, the grandson of the vicar, Thomas Swift, though there is no record of his baptism in the parish register. The family's more famous writer, Jonathan Swift (1667–1745), was a cousin of his father. His poetry, which appeared in several periodicals, is mostly concerned with exposing the follies of mankind.

SWINTON E D
See OLE-LUK-OIE

SYLVESTER James
b.1858 poet and hymn writer. He was
born in West Bromwich, where he is
best known perhaps for the poem
'West Bromwich Town', written in
1882 on the occasion of the town's
incorporation. His other work includes
Wayside Poems (1900) and *Hymns on
the Church Catechism* (1914).

SYLVESTER Philip
See WORNER, Philip

SYMONDS William Samuel
1818–87 novelist. He was born in
Hereford. From 1843 to 1845 he was

curate at Offenham near Evesham.
Having become rector of Pendock in
1845, he shortly afterwards inherited
Pendock Court. His two historical
novels, *Malvern Chase* (1881), about
the Wars of the Roses, and *Hanley
Castle* (1883), about the Civil War,
are set in the district.

SYMONS Annie Colenso
early 20th C poet. Born in Walsall,
she was the author of *A Lay of Japan
and Other Poems* (1909), a volume
which is much concerned with royalty
and literary figures. She was also a
contributor to Alfred Moss's*, *Songs
from the Heart of England* (1920).

T

TACITUS Caius Cornelius
?55–120 AD historian and orator. He
visited the west midland area in order
to learn about the Silurii who at that
time inhabited what is now Herefordshire. The final defeat of the tribe's
leader, Caradoc, almost certainly took
place at Coxall Knoll near Leintwar-
dine. His findings were written in the
biography of his father-in-law, Julius
Agricola, (c98). He is now regarded as
the last great classical historian.

TALFOURD Sir Thomas Noon
1795–1864 poet. A judge and the
author of the forgotten blank-verse
tragedies, *Ion* (1836), *The Athenian
Captive* (1838) and *Glencoe* (1840),
he died while attending on the judges'
bench at the crown court in Stafford.

TARLTON Richard
1530–88 actor and playwright. He
was born at Condover in Shropshire.
A member of the Queen's Company
of Players and possibly the original of

several of William Shakespeare's*
jesters, he is known to have written at
least one play, *The Seven Deadly Sins*
(1585), which was performed by his
own company. *Tarlton's Jests*
(published posthumously in 1611) is a
valuable source of biographical and
sociological information.

TATE Joanna
mid-20th C children's writer. A
prolific writer of children's fiction,
including *Luke's Garden* (1967),
Ginger Mick (1974) and *The Runners*
(1974), she now lives in Shrewsbury.
Her work has been described as about
'real characters in real situations'.

TATWIN
d.734 poet. A monk at Bredon, he
became archbishop of Canterbury in
731. His poem, *Aenigmatu*, is written
in Latin hexameters.

TAYLOR Boswell
mid-20th C novelist. He was headmaster at a school in Birmingham and

lived in Warwickshire. *Dust on the Lathes* (1947), which describes the conflicts between old skills and the new technology, is set in an engineering works in Birmingham.

TAYLOR John
1580–1653 poet. A visitor to the west midland area, he made famous one Thomas Parr of Alberbury in Shropshire. In the poem, 'Old Parr', he claimed this personage lived from 1483–1635. *The Peerless Pilgrimage* (1618) describes his walk from Edinburgh to Braemar.

TENNYSON Alfred Lord
1809–92 poet. After visiting Coventry in 1840 he retold the legend of Lady Godiva in his poem, 'Godiva'. Now enjoying something of an appreciative re-estimation, he is probably best known for *In Memoriam* (1850) and *Idylls of the King* (1857).

TERRY Ellen
1848–1928 actress and letter writer. She was born in Coventry into a family of actors. Her letters were published in 1931 as *Ellen Terry and Bernard Shaw: A Correspondence*.

TERSON Peter
b.1932 playwright and children's writer. He is associated with Stoke-on-Trent's Victoria Theatre. *A Night to Make the Angels Weep* (1964), *The Mighty Reservoy* and *Mooney and His Caravans* (1966, on TV; 1968, on stage) were among the first of his plays to be performed. Early publications include *The Apprentices* (1968) and *Zigger Zagger* (1970). *The Fishing Party* was produced on television in 1972 to much critical acclaim. He has also written one-act plays for schools. He continues to write, specialising in gentle pathos and a pervasive kind of pragmatic morality.

TEY Josephine
1897–1952 (pseudonym of Elizabeth Mackintosh, who also wrote under the name of Gordon Daviot) playwright and novelist. She spent three years as a student at the Anstey Physical Training College in Birmingham. Her play, *Richard of Bordeaux* (1932), in which John Gielgud starred, was an instant success. *The Franchise Affair* (1948) and the investigative *Daughter of Time* (1951), in which she sets out to prove that Richard III was the victim of a Tudor smear campaign, are her best-known novels. Her work has been adapted for television – with mixed results.

THARP Henry
1853–73 poet. He lived in Walsall. His collection, *The River of Sighs*, appeared in 1872.

THIMELBY Mrs Henry
b.1608? poet. A contributor to Arthur Clifford's*, *Tixall Poetry*, she was born in Staffordshire, the fourth daughter of Sir Walter Aston.

THOM Robert W
mid-18th C poet. He lived for a while in Coventry. Many of the poems in his collection, *Coventry Poems* (1860), were written for special civic occasions in the city.

THOMAS Craig
b.1942 novelist and short story writer. He taught for a while in schools in Stratford-upon-Avon (1966–68), Lichfield (1968–73) and Walsall (1973–77). Some of his short stories had previously been published in various periodicals; but his first novel, *The Rat Trap*, did not appear until 1976. More recent work includes several politically aware thrillers, including the bestseller, *Firefox*

(1977), which in 1981 was made into a film starring Clint Eastwood. *Playing with Cobras* appeared in 1993.

THOMAS D M
b.1935 novelist and poet. He lives in Hereford. His first collection of poems, *Two Voices*, appeared in 1968. Other verse, mainly concerned with the themes of life and death, includes *Logan Stone* (1971) and *Lilith-Prints* (1973). He has received the Cholmondeley Award for Poetry; *The Flute Player* (1979) won the Gollancz Pan/Picador Fantasy Award; *The White Hotel* won the Cheltenham Prize in 1981. Later work includes the novels, *Swallow* (1984) and *Summit* (1987), and the book of poetry, *Dreaming in Bronze* (1981). *Eating Pavlova* appeared in 1994.

THOMAS Edward
1878–1917 poet, essayist, nature writer, biographer and novelist. In 1912 he stayed with Robert Frost* near Ledbury and was encouraged by him to contribute his poems to magazines and periodicals. He wrote them under the name of Edward Eastaway, his own name being at the time associated with hack writing. Not until after he was killed in France was it realised what an original poetic voice his was – clear, concise, unstrained. *The Collected Poems* was published in 1920.

THOMAS Jill Penelope
b.1938 poet. A district nurse and member of the Attingham Writers' Group, she lives in Telford. The first collection, *Night Occupation* (1974), intimated that here was a fresh and perceptive poetic voice.

THOMSON James
1700–48 poet, playwright, translator and essayist. In 1743 he stayed at Hagley Hall, the home of Lord Lyttelton*. While there, he added lines concerning his host and his host's home to the text of the section, 'Spring', in his long poem, 'The Seasons'. A revised version of 'The Seasons', a precursor of the later very popular topographical poetry, appeared in 1744. Other work includes the tragedy, *Sophonisba* (1730), and the verse allegory, *The Castle of Indolence* (1748).

THOMSON Phillip
mid/late 20th C poet. He lives in Walsall and works as a freelance graphic artist. Two of his collections of poems, *The Grotesque* and *Listening for Clouds*, were published in 1972. His work combines the fey with the visceral, and is rather unnerving.

THOMSON William
1670–1738 poet and historian. Though the vicar of Exhall, he chose to live in a property of his wife's at Atherstone-upon-Stour. In 1721 they moved to Worcester. His much enlarged edition of Dugdale's *Warwickshire* appeared in 1730; but his researches into the churches and estates of Worcestershire never appeared; and the collection of his verse, *Poems*, was not published until 1911.

THORNEYCROFT Thomas
1822–1903 poet, playwright and essayist. He was born at Willenhall, the son of an ironmaster who was the first mayor of Wolverhampton and later moved to Tettenhall. His work is multifarious and includes accounts of five patents and thirty inventions as well as a three-act opera, *The Thorneycroft Cousins* (1886). The long narrative poem, *A Trip to America,*

appeared in 1869 complete with photographs of his travels. His verses, *Some Love in Foreign Lands to Roam*, have been set to music.

THORPE Sylvia
b.1926 novelist. She lives in a village near Ross-on-Wye. Her novels, mainly of the historical and/or romantic kind, as their titles might suggest, include *The Sword and the Shadow* (1951), *The House at Bell Orchard* (1962) and *The Scarlet Domino* (1970).

Hester Thrale

THRALE Mrs Hester Lynch
1741–1821 letter writer and diarist. She and her husband were friends of Dr Johnson* and travelled extensively with him in the west midland area. In 1774 they are known to have visited Hagley Hall, the home of the Lyttelton family. The collection, *Anecdotes of the Late Samuel Johnson*, was published in 1786. *Thraliana*, a hotchpotch of literary jests, diary entries, verse and anecdotes, was edited by K C Balderston and published in 1942.

THURSFIELD Richard
1827–1906 poet. Born at Wednesbury, as a boy he often visited his grandfather at the vicarage in Pattingham. Originally trained as a solicitor, he was ordained in 1854 and eventually returned to the west midland area in 1872 where he became successively vicar of Ullenhall and vicar of Bredwardine. His book of verse, *Bethany: or, Thoughts in Verse on John XI, and Other Subjects*, was published in 1864.

TILDESLEY Cecil James Croydon
1877–1963 poet. Born at Penkridge, he was the younger son of the following. His reputation rests on the poem, *Cannock Chase*, which appeared in *Chambers' Journal* in 1918.

TILDESLEY James Carpenter
1840–1907 poet and essayist. Born in Willenhall and educated at Old Hall in Wellington, he became a lock manufacturer, chairman of Wolverhampton Chamber of Commerce, chairman of Willenhall Urban Sanitary Council and a county magistrate. He contributed articles and poems, chiefly to do with local life and concerns, to various publications including the *Birmingham Gazette* and the *Gentleman's Magazine*. He and his son figure largely in Norman Tildesley's study, *Family of Tildesley of Staffordshire*.

TILTMAN Mrs Marjorie Hessell
mid-20th C novelist. As a child she lived in Birmingham. Her two books, *Quality Chase* (1939) and *Quality Chase's Daughter* (1955), relate to the city.

TIMS Hilton
mid/late 20th C novelist. He was born in Ellesmere in Shropshire. His historical novel, *All the Pride of Power*, was published in 1973. He continues to write – mainly in the history/romance genre.

TIPPER John
d.1713 poet and actor. A native of Coventry, he became a master at the city's Bablake School in 1699. Though chiefly remembered for his founding of various periodicals, including the *Ladies' Diary* (1704), *Delights for the Ingenious* (?1706) and *Great Britain's Diary, or the Union Almanack*, he also wrote a verse entertainment which was performed in 1706 by the boys of Bablake School at a thanksgiving celebration for the victories in Flanders and Spain.

TIPTAFT Norman
1883–1970 novelist and religious and topographical writer. A member of Birmingham City Council, he is known to have written one novel, *The City Father* (1925), which is set in Birmingham.

TIPTON David
b.1934 poet. He was born in Birmingham. His first collection, *Poems in Transit*, appeared in 1960, to be followed by *City of Kings* (1967) and *Millstone Grit* (1972). He now writes both prose and verse. *Millstone Grit and Other Poems* appeared in 1993.

TOCZEK Nick
b.1950 poet. He studied industrial metallurgy at the University of Birmingham and has lived for a time in Moseley. Two of his volumes of poetry were published before the end of 1974, *Because the Evenings* (1972) and *The Book of Numbers* (1973). He continues to write about life's horrors and sillinesses in both prose and verse – frequently in a sharply humorous manner. *Bigger Tory Vote* appeared in 1991.

TOFT John
b.1933 novelist and short story writer. Born in the Potteries, the son of a Marxist steel worker, he was educated at the local grammar school. His work includes *The Bargees* (1969), *The Wedge* (1971) and *The House of the Arousing* (1973). Much of his later work, including *The Dew* (1981), has a west midland setting.

TOLKIEN J R R
1899–1973 novelist and academic. The son of a banker, at the age of four he came to Birmingham from South Africa and was later educated at King Edward's School. He lived in various parts of the city, including Wake Green Road and from 1902 to 1910 at Five Ways (marked by a plaque). The inspiration for his most popular books, *The Hobbit* (1937) and *The Lord of the Rings* (1954 and 1955), is supposed to have come in part from the area near Sarehole Mill.

TOMKINS Samuel
mid-19th C novelist and poet. Born in Handsworth, he was educated at the local church school and later became a clerk in a factor's warehouse. In 1867, after he had moved to Wombourne near Wolverhampton, he published a novel entitled *Woodland and Woodbee, a Tale of Manly Virtue*. He had moved to Trysull in Staffordshire by the time *Worth and Wealth, A Poem* appeared in 1869. His work is lyrically pleasing, if not especially original in subject matter.

TOMKINSON Thomas
1631–1710 poet. Born at Sladehouse in Ilam, Staffordshire, the son of a farmer, he later belonged to the Muggletonian religious sect. It was his beliefs which inspired the 26-stanza poem, 'Joyful News from Heaven, for the Jews are Called'.

TOMLINSON Charles
b.1927 poet. Born in Stoke-on-Trent, he was educated at Longton High School. His first book, *Relations and Contraries*, appeared in 1951 and since then he has published several volumes of verse. In 1957 he received the Hokin Poetry Prize from the magazine, *Poetry* (Chicago), for 'The Necklace' (1955); and in 1960 he won their Blumenthal-Levitson Award. All his work is marked by a strong visual element, his best collection being *The Way of the World* (1969).

TOMLINSON John Wickes
1801–57 poet and hymn writer. Born in Stoke-on-Trent and educated at Rugby School, he was later to become rector in the city. The book, *Poems, an Addition to the Book of Psalms and Hymns in Use at the Parish Church of Stoke-on-Trent*, appeared in 1835. Other work includes *The Bride's Melody* (1836) and *The Rock of Nice; Historic and Descriptive Poem* (1855).

TOONE Mary
late 19th C poet. She lived in Leamington Spa. A collection of her verse entitled *Poetry* appeared in 1874.

TOTTEN Malcolm
journalist, playwright and broadcaster. He worked for the *Birmingham Post* as news editor. With Jon Raven* he wrote *Up Spaghetti Junction*, a musical review of the life and times of Birmingham, which was presented in February 1973 at the Birmingham Repertory Theatre. A man of many parts, he also wrote a history of the Metal Mechanics Union called *Founded in Brass*. He continues to write.

TOY John
1611–63 poet. He was born in Worcester. Successively he was chaplain to the Bishop of Hereford, headmaster of Worcester Free School and in 1643 headmaster of King's School. He held this office, together with the living of Stoke Prior, until his death and is buried in Worcester Cathedral. His two best-known works are *Worcester's Elegie and Eulogie* (1638), which describes the plague years of 1637 and 1638 in the city, and the collection, *Quisquiliae Poeticae* (1662).

TOZER Basil John
1872–1949 novelist. His only known work, *Riddle of the Forest* (1934), which concerns ghostly experiences in the rural 1890s, is set in Acton Burnell Park, ten miles or so from Shrewsbury. He dedicates the novel to Barbara Cartland* 'for her encouragement'.

TRAHERNE Thomas
1637–74 poet, essayist and divine. He was born in Hereford, the son of a shoemaker. After his father's death he and his brother were brought up by an uncle, Philip Traherne, a prosperous innkeeper who twice became mayor of Hereford. Thomas was rector of Credenhill from 1657 to 1667, though he did not go to live in the parish until 1661. His best-known work, *Centuries* (1674), was a collection of meditations written for a pious community in Kington which was led by Susanna Hopton. In 1896 Bernard Dobell discovered manuscripts of more of his poems which he edited and published in 1903. Much of Traherne's work combines a fascination for new ideas with a serene spiritual joy.

TRAILL Peter
1896–1968 (pseudonym of Guy Mainwaring Morton) novelist. He was educated at Rugby School. His

many novels include *Woman To Woman* (1924), *Here Lies Love* (1932) and *Mutation Mink* (1950).

TRAVIS Elijah
late 18th C poet. The author of *Original Poems for Children* (1877), he was born in Staffordshire.

TRAVIS Peter
mid/late 20th C short story writer. He lives in Newcastle-under-Lyme. The collection, *Run Like the Wind and Other Stories*, appeared in 1972.

TREASE Geoffrey
b.1909 novelist, biographer and children's writer. After frequently visiting Herefordshire on walking tours in his youth, in 1954 he decided to settle in Colwall where he lived until a few years ago. *The Maythorn Story* (1960) and its sequel, *Change At Maythorn* (1962), depict thinly disguised Colwall and the Malvern Hills. His autobiography, *Laughter at the Door*, was published in 1974. An extraordinarily prolific writer of children's adventure stories, he also published *Tales Out of School* (1949), a critical survey of children's fiction.

TREECE Henry
1911–66 novelist, children's writer and poet. Born in Wednesbury, he was educated there and in Birmingham. For some years he taught at Cleobury Mortimer. A writer of very many novels, including *The Eagles Have Flown* (1954) and *The Children's Crusade* (1958), which combine adventure with vivid historical settings, he was also the founder of a group known as 'The New Apocalypse' whose members described themselves as 'anti-cerebral'. With James Findlay Hendry, he edited two of their anthologies, *The White Horseman*

(1941) and *The Crown and the Sickle* (1945).

TRENEER Ann
mid-20th C novelist and short story writer. For several years she was on the staff of King Edward's High School for Girls in Birmingham. *Reminiscences* appeared in 1944; *Happy Button and Other Stories* in 1950. *A Stranger in the Midlands* tells of her experiences, an exile from Exmouth, in the city of Birmingham and in Shropshire and Worcestershire.

TREVOR Meriol
b.1919 children's writer. *Lights in a Dark Town* (1964) refers to Cardinal Newman's* life in Birmingham where she is believed to have lived for a time.

TRUMPER Dr H B
See BAGSTER, Hubert

TUNSTALL Beatrice
mid-20th C novelist. She has many associations with the west midland region, and is believed to have lived in Bunbury in Shropshire – the place made famous by Algernon Moncrieff in Oscar Wilde's play, *The Importance of Being Earnest* (1895). *The Long Day Closes* (1934) relates to Shropshire; *The Shiny Night* (1934) to Staffordshire; and *The Dark Lady* (1939) to Warwickshire.

TURNBULL Ann
b.1943 children's writer. She lives in Madeley in Shropshire. Her first book, *The Frightened Forest*, appeared in 1974. Since then she has written several books, many for young children, including *Pigeon Summer* which is set in a fictionalised mining village based on her home town.

TURNBULL Gael
b.1928 poet. From 1964 he lived for

nearly twenty years in Malvern, writing and working as a GP and an anaesthetist. Founder of the Migrant Press (for poetry) in 1957, he wrote many pieces for local performances in the Malvern area. Early collections of poetry include *A Trampoline* (1968) and *Scantlings* (1970). Since then he has published several volumes of verse. The collection, *A Gathering of Poems 1950–1980*, appeared in 1983. His work always shows an inventive technical skill.

TURNER David
b.1927 playwright, adaptor and poet. He lived for a time in Solihull. His play, *Semi-Detached*, one of the mainstays of amateur dramatic groups, was first performed in 1960 and his adaptation of *The Servant of Two Masters* in 1973. A version of *The Beggar's Opera* appeared in 1982.

TURNER David
b.1952 poet. He was born and educated in Birmingham. At the age of eighteen he started writing poetry which appeared in several periodicals, though his collection, *The Buzzard*, did not appear until 1976. So far as is known, he continues to write.

TURNER Joseph
b.1871 poet. He was for many years assistant master at Croft Street Council School in Walsall. His work, which often describes local places, appeared in Alfred Moss's*, *Songs from the Heart of England* (1920).

TURNER Philip
b.1925 children's writer and radio playwright. Born in Canada and brought up in the west midland area, he spent some years teaching in Droitwich High School before leaving the district in 1973. He later returned

to the area to live in Malvern. A prolific writer, he often includes a well-researched historical element in his work. Among his published books are *Sea Peril* (1966), *Devil's Nob* (1970) and *Colonel Sheperton's Dock* (1974). His passion play, *Christ in a Concrete City*, was broadcast on radio in 1969. He continues to write, mainly for children.

TURNER Raymond
b.1920 poet. A former local government officer, he lives in Wolverhampton. The collection, *Flies in Amber*, was published in 1971 and *The Garden of Cain* in 1973. His poetic voice, though often straightforward and unambiguous, on occasions takes off into the distinctly surreal.

TURNERELLI Edward Tracey
1813–96 novelist, short story writer and poet. From 1854 he lived in Leamington Spa. His work, which includes *A Night in a Haunted House* (1859) and *Christmas Tales for Christmas Charities* (1873), has a tendency to dwell on things that go bump in the night.

TWAIN Mark
1835–1910 (pseudonym of Samuel Clemens) novelist. An American, he visited Stratford-upon-Avon in 1907 on a pilgrimage to William Shakespeare's birthplace and to see Harvard House where the mother of the founder of Harvard University had lived. Marie Corelli*, who had helped to rescue the house from redevelopment, was his guide. In this country *The Adventures of Tom Sawyer* (1877) and its sequel, *The Adventures of Huckleberry Finn* (1884), are his best-known novels.

TWIGG Douglas C R
late 20th C poet. He lives in Stoke-on-

Trent. His collection, *Timeless Hour*, subtitled 'a poetic exercise in metaphysics', was published in 1973. It is not known whether he continues to write.

TWYCROSS-RAINES John B
late 19th C novelist. His only known work, *Aston Hall: A Tale of the Civil War* (1882), is set in Birmingham.

TYNAN Kenneth
1927–80 essayist and theatre reviewer. He was born and educated in Birmingham. His championship of naturalistic drama helped to promote the British theatrical renaissance of the 1950s and 1960s. The four collections of his essays and reviews, *He That Plays the King* (1950), *Curtains* (1961), *Tynan Right and Left* (1968) and *A View of the English Stage* (1974), show how criticism in his hands is taken out of the world of journalism and into the realms of literature.

U

UNDERHILL E A
1869–1944 poet. He was born in Upper Gornall in Staffordshire where his family had lived for more than 400 years. On becoming a teacher in Bilston, he moved to Dudley. The collection, *Patchwork* (1932), which includes 'Around the Beacon (Sedgley)' as well as other poems on the locality, has a foreword written by the principal of Dudley Training College.

UNDERHILL Edward
mid-16th C poet. Known as the 'hot-gospeller', he was born in Eatington in Warwickshire. All his work, which was published in pamphlets and broadsheets, is characterised by an anti-papist flourish and a disregard for grammar.

URBAN Sylvanus
See CAVE, Edward

V

'V'
See CLIVE, Caroline

VAUGHAN Robert Alfred
1823–57 poet. Born in Worcester, the son of a Congregational pastor, he himself was for a time a Congregational minister – in Birmingham. *Poems* (1844) and *Hours with the Mystics* (1856) are his main works.

VAUGHAN Rowland
early 17th C poet and agriculturist. A landowner at Bacton in Herefordshire's Golden Valley, he describes a fictional community in his treatise (1610) with the leisurely title, *Most approved, and long experienced Waterworkes. Containing, The manner of Winter and Summer-drowning of Medow and Pasture, by the advantage of the least, River, Brooke, Fount, or Waterprill adjacent; there-by to make those grounds (especially if they be drye) more Fertile Ten for One. As also demonstration of a project for the great benefit of the Common-wealth generally, but of Hereford-shire especially.*

VERNAL J
mid-19th C novelist. He is believed to have lived in Birmingham where his novel, *Recollections of a Tradesman* (1864), is set.

VERNON Marjorie
mid-20th C (pseudonym of Miss M Cottam) novelist. She was born in Wolverhampton and lived in Harborne Road in Warley Woods. Her first novel was published in 1946. Most of her work, which belongs to the romantic genre, is inspired by travel and set abroad.

VERNON William
b.1756 poet and soldier. Born in Wolverhampton and brought up to the buckle-making trade, he found the work uncongenial and left to find his fortune in London – later becoming a soldier. There are only two authenticated volumes of his poems, which are concerned mainly with local places, nature and rural journeys. The first was published in 1775.

VERSCHOYLE Catherine M
early 20th C novelist. She lived in Ross-on-Wye. Her only known novels are *Oldham* (1927) and *Willow and Cypress* (1929).

VIRR John J
1933–84 poet. He was brought up in Pedmore near the Clent Hills in Worcestershire – the inspiration of much of his early poetry which, with his later work, was published in the volume entitled, *Collection of Poems*.

VITALIS Ordericus
1075–1143 chronicler. He was born at Atcham in Shropshire and baptised by his godfather, the priest Orderic, in St Eata Church. Having completed his education, begun at the age of five in Shrewsbury, he became a clerk in the church of St Peter and St Paul. Though he spent most of his life in Normandy, he visited England frequently to collect material for his *Historia Ecclesiastica* (1123–41), a gossipy chronicle in thirteen books about the life and times of Normandy and England which makes many sentimental references to the author's 'Severnside' origins.

W

WADDINGTON-FEATHER John
b.1933 novelist, children's writer and playwright. A teacher, he lives at Lyth Bank in Shrewsbury. In 1966 he was awarded the Bronte Society prize; and in 1973 he won the Cyril Hodges Poetry Award. Included in his many works are the verse dramas, *Garlic Lane* (1970) and *Easy Street; a Modern Morality Play* (1973), and the volume, *A Collection of Verse* (1963). Much of his later work for children describes the fortunes of Quill, an adventurous hedgehog.

WADLEY Thomas Proctor
1826–95 poet. He became rector of Naunton Beauchamp in Worcestershire in 1874. Though his chief interest was in genealogy, he also contributed poems to various periodicals.

WAIN John
1925–94 novelist, poet, short story writer and critic. The son of a dentist, he was born in Stoke-on-Trent and from 1934 to 1942 he attended Newcastle-under-Lyme High School. His first novel, *Hurry On Down*

(1953), detailing the experiences of the unconforming Charles Lumley, placed him in the 'angry young man' camp (see OSBORNE, John). He also published several volumes of poetry, collected in *Poems 1949–79* (1981), two volumes of short stories, *Nuncle* (1960) and *Death of the Hind Legs* (1966), and a number of other novels. *Sprightly Running* (1962) is autobiographical. A Movement poet (see FISHER, Roy), in 1953 he broadcast 'First Reading', a BBC radio series which introduced to the listening public young poets such as Philip Larkin*, D J Enright* and Kingsley Amis who, like him, had reacted against the opacity and literariness of pre-1930s poetry.

WAINWRIGHT Jeffrey
b.1944 poet. He was born in Stoke-on-Trent. A collection of verse, *The Important Man*, appeared in 1971. His poetic voice continues – political and questioning – in a language that is both unadorned and compassionate. *Red-headed Pupil and Other Poems* appeared in 1994.

WAKEFIELD George
1821–88 poet. Born at Uttoxeter, the son of a carpenter and joiner, he was educated briefly at 'an old grandame's of the name of Shenton'. He became successively a shoemaker, a railway nightwatchman, a porter and a station master. He is now best known for his long rural poem, *The River Dove and Human Life Compared* (1856), in which he found delight in charting the connections between literary characters and the age-old serenity of the river.

WALEY Arthur
1889–1966 translator and poet. He was educated at Rugby School. An authority on Chinese and Japanese

poetry, he published his most popular work, *One Hundred and Seventy Chinese Poems*, in 1918. His scholarship and enthusiasm helped to generate the 1920s' interest in things and ideas Oriental.

WALKER David
b.1911 novelist, children's writer and short story writer. He was educated at Shrewsbury School. His work, which includes the novels, *The Storm and the Silence* (1949) and *Geordie* (1950), was published after he had settled in Canada.

WALLACE Doreen
b.1897 (pseudonym of Doreen Rash, adopted as a mark of her admiration for the work of Edgar Wallace) novelist. She was educated at Malvern. Her novels, which number over thirty and are usually to do with family affairs, include *A Little Learning* (1931), *Green Acres* (1941) and *Mayland Hall* (1960). Most of her life was spent with her farmer husband near Diss in Norfolk.

WALLACE Edgar
1875–1932 novelist and playwright. He worked for a while on the staff of the *Birmingham Gazette*. A prolific and prosperous writer, in 27 years he produced over 150 novels, beginning with *The Four Just Men* (1906). At the time of his death, in Hollywood, USA, he was working on the script for the film, *King Kong*.

WALPOLE Horace
1717–97 poet and novelist. In 1753 he visited Hagley Hall, the home of Lord Lyttelton*, and praised the garden fulsomely. He is perhaps best known now for his gothic novel, *The Castle of Otranto* (1764). Recent research suggests he was in no way responsible for Thomas Chatterton's suicide.

WALSH William
1663–1708 poet. Born in Abberley
Lodge, he lived there all his life,
entertaining many literary figures,
among them John Dryden*, Joseph
Addison* and Alexander Pope*. He
was for a time MP for Worcester and
is buried in the Saxon church at
Abberley. He collaborated with John
Vanbrugh in an adaptation of
Molière's plays. 'The Despairing
Lover' is perhaps the best known of
his poems, which were collected and
published posthumously in 1716.
Another collection, *Works in Prose
and Verse*, appeared in 1736. (See
BUTT, George.)

WALTER Elizabeth
mid-20th C novelist. She grew up in
Hereford. All her work is in the
mystery/crime genre, *The More
Deceived* being her first novel.

WALTERS Bryan
See CYNFYN

WALTERS Hugh
b.1910 (pseudonym of Walter
Llewellyn Hughes) children's writer.
He lives in Bilston. His work, which
includes *Blast Off At Woomera*
(1957), *Destination Mars* (1963),
Journey to Jupiter (1965) and
Passage to Pluto (1973), belongs to
the space adventure genre and has
been described by *The Guardian* as
combining 'an artful mounting
tension with a mass of fascinating
technical detail'. Later work, which
includes *First Contact* and *Murder on
Mars*, has introduced a detective
element.

WALTON Elisha
1843–1914 poet and folklorist. He
was born in Burslem. His works
include *The Romance of the Hills –
Tales of the Staffordshire Moorlands*

and various poems and ballads,
collected in 1928, among which is one
describing Dieu-la-Cresse Abbey in
Leek.

WALTON Izaak
1593–1683 angler, essayist and
biographer. Born in Eastgate Street,
Stafford (commemorated by a
plaque), he was baptised in St Mary's
Church where there is a commemorative bust. In 1654 he bought a cottage
in Shallowford, now a museum,
where he used occasionally to stay on
his retirement from London. He and
his friend, Charles Cotton*, are
known to have visited Ilam Hall, the
home of Robert Port. From 1660 to
1662 he lived in Hartlebury Castle in
Worcestershire, as Bishop Morley's
steward. There is an inscription by
him in Worcester Cathedral on the
tablet commemorating his first wife's
death. He is chiefly known now for
his discourse on fishing presented in
dialogue form in *The Compleat
Angler* (1653). Among his *Lives* are
included those of John Donne* (1640)
and George Herbert* (1670).

WALTON Stella V
b.1905 poet and journalist. Her
parents brought her to live in Wolverhampton when she was six. She later
contributed a series of Black Country
poems to the *Express and Star* and,
under the name of Joan Slade, wrote
the woman's column in the same
paper.

WANLEY Nathaniel
1634–80 poet. In 1632 he became
vicar of Holy Trinity Church in
Coventry. Though a manuscript
version of his poems, which included
'The Witch of Endor' and 'Lazarus',
appeared in 1667, they were not
published until 1928. *The Little
Wonders of the World* (1678) earned

him £10 from the Council of Coventry.

WANLEY Humphrey
1672–1726 diarist. The son of Nathaniel Wanley (see above), he was born in Coventry. He began work apprenticed to a limmer, but eventually became a respected librarian in the city. From 1714 until his death he kept a journal, recording in particular his work in the Harleian Library of Edward, Earl of Oxford.

WARD Mrs Humphrey
1851–1920 novelist and essayist. Born in Tasmania, the daughter of Dr Thomas Arnold's second son, she came to England with her family in 1856. From 1861 to 1865 she attended the Rock Terrace School for Young Ladies in Shifnal – a far from pleasant experience which she was to draw on in her novel, *Marcella* (1894). Most of her work embodies, in fictional form, her own belief in the virtue of Christian charity.

WARING Robert
1614–58 poet. He was born at Lea near Wolverhampton. During the Civil War he found refuge at Apsley in Shropshire in the home of Sir William Whitmore. Regarded as one of the great wits and orators of his day, he is best known for the collection, *Amoris Effigies*.

WARMSTRY Gervase
1604–41 poet. Born into an old Worcestershire family, his father being chief registrar of the diocese, he was educated at King's School in Worcester. In 1630 he succeeded his father as registrar. He is buried in the cathedral. His only work of note, *Virescit Vulnere Virtus: England's Wound and Cure* (1628), was political in nature.

WARNER Rex
1905–86 poet, novelist and classical scholar. He was born in Birmingham. The collection of his verse, *Poems*, was published in 1937. His novels, which include *The Wild Goose Chase* (1937), *The Aerodrome* (1941) and *The Vengeance of the Gods* (1954), reveal his bleak, often harsh voice. Other work includes translations of ancient Greek poetry.

WARNER William
1552–1609 poet. He was the son of the vicar of Radway in Warwickshire. Known as one of the most sententious of poets, in 1592 he published *Albion's England* – an epitome of British history extending over thirteen books expressing much patriotic feeling.

WATTS Stanley G
mid-20th C children's writer. He was born in Kidderminster and lived there for several years. *Number 21* (1966), *The Scop's Apprentice* (1967) and *The Breaking of Arnold* (1971) are set in Bedminster, a fictionalised Kidderminster. *Spaceship in Paradise* (1979) was dedicated to C S Lewis*, his tutor at Oxford.

WEAVER Thomas
1616–63 playwright. He was born in Worcester. Though charged with treason for his political skit, *Zeal Overheated*, he was acquitted by the trial judge who was loath 'to condemn a scholar and a man of wit'.

WEBB Henry Bertram
See CLAYTON, John

WEBB Jane
1807–58 novelist. Born in Birmingham, she was the daughter of a businessman who in 1820 took his family to live in Bartley Green. She later married John Claudius Loudon, who

View from Wenlock Edge

designed Birmingham's Botanical Gardens. Her only known work is the deliciously gothic, *The Mummy! A Tale of the Twenty-second Century*, which appeared anonymously in 1827. Where would the horror-film industry be without it?

WEBB Mary

1881–1927 novelist. She was born at Leighton Lodge in Leighton-under-Wrekin and was christened in St Mary's Church at Leighton Hall. In 1882 the family moved to The Grange, a house just outside Much Wenlock, where she was educated at home. In 1896 the family again moved, this time to the Woodlands in Stanton-upon-Hine-Heath, and from 1902 until her marriage to Henry Webb in 1912 she lived at Maesbrook, the family home in Meole Brace. (A brass plate on one of the pews in the village church commemorates her worshipping there.) Though she and her husband went to live in Weston-super-Mare, she could not bear being away from her beloved Shropshire and they returned in 1914 to rent Rose Cottage in Pontesbury. Here, inspired by Stiperstones, she completed her first novel, *The Golden*

Arrow (1916). Though she made several sorties onto the London literary scene, she always returned to her homeland and is buried in Shrewsbury cemetery. Her two best-known novels are *Gone to Earth* (1917), in which the miners' chapel at Snailbeach figures, and *Precious Bane* (1924). In her work Shrewsbury is represented as Silverton, Church Stretton as Shepwardine, Ratlinghope as Slepe, Bishop's Castle as Mallard's Keep, Clun as Dysgwlfas-on-the-wild-moors and there are many more connections.

WEBSTER Leonard

late 20th C poet and children's writer. Born in Birmingham, brought up in Smethwick, he was educated at the town's grammar school and at the University of Warwick. He now lives in Warley. The collection, *Behind the Painted Veil*, was published in 1972. His more recent work, including the children's novel, *The Turban Wallah*, covers many contemporary issues.

WEDDUP Jan

late 20th C poet. *Edgehill* (1974) describes the first battle of the Civil War, which took place in Warwickshire. The poems and drawings 'are separate responses to the fear and terror the fields of Edge Hill have witnessed, and still, in some strange way, retain'.

WEIGALL Arthur
1880–1934 novelist, biographer and lyricist. He was at school in Malvern. Compared to his serious work as an Egyptologist, his novels, which include *Saturnalia in Room 23* (1927), are in a distinctly lighter vein.

Fay Weldon

WELDON Fay
b.1933 novelist and television playwright. She was born and brought up in Worcester. Her books, which include *The Fat Woman's Joke* (1967) and *Down Among the Women* (1971), are mainly concerned with the tragicomic business of being female in modern society – a theme she has continued to explore in her later novels and novellas. Many of these, such as *The Life and Loves of a She Devil* (1983), have been adapted for television. Recent work includes *The Rules of Life* (1987), *The Hearts and Lives of Men* (1987) and *The Affliction* (1994).

WESTALL Robert
1929–93 poet, children's writer and critic. From 1957 to 1958 he taught art at Erdington Secondary Modern School in Birmingham. Though his first book, *The Machine-Gunners*, did not appear until 1975, he was in print from 1970 as Northern Art Critic for *The Guardian*. During the 1970s and 1980s this much respected writer published a number of books for children and teenagers – some controversially bleak and violent.

WETENHALL Edward
1636–1713 poet and religious writer. The author of *The Wish, Being the Tenth Satyr of Juvenal in Pindarick Verse*, he was born at Lichfield.

WEYMAN Stanley
1855–1928 novelist. The son of a solicitor, he was born in Broad Street in Ludlow, where he lived until his marriage in 1895, and was educated at Ludlow Grammar School and Shrewsbury School. His historical romances, among them *The Red Cockade* (1895) and *Under the Red Robe* (1896), were very popular. An earlier novel, *The New Rector* (1891), though purporting to be set in Warwickshire, has scenes in it which more closely recall Ludlow. He returned to Ludlow after his retirement and stayed there until the early 1890s. His twenty-first novel, *The Great House*, was published in 1922.

WHALLEY Peter
1722–91 poet and proofreader. Born in Rugby, he not only wrote commentaries on William Shakespeare* and Ben Jonson* and corrected the proofs of Alexander Pope's* *Shakespeare*, but also produced much original verse which was often concerned with contemporaneous poets and poetry.

WHATELEY Mary
See DARWALL, Mrs Mary

WHEELER Richard
d.1979 poet. He lived in Clun.
Remembering Summer, which
describes and celebrates many places
in South Shropshire, was published in
1968. His later poetry, published in
various magazines, shows a great
range of subjects and poetic forms.

WHEWAY John
b.1943 poet, novelist and playwright.
He read philosophy at the University
of Warwick. *The Green Table of
Infinity*, a collection of prose pieces
dedicated to Gavin Bantock*, was
published in 1972. Other work
includes a novella, *Poborden*, and a
play, *Cadenza*.

WHISTLER Charles W
1856–1913 novelist. *A King's
Comrade* (1904), based on the life of
King Ethelbert, is subtitled *A Story of
Old Hereford*. Other work, most of it
in historical vein, includes *For King
and Empress*, *Havelok the Dane* and
King Alfred's Viking.

WHITE James
1775–1820 humorist. He was born in
Bewdley. His one great work, *The
Original Letters etc of Sir John
Falstaff and His Friends* (1796),
inspired by his admiration of the
'great' man, was very popular in its
day.

WHITEHOUSE A W
late 19th C poet. He was born and
lived all his life in Wednesbury. Many
of the poems in *Poems, Grave and
Gay* (1885), which are generally in a
religious cast, first appeared in the
Midland Advertiser.

WHITEHOUSE Walter G
early 20th C novelist. He is believed
to have lived in Malvern. His book,
The Straits of Malvern (1906), is set
in the area.

WHITTAKER Joseph
b.1871 novelist and poet. He was
born in one of Wolverhampton's
slums. When he was four his parents
moved to Townwell-fold where, at the
age of twelve, having been educated
at the local church school, he started
work as a pawnbroker's assistant.
Later he became a warehouse clerk. In
1892 he published the first of his six
volumes of poetry, entitled *Poems*. At
the same time several of his articles
appeared in the *Express and Star*. His
novel, *Tumble-fold*, details the hard
lives of the town's poor in the 1870s
and 1880s.

WHYTYNTON Robert
b.1480 poet and grammarian. He was
born and educated at Lichfield.
Involved in several instances of
'warfare of epigrams', many of his
'missiles' being written in verse, he
also published widely on rhetoric and
grammar.

WIGGIN Maurice
b.1912 television critic and essayist.
Born in Bloxwich in Staffordshire, he
was educated at Queen Mary's
Grammar School in Walsall. In 1938
he became editor of the *Birmingham
Gazette*. Most of his writing, which
includes the collections of short prose
pieces, *In Spite of the Price of Hay*,
The Memoirs of a Maverick (1968)
and *A Cottage Idyll* (1969), is autobiographical.

WILDING Michael
b.1942 novelist and short story
writer. From 1967 to 1968 he worked
in the English Department of the
University of Birmingham. He now
lives in Australia. The collection of
short stories, *Aspects of the Dying
Process*, appeared in 1972 and the
novel, *Living Together*, in 1974. His
work continues to show both literary

awareness and an interest in contemporary issues and preoccupations.

WILKINSON Edith
mid-20th C poet. She lived in Coventry. The first poem in her collection, *Bright Flame* (1968), is concerned with the city's three spires.

WILKINSON Edward
d.1900 poet. He lived in Leamington Spa. In memory of his sister, Eliza, who was the founder of the Unmarried Women's Institute, he wrote the poem, 'Reverie At Home' (1883).

WILLETTS Ronald Frederick
b.1915 poet and academic. He lives in Birmingham and from 1946 to 1981 was successively lecturer, reader and Professor of Greek at the University of Birmingham. His first volume of poetry, *The Trobriand Islanders*, appeared in 1960 and he was co-author of *New Poems* (1965). Much of his work is inspired by myth and legend.

WILLIAMS Alfred Rowberry
early 20th C novelist. He lived in Walsall. In *The Cornfield* (1924) his 'chief aim has been to visualise the atmosphere in which countryfolk live'. He was also the compiler of *Legends of the Severn Valley* (1925). *Wallchester in The Minutes* (1927), a fictional representation of civic life, is set in a thinly disguised Walsall.

WILLIAMS Charles Hanbury
1709–59 poet. He was MP for Leominster from 1754 until his death. His volume of poems, *Odes*, was published posthumously in 1775.

WILLIAMS John Bickerton
1792–1855 poet and religious writer. Born at West Felton in Shropshire, he practised as a solicitor in Shrewsbury and was mayor in 1836. After his retirement he lived at The Hall in

Wem. His poems were published in several periodicals.

WILLIAMS Joseph
1692–1755 diarist. He was born and lived all his life in Kidderminster. Extracts from his diary, which described many aspects of the town as well as his personal life, were published posthumously in 1816.

WILLIS Nathaniel Parker
1806–67 poet and playwright. An American, in 1828 he stayed at the Red House in Bridge Street, Stratford-upon-Avon, in the room where his compatriot, Washington Irving*, had stayed ten years earlier. The record of his visits to England was published in two books, which make mention of a poker inscribed with Irving's name and a battered copy of the *Sketches* shown him by his landlady.

WILLMORE Frederic William
1848–1902 poet and historian. He was born at West Bromwich and completed his education at Queen's College in Birmingham. Best known for his *History of Walsall and Its Neighbourhood* (1887), he also wrote occasional verse. Alfred Moss* included 'The Chieftan's Grave' in his anthology, *Songs from the Heart of England* (1920).

WILSON Clive
late 20th C poet. He lived in Eccleshall. Many of the poems in his only known collection, *The Dark Kiss* (1974), were written during 'the stress and tragedy of war'.

WILSON Guy
mid/late 20th C novelist. *The Industrialists* (1968), a novel set in the contemporary industrial midlands, centres on problems of the owner/worker relationship. It is believed he continues to write.

WILSON Harrison Corbet
mid-18th C publisher and poet. He lived in Leamington Spa. *Leamington, a Poem* appeared in 1843 and *England's Queen and Prince Albert, a poem in two cantos* in 1849.

WILSON Keith Stewart
b.1951 poet. During his time as a student at the University of Birmingham he edited the *Poetry Maga* and was a member of the group of writers named 'Second City Poets'. His collection, *The Tragic Roundabout*, was published in 1972. He is a frequent contributor to the magazine, *Midland Read*.

WILSON JONES J
mid-20th C poet. He is believed to have lived for a time in the Black Country. His only known collection, *A Midland Bouquet*, was published in 1951.

WINDSOR George R
late 19th C novelist, historian and patent medicine vendor. He either lived, or stayed for a period of time, in All Stretton. His novel, *Laura Heathjohn; a Tale of Church Stretton* (1885), is based on a local murder which took place in the town a few miles to the south of his home.

WINDSOR-GARNETT J R
early 20th C novelist. He is believed to have associations with Wolverhampton. *The Village* (1931) is set in the Black Country.

WITHY Nathaniel
late 18th C poet. Born in Wolverhampton, he taught himself to read and write and later went to live in a cottage on the Hagley Hall estate under the patronage of Lord Lyttelton. The collection, *Miscellaneous Poems* (1778), shows considerable intellectual force.

WODEHOUSE P G
1881–1975 novelist and playwright. His father having retired to Stableford, he was a frequent visitor to Shropshire from 1895 to 1902 during his school holidays. Several of his novels draw on settings he would have known from these visits. Blandings Castle, the country seat of the character Clarence, Earl of Emsworth, which figures largely in several stories, is situated in Shropshire. Long recognised as a comic genius, Wodehouse is best known for the series of Jeeves and Bertie Wooster novels made up of *My Man Jeeves* (1919), *The Inimitable Jeeves* (1923) and many more.

WODEN G
1884–1978 (pseudonym of G W Slaney) novelist and playwright. Born in Wednesbury, he was educated at Queen Mary's Grammar School in Walsall. The following novels, all much in the rattling good yarn mould, make reference to Birmingham: *The New Dawn* (1915), *Paul Moorhouse* (1915), *The Great Cornelius* (1926), *The Parson and the Clerk* (1930) and *Holiday Adventure* (1939).

WOLSELEY Robert
1649–97 poet. He was born at Wolseley Hall in Staffordshire, the eldest son of the Cromwellian Sir Charles Wolseley. Best known for his poetical battle with Wharton that ended in a duel in which Wharton was fatally wounded, he also wrote several poems, including 'A Character of the English' – an allusion to the *De Vita Agricolae* of Tacitus*.

WOOD Mrs Henry
1814–87 novelist. The daughter of a wealthy glove manufacturer, she was born in Worcester and lived there until her marriage in 1834. The city is

represented as Helstoneleigh in those of her novels that are set in the area – such as *Mrs Halliburton's Troubles* (1862) and the 'Johnny Ludlow' short story series (1868–89). Although she is most famous for *East Lynne* (1861), a novel based on a true Worcester story which has frequently been adapted for stage and film, she considered *The Shadow of Ashlydat* (1863) to be her best novel.

WOOD Robert Henry
b.1923 children's writer. Born in Brierley Hill and educated at King Edward VI Grammar School in Stourbridge and the University of Birmingham, he now lives in Kingswinford. His many plays for children include *King's English, Three Gentleman of China* and *Post Early for Christmas*.

WOOD William Arthur
b.1857 poet. Born in Lichfield and educated at the grammar school, he became a pillar of city society and attained the position of sheriff of the county in 1908. Many of his poems were published locally, though his *History of Lichfield in Verse* was never completed.

WOODHOUSE Isaiah
early 20th C poet. He lived in Bloxwich. His only known work, *Original Poems on Doctrine, Experience and Practice*, appeared in 1927.

WOODHOUSE James
1735–1820 poet (known, not altogether propitiously, as the 'Cobbler Poet'). Born at Rowley Regis and apprenticed to a shoemaker, he later taught in a local endowed school until he found a patron in William Shenstone*. *The Life and Lucubrations of Crispinus Scriblerus*, his long autobiographical poem, characterised by a gloomy tone and infelicities of

metre and rhyme, is his magnum opus.

WOODS Margaret L
1856–1945 poet and novelist. She was born in Rugby, and educated there and at Leamington Spa. *Collected Poems* appeared in 1913 and her most popular novel was the very moving, *A Village Tragedy* (1887).

WORBOISE Emma J
1825–1918 novelist and poet. She was born in Birmingham and after a brief stay in Bristol returned with her parents to live in Edgbaston. She later kept a school in Aston. The author of over fifty books, she published her first, *Alice Cunningham*, in 1846. Much of her work relates to the Birmingham area: *Overdale, or the Story of a Pervert* (1869) is set in Erdington and district where she lived from 1865 to 1869; *Evelyn's Story, or Labour and Wait* (1876), *His Next of Kin* (1887), *Violet Vaughan, or the Shadow of Warneford Grange* (1903) and *A Woman's Patience* (1905) are all set in Birmingham; the undated *Our New House, or Keeping Up Appearances* is set in Ashted and Gravelly, or Copely, Hill; and the undated *Sir Julian's Wife, or Hopes and Misgivings* is set in Palmer Street Chapel, Birmingham. She also published a volume of poetry.

WORDSWORTH William
1770–1850 poet. He and his sister, Dorothy, often stayed with his wife's brother at Brinsop Court in Herefordshire. While there in 1835 he visited Bishopstone and wrote a sonnet on the Roman antiquities discovered in the village. He also visited Ledbury, finding in the story of St Catherine – her interpreting the sound of the bells rung without human aid as a sign she

should settle in the town – a fit subject for another sonnet. On another visit to Brinsop in 1843 his maid and friend, Jane, became ill and died. Perhaps it was on this occasion that he planted the cedar tree on the lawn – which was seen and mentioned by Francis Kilvert* in 1879. *Lyrical Ballads* (1798), produced with Samuel Taylor Coleridge*, remains a landmark in the history of English poetry. *The Prelude* (1805) is now generally considered to be his best work.

WORNER Philip

b.1910 poet and playwright. (Also writes as Philip Sylvester and Philip Incledon.) He was tutor at Worcester College of Education from 1949 to 1970, and still lives in the city. His first collection of verse, *Eros and Psyche*, appeared in 1933. Other work includes *All Dreaming Gone* (1940), *The Cactus Hedge* (1951), *Wrack* (1971) and *His Star Returns* (1979).

WOUIL George

early 20th C novelist. He lived in Walsall which, disguised as Walshaw, is the setting for his only known novel, *Sowing Clover* (1913).

WRATISLAW Albert Henry

1822–92 poet and translator. Born in Rugby, the son of a solicitor and grandson of Count Marc Wratislaw von Mitrowitz, a Bohemian nobleman, he was educated at Rugby School. In 1852 he published translations of a number of ancient Bohemian poems under the title of *The Queen's Court Manuscript*.

WRATISLAW Theodore

b.1871 poet. The son of Albert Henry Wratislaw*, he was born in Rugby and educated at Rugby School. His collections of verse – which include *Love's Memorial and Some Verses*

(1892), *Caprices* (1893) and *Orchids* (1896) – reveal the fin-de-siècle influence of Oscar Wilde and Aubrey Beardsley rather than that of Warwickshire.

WRIGHT R Lewis

1889–1985 poet and novelist. He was born in Tettenhall and educated at a public school. In 1937 he returned from working abroad as a banker and published his first novel in 1940. Though completed during 1937, when he was bedridden at the family home in Wolverhampton after a riding accident, *The Katty Letters* (written in phonetic script, and purporting to be from his cat to his daughter) was not published until 1977. He retired in 1953 and returned to live at Nags Hill, Burntwood. In his will he left money to Tettenhall College and Chase Terrace High School for competitions to help preserve good English.

WRIGHT Robert

b.1823 poet. A watchmaker by trade, he lived in Coventry. The collection, *Poems and Abbreviations on the Mysterious passages in the Bible*, appeared in 1860.

WRIGHT Thomas

1810–77 essayist, biographer and historian. Born at Tenbury Wells in Worcestershire, he was educated at Ludlow Grammar School. In 1859 he returned to Shropshire briefly as superintendent of the Roman excavations at Wroxeter. *Biographia Britannica Literaria* (1842 and 1846), a biography of literary characters, remained uncompleted at his death. He was also the author of more than eighty works of scholarship including *Queen Elizabeth and Her Times* (1838) and *The History of Domestic Manners and Sentiments in England During the Middle Ages* (1862).

WROTTESLEY Edward John
1814–1901 poet. Born at Codsall, he returned to Staffordshire as curate for Tettenhall. Later, in 1863, he became vicar of Brewood. He published a volume of poems in 1851 which was dedicated to the ladies of Tettenhall.

WYATVILLE George
late 19th C poet. He lived in Birmingham. His only known collection of verse, *Victoria – Regina et Imperatrix and Other Poems* (1897), was published by a Birmingham firm.

WYCHERLEY William
1640–1716 playwright. Born at Clive Hall, Preston Brockhurst in Shropshire, he often returned to the house after his education in France and at Oxford, inheriting the estate on his father's death in 1697. *The Country Wife* (1675) and *The Plain Dealer* (1676) are his best-known plays. Publication of *Miscellany Poems* in 1704 led to a meeting with Alexander Pope* which blossomed into friendship.

WYNDHAM John
1903–69 (pseudonym of John Benyon Harris) novelist and short story writer. He was born and brought up in Edgbaston, the son of a barrister. *The Day of the Triffids* (1951) began a long and successful career as a writer of what he called 'logical fantasies'. *Consider Her Ways and Others* (1961) is a collection of short stories.

WYRLEY William
1565–1618 poet and essayist. He was born in Wyrley in Staffordshire. Having become a copyist for Samson Erdeswicke, he wrote a treatise on armoury which was published in 1592. The first part of the book is in prose and describes the uses of armoury; the second is made up of two poems celebrating the lives and deaths of Sir John Chandos and Sir John de Gralhy.

Y

YATES Richard
b.1947 poet. Born in Erdington in Birmingham, he lived in Sutton Coldfield and worked for a while in Leamington Spa. His volume of ten poems, *Sinister Vintage*, appeared in 1973.

YOUNG Francis Brett
1884–1954 novelist and poet. He was born at The Laurels, Halesowen, the son of a doctor who later became medical officer of health for the borough. At the age of seven he went to a small private school in Sutton Coldfield, called Iona. In 1901 he became a medical student at the University of Birmingham. He married Jessica Hankinson from Alvechurch in 1908. After many years away from the west midland area he returned in 1932 to live at Craycombe House near Evesham. Ill health forced him to go abroad, but he managed to return in 1950 to accept the honorary degree of D.Litt from the University of Birmingham. His ashes are interred in the north transept of Worcester Cathedral. Very many of his novels, the best known of them being *Portrait of Clare* (1927) and *My Brother Jonathan* (1928), have a west midland setting.

The west midland counties

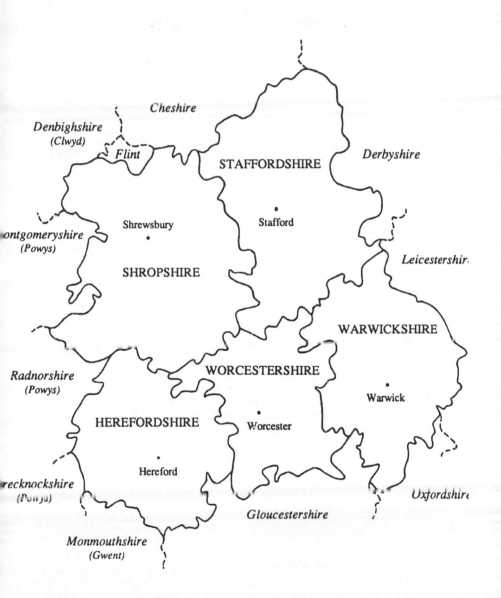

A–Z of places (by county)

HEREFORDSHIRE

BACTON Rowland Vaughan

BISHOPSTONE William Wordsworth

BOSBURY Edna Lyall

BREDWARDINE Francis Kilvert, Richard Thursfield

BRINSOP Francis Kilvert, William Wordsworth

BYTON Josephine Bromley

COLWALL Ernest Ballard, E Barrett Browning, Rosemary H Jarman, William Langland, Geoffrey Trease

CREDENHILL Thomas Traherne

DINMORE John Leland

DOWNTON Richard P Knight

EYE Jeremy Sandford

FOXLEY Uvedale Price

GOODRICH Theophilus Swift

HAMPTON John Leland

HEREFORD John S Arkwright, Geoffrey Bright, John Davies, Daniel Defoe, Richard Edes, Catherine Fellows, Roger Garfitt, David Garrick, Francis Godwin, Norman Hidden, John S Hoskins, James H James, Edward Kaulfuss, George S Kemble, John Leland, Arthur Machen, Map (or Mapes), John Masefield, John Philips, William Powell, Graham Price, Robert of Gloucester, Alick Rowe, William S Symonds, D M Thomas, John Toy, Thomas Traherne, Elizabeth Walter, Charles W Whistler

HOLME LACY John Aubrey

KENCHESTER John Leland

KINGTON George S Kemble, Isobel Lambot, Alick Rowe, Thomas Traherne

LEDBURY Ernest Ballard, Robert Frost, William Langland, John Masefield, Edward Thomas, William Wordsworth

LEOMINSTER Geoffrey Bright, Daniel Defoe, Richard P Knight, John Leland, Charles H Williams

LONGTOWN Gwyn Davies

MADELY Leslie Paul

MONKLAND Henry W Baker

MORDIFORD Michael Drayton

MUCH MARCLE Geoffrey Mason, Malcolm Munthe

NETHERWOOD Robert Devereux

ORCOP Frances Horovitz

PEMBRIDGE John Aubrey

PUDDLESTON John Osborne

RICHARD'S CASTLE Richard Gifford

ROSS-ON-WYE John Aubrey, Robert Bloomfield, S Taylor Coleridge, Daniel Defoe, Charles Dickens, Alfred Duggan, James Parry, Alexander Pope, Dennis Potter, Sylvia Thorpe, Catherine Verschoyle

RUSHALL William H Robinson

STOKE EDITH Celia Fiennes

STRETTON GRANDISON Celia Fiennes

STRETTON SUGWAS John Aubrey

TEDSTONE-DE-LA-MERE Luke Booker

WALFORD Thomas D Fosbroke

WESTON-UNDER-PENYARD Mayne Reid

WHITBOURNE Francis Godwin

WHITFIELD Caroline Clive

WITHINGTON John Philips

WOONTON George Evans

WORMSLEY Richard P Knight, Map (or Mapcs)

THE COUNTY IN GENERAL
John Aubrey, Hubert Bagster, William Black, William Camden,
T H Chetwynd, Alfred J Church, Thomas E Cole, Arthur O
Cooke, Donald Davie, Daniel Defoe, Michael Drayton, Thomas
Fuller, Robert J Gibbings, Roy Holland, John Leland, Harold J
Massingham, John Shane, Tacitus

SHROPSHIRE

ACTON BURNELL Basil J Tozer

ALBERBURY John Taylor

ALBRIGHTON G William S Sparrow

ALKINGTON Roger Cotton

ALL STRETTON Hesba Stretton, George R Windsor

APSLEY Robert Waring

ATCHAM Anna B Kingsford, Ordericus Vitalis

ATTINGHAM E M Almedingen, Margery Lea, Jill P Thomas

BADGER Isaac H Browne (1705), Isaac H Browne (1745)

BECKBURY Wilfred Byford-Jones

BISHOP'S CASTLE Gerald Adams, A Cotman, Richard Gifford,
Mary Webb

BOSCOBEL William H Ainsworth, George L Banks

BRIDGNORTH Richard Baxter, Lord Berners, Isaac H Browne (1745), Cynfyn, Edward Hall (or Halle), Thomas Irving-James, Francis Moore, Thomas Percy

BROSELEY Mrs F L Mortimer, Thomas A Peate-Hughes

BUNBURY Beatrice Tunstall

CHURCH STRETTON E M Almedingen, Kenneth Bird, Henry Kingsley, Oliver Sandys, Hesba Stretton, Mary Webb, George R Windsor

CLAVERLEY Hesba Stretton

CLEETON ST MARY Mrs E Hewins

CLEOBURY MORTIMER Nicholas Brennon, Simon Evans, William Langland, Henry Treece

CLUN Richard Ball, Paul Chadburn, E M Forster, Sir Walter Scott, Mary Webb, Richard Wheeler

COALBROOKDALE Arthur C Fox-Davies, Edith Pargeter

COLD HATTON Alan and Frank Manford

CONDOVER Mary Cholmondeley, Richard Tarlton

CRAVEN ARMS Mona Rimmer

DALLICOTT Rosa M Kettle

DAWLEY John Clayton, John Petty

DIDDLEBURY Edward Herbert

DONNINGTON Goronwy Owen

DONNINGTON WOOD Lucy Cameron

EDGMOND Richard Barnfield, Pattie Hinsull

ELLESMERE John Ayscough, Austin Stevens, Hilton Tims

EYTON-ON-SEVERN Edward Herbert, George Herbert

HADNALL Charles Hulbert

HAUGHMOND John Audelay

HAWKSTONE Samuel Johnson

HIGH ERCALL Richard Baxter

HINSTOCK Charles B Ash

HODNET Charles B Ash, Mary Cholmondeley, Reginald Heber, Cyril H Percy

IGHTFIELD Arthur Mainwaring

IRONBRIDGE Sarah Barker

KINNERSLEY John Masefield

LAWLEY Thomas Ragg

LEIGHTON-UNDER-WREKIN Mary Webb

LILLESHALL John Myrk (or Myrkes)

LITTLE STRETTON Beatrice Harraden, Ian MacLaren, Peter Reading, Oliver Sandys

LUDFORD Armel O'Connor, Violet O'Connor

LUDLOW Donald H Barber, Violet Bullock-Webster, Samuel Butler (1612), Abraham Fraunce, A E Housman, Henry James, Richard P Knight, John Milton, Armel O'Connor, Violet O'Connor, Sheena Porter, Philip Sidney, Stanley Weyman, Thomas Wright

LUTWYCHE George Benson, Stella Benson, Nicholas de Toulouse Savine

MADELEY Edith Pargeter, Ann Turnbull

MADELEY WOOD Joseph Anstice

MAESBURY Richard Ball

MALIN'S LEE Thomas Ragg

MEOLE BRACE Lucy Bather, Samuel Butler (1835), Gavin Gibbons, Mary Webb

MINSTERLEY Arthur Allwood

MORTON Charlotte S Burne, Florence Henniker

MUCH WENLOCK Isaac H Browne (1705), Hugh Farley, Catherine M Gaskell, Henry James, Alec Lea, Mary Webb

NEWPORT Thomas Brown, Charles Dickens

NORBURY Richard Barnfield, John Harris

NORTHWOOD Harriet Fourdrinier

OSWESTRY Richard Ball, Charles W S Brooks, Edward M Darling, John F M Dovaston, Isaac Hughes, Wilfred Owen, Barbara Pym, Richard Richards, T Salway

OTELEY Francis Kynaston

PLAISH William Leighton

PONTESBURY John Clayton, Mary Webb

PRESTON BROCKHURST William Wycherley

PULVERBATCH Georgiana F Jackson

RATLINGHOPE Mary Webb

ROWTON Richard Baxter

RUYTON-OF-THE-ELEVEN-TOWNS A Conan Doyle

SELATTYN Goronwy Owen

SHIFNAL Thomas Brown, Charles Dickens, Thomas Percy, Mrs H Ward

SHREWSBURY A T Agnew, C A Alington, Arthur Allwood, James Amphlett, Mrs E J Burbury, Samuel Butler (1835), Jeffrey Caine, Thomas Churchyard, Desmond Coke, S Taylor

Coleridge, Wilkie Collins, Edmund Crispin, Edward Moore
Darling, W A Darlington, Elizabeth Darwall, Thomas Day,
Daniel Defoe, Paul Dehn, Charles Dickens, Benjamin Disraeli,
John F M Dovaston, Frances Eager, Frederick W Faber, George
Farquhar, Celia Fiennes, E M Forster, Abraham Fraunce, Gavin
Gibbons, Fulke Greville, F Bayford Harrison, Nathaniel
Hawthorne, William Hazlitt, William W How, Charles Hulbert,
C A Hulbert, Thomas Ingoldsby, Margaret A B Jones,
Benjamin H Kennedy, Charles R Kennedy (1808), Ernest G
Lee, John Lovelace-Street, Arthur Mainwaring, M
Montgomery-Campbell, Gerard Moultrie, Job Orton, Wilfred
Owen, Edith Pargeter, Ambrose Philips, Sheena Porter, Lester
Ralph, John Reynolds, John H Reynolds, Campbell H Sadler,
Owen Seaman, Neville Shute, Philip Sidney, Silverpen, David
Simons, Joanna Tate, Ordericus Vitalis, John Waddington-
Feather, David Walker, Mary Webb, Stanley Weyman, John B
Williams

SILVINGTON Mrs E Hewins

SNAILBEACH Mary Webb

STABLEFORD P G Wodehouse

STANTON-UPON-HINE-HEATH Mary Webb

STOKESAY Henry James

TELFORD Margaret A B Jones, Martin Pescador, E Stevens, Jill P
Thomas

TONG Charles Dickens

TUCK HILL Arthur Brockhurst

UPPINGTON Richard Allestree, Goronwy Owen

WELLINGTON Keri Berne, Patrick Bronte, Philip Larkin, William V
Moorhouse, Hesba Stretton, James C Tildesley

WEM S Taylor Coleridge, William Hazlitt, John B Williams

WEST FELTON John F M Dovaston, Benjamin H Kennedy, John B
Williams

WHITCHURCH Daniel Defoe, Celia Fiennes, Reginald Heber

WHITTINGTON William W How

WITHINGTON Rann Kennedy

WORFIELD E M Almedingen

WROCKWARDINE Sheila Jack

WROXETER Richard Allestree, Richard Baxter, Charles Dickens, H Lang Jones, Thomas Wright

THE COUNTY IN GENERAL
Richard Austin, Sarah Barker, Anthony Barnett, Barrington J Bayley, Josephine Bell, John Betjeman, William Black, Charlotte S Burne, William Camden, Arthur O Cooke, Augustine D Crake, Donald Davie, Daniel Defoe, Michael Drayton, Celia Fiennes, J Fogerty, Hollis Freeman, Thomas Fuller, Leonard Galletley, Geraint Goodwin, Geoffrey Grigson, Nathaniel Hawthorne, Mary C Hay, G A Henty, Charles Hobday, Samuel Horton, A E Housman, William H Hudson, Margaret A B Jones, Leslie Kark, Henry Kingsley, John Leland, Audrey E Lindop, Frederic Manning, Hugo Manning, John Masefield, Sheena Porter, Roger Rehm, Stephen L Robertson, Malcolm Saville, John Shane, Emma Smith, Mrs H L Thrale, Ann Treneer

STAFFORDSHIRE

ABBOT'S BROMLEY Henry Francis Cary

ABBOT'S HAY Charles J B Masefield

ACTON TRUSSELL James R Alsop, Margaret Mayo

ADBASTON Charles Bowker Ash

ALDRIDGE Alfred Moss, William H Robinson, Henry Shore

ALTON TOWERS Benjamin Disraeli, Thomas Moore

ANSLOW Michael Brassington

BARTON-UNDER-NEEDWOOD Thomas Gisborne

BEDNALL George P R Alsop, James R Alsop

BERESFORD Charles Cotton

BIDDULPH Arthur Berry

BILSTON David Bailey, Fred R Bartlett, George Beardmore, Julia Berrington, Jeannie G Bettany, G C Daley, John Dangerfield, Emily Edridge, Malcolm S Fellows, John Freeman, Charles F Forshaw, George T Lawley, Thomas Moss, Henry Newbolt, Harriet Nokes, Frederick Price, George Price, E A Underhill, Hugh Walters

BLITHFIELD Lewis Bagot

BLOXWICH Harold Parry, Maurice Wiggin, Isaiah Woodhouse

BOBBINGTON Cuthbert Bede

BONEHILL James R Alsop

BREWOOD W H Ainsworth, James Amphlett, Edward Banks, Charles L Brain, Alfred Hayes, Edward J Wrottesley

BRIERLEY HILL Noah Cooke, Eustace B Cropper, Paul Darby, Charles Hatton, Archie Hill, Tim Longville, Thomas Moss, Robert H Wood

BROOME HILL J Eric Roberts

BURNTWOOD R Lewis Wright

BURSLEM Thomas Baker, Marjorie Boulton, Mrs Brettell, John Davenport, Frederick Harper, Noah Heath, A Bernard Hollowood, Philip Oakes, Elisha Walton

BURTON-ON-TRENT Frederick Attenborough, Isaac H Browne (1705), John Coleman-Cooke, William Coxon, Brenda M Draper, F S Hill, George Stayley

CALWICH Mrs M Delaney, Jean-Jacques Rousseau

CAN LANE John Cornfield

CANNOCK Bruce Beddow, Henry F Cary, Thomas Cotterill, A E

Dudley, Leonard Galletley, G A Henty, J Eric Roberts, William H Robinson, Cecil J C Tildesley

CAVERSWALL Robert W Buchanan

CHAPEL ASH Alfred Hayes, Alfred Noyes

CHASETOWN Charles L Brain

CHEADLE Thomas Bakewell, Samuel J Looker

CHILLINGTON W H Ainsworth

CODSALL Marjorie Crosbie, Audrey E Lindop, Edward J Wrottesley

COLTON Robert E Landor

COLWICH Samuel J Stone

COSELEY R W Earp, Jim W Jones

CRADLEY HEATH Florence A Clee

CROXTON Maud Randall

DARLASTON E Baker, Richard Barnfield, George Fisk, Roger Ormerod

ECCLESHALL Charles B Ash, Clive Wilson

EDIAL David Garrick, Samuel Johnson

ELFORD Francis E Paget

ELLASTONE Arthur E Dodd, George Eliot

ENDON T E Hulme

FAR GREEN Noah Heath

FINCHFIELD Winifred Mantle

GRATTON George Heath, T E Hulme

GRATWICH John R Palmer

GREAT FENTON William Fernyhough

HAMSTALL RIDWARE Francis G Cholmondeley

HANLEY Thomas H Allbut, William Allbut, Bernard Batigan, Arnold Bennett, Mrs Craik, Elijah Fenton, A Bernard Hollowood, Elijah Jones, Isaac Keeling, Thomas Mills, Samuel Pattison, John Ridgeway, Edward Swaine

HARTWELL C F Keary

HAUGHTON John Darwall

HEDNESFORD Nancy Foster

HIGHFIELD George A H Eades

HORSELEY HEATH Ben Boucher

HORTON George Heath

HUGGERSTON Samuel J Stone

ILAM William Congreve, Samuel Johnson, Thomas Tomkinson, Izaak Walton

IPSTONES Elijah Cope

KEELE Roy Fisher, Philip Higson, John I Jones, Ralph de Tunstall Sneyd

KIDSGROVE Elizabeth A Needham

KINGSTONE John R Palmer

KINGSWINFORD Charles Hatton, Thomas Moss, Robert H Wood

KINVER Sabine Baring-Gould, Harold Parsons, Nancy Price

LEA Robert Waring

LEEK Richard Badnall, Nellie Birch, Muriel H Brown, William Challinor, Elijah Cope, Edward A Deacon, A L Gee, Abraham K Killminster, Thomas Marsden, William K Parkes, Ralph de Tunstall Sneyd, Elisha Walton

LEEKFRITH Alfred Hine

LICHFIELD Joseph Addison, Elias Ashmole, Muriel Austin, John Ayscough, Isaac H Browne (1705), William Buckley, George Butt, Geoff Charlton, Edward M Darling, Erasmus Darwin, Geoffrey Dennis, Thomas Dilke, George Farquhar, George Fisk, Richard Garnett, David Garrick, Nathaniel Hawthorne, Samuel Johnson, Richard Jones, Benjamin H Kennedy, Isobel Lambot, Thomas H Lister, Thomas L F Livingstone, Mary W Montagu, George T Neville, Thomas Newton, Priscilla Pointon, Alexander Pope, Henry Salt, Sir Walter Scott, Anna Seward, Craig Thomas, Edward Wetenhall, Robert Whytynton, William A Wood

LINLEY WOOD Mrs A Marsh-Caldwell

LONGSDON Arthur E Dodd

LONGTON Thomas Cotterill, William Cyples, Robert Garner, Jock o'Hazeldean, Thomas L F Livingstone, Edith Morris, Frank Smith, Charles Tomlinson

LONGWOOD Alfred Moss

MADELEY Dave Rowley

MEIR David Johnson

MERRIDALE Edward Banks

NEEDWOOD F N C Mundy

NEWCASTLE-UNDER-LYME Philip Astley, George Beardmore, Arnold Bennett, Vera Brittain, George Cooper, Mrs Craik, Sir John Davies, Arthur E Dodd, Elizabeth Elstob, Elijah Fenton, Robert Fenton, Celia Fiennes, Sylvester Harding, Philip Higson, T E Hulme, David Johnson, Richard Jones, Isaac Keeling, Nellie Kirkham, Edward Knight, Arthur Leech, Oliver W F Lodge, Dave Rowley, Peter Travis, John Wain

OAKAMOOR Samuel J Looker

OXLEY Ashley Milner

PATTINGHAM Richard Thursfield

PENDEFORD William Pitt

PENKRIDGE Cecil J C Tildesley

PENN Vera I Arlett

PENN FIELDS Marjorie Crosbie

QUARNFORD Miss J Dakeyne

REDMERE Edward J Shaw

ROWLEY PARK Paul Butters

ROWLEY REGIS James Woodhouse

RUDYARD Elijah Cope, George Heath

RUGELEY Mary Knowles, John Porter

SEDGLEY David Bailey, Eustace B Cropper, Robert Garner, Jim W Jones, E A Underhill

SHALLOWFORD Izaak Walton

SHENSTONE Florence L C Barclay

SMALLTHORNE Arthur Berry

SMETHWICK Sydney Fowler, Herbert Glyn, Henry Pettitt, Leonard Webster

SNEYD GREEN Noah Heath

STAFFORD Geoffrey Adkins, James Amphlett, George Borrow, George Butt, Paul Butters, Charles S Coldwell, Charles Dickens, George W Gough, Jim Hunter, T E Jackson, Edward Knight, R B Sheridan, Ralph de Tunstall Sneyd, William Somervile, George Swann, Thomas N Talfourd, Izaak Walton

STALLINGTON John A Harvey

STOKE-ON-TRENT George Beardmore, Arnold Bennett, Arthur Berry, Havergal Brian, Pauline Devaney, Arthur E Dodd, Robert Garner, Paul Gater, Frederick Harper, John A Harvey, John Hind, A Bernard Hollowood, Jane M Hollowood, Nellie

Kirkham, Alexander Pope, Austin Stevens, Peter Terson, John Toft, Charles Tomlinson, John W Tomlinson, Douglas C R Twigg, John Wain, Jeffrey Wainwright

STONE Thomas Bakewell

STOURTON Francis Grazebrook

STRETTON William Congreve

SWYTHAMLEY Gage E Freeman

TAMWORTH Edward Farmer, Gage E Freeman, Mary K Roby

TETTENHALL Joyce Coombes, John Pearson, William Pitt, Jon Raven, Thomas Thorneycroft, R Lewis Wright, Edward J Wrottesley

TIPTON Edith Cotterill, Harry Harrison

TIVIDALE Susan Price

TIXALL Arthur Clifford, Georgiana Fullerton, Mrs H Thimelby

TOWNWELL-FOLD Joseph Whittaker

TRENTHAM Thomas Bakewell, George Beardmore, Benjamin Disraeli, William Fernyhough, Paul Gater, Thomas Moss, Frank Smith

TRYSULL Samuel Tomkins

TUNSTALL Hugh Bourne

TUTBURY Thomas Cotterill

UPPER GORNALL E A Underhill

UPPER MAYFIELD Thomas Moore

UTTOXETER Samuel Bentley, William T Birch, Mrs A Harrison, Nathaniel Hawthorne, Mary Howitt, Samuel Johnson, Francis Redfern, George Wakefield

WALSALL A T Agnew, James A Aldis, Dorothy Baker, A Sedgwick Barnard, Harold M Barrows, Herbert Bennett, Charles L Brain,

Arthur Brockhurst, David Calcutt, Alfred A Cole, Constance Cotterell, George Cotterell, Mrs M Cotterell, John F Crump, Edward M Darling, Elizabeth Darwall, John Darwall, Mary Darwall, Mary Davis, Eric R Day, Geoffrey Dennis, Noreen Dilcock, Joseph Dixon, Sister Dora, Margaret Eastvale, George Evans, William Everton, Catherine Fellows, George Fisk, Arthur B Frost, Alexander Gordon, Marjorie Green, Arthur C Harrison, Hubert D Harrison, Madeline Hindsley, Jerome K Jerome, Peter Jones, John Kilbourn, Frank G Layton, Robert Leach, A Hampden Lee, John MacMillan, Kathleen H Mason, Alfred Moss, Henry Newbolt, Stella Nowell, Douglas Orgill, Francis P Palmer, Harold Parry, John Petty, Aileen Quigley, John Reynolds, A M Roe, Jessie L Shannon, Edward J Shaw, Gordon Smith, Elijah Stanley, Charles Strong, Annie C Symons, Henry Tharp, Craig Thomas, Phillip Thomson, Joseph Turner, Maurice Wiggin, Alfred R Williams, Frederic W Willmore, G Woden, George Wouil

WARLEY Leonard Webster

WARLEY WOODS Marjorie Vernon

WEDNESBURY Thomas F Bissell, David Calcutt, John Goddard, Emillie Hammond, David C Murray, Richard Thursfield, Henry Treece, A W Whitehouse, G Woden

WEDNESFIELD John Morrison

WEST BROMWICH W W Hackett, David C Murray, Edwin Radford, James Sylvester, Frederic W Willmore

WHITMORE Samuel J Stone

WIGGINTON Gene Kemp

WILLENHALL Stephen Chatterton, Thomas Thorneycroft, James C Tildesley

WOLSELEY William Somervile, Robert Wolseley

WOLSTANTON Sid Rowe

WOLVERHAMPTON Julia Berrington, J Bevan, Luke Booker, Henry Bull, Florence Burleigh, H Herman Chiltern, Edward Chitham,

Helen Cockerill, Elisha Coles, Joyce Coombes, John D Cooper, Emily Edridge, Thomas Edwards, Susan Fearn, Frank P Fellows, Ellen T Fowler, Emillie Hammond, Derek Harris, Alfred Hayes, Pamela J Hodgson, Sheila Jack, Jim W Jones, Margery Lawrence, Audrey E Lindop, Winifred Mantle, Stanley Mason, Lawrence Meynell, Keith Miles, Stephen Morris, John Morrison, Thomas Moss, Philip Oakes, Roger Ormerod, Harold Parsons, John Pearson, Enoch Powell, Benjamin Purshouse, Maud Randall, Dorothy Reynolds, John Reynolds, Henry Siddons, Annie S Swann, Thomas Thorneycroft, James C Tildesley, Raymond Turner, Marjorie Vernon, William Vernon, Stella V Walton, Joseph Whittaker, J R Windsor-Garnett, Nathaniel Withy, R Lewis Wright

WOMBOURNE Samuel Tomkins

WOOTTON Jean-Jacques Rousseau

WYRLEY William Wyrley

YOXALL Thomas Gisborne

THE COUNTY IN GENERAL
John Addison, Georgiana Bennet, Pearl Binder, Les G Bishop, William Black, William Butt, William Camden, W H Canaway, Alfred J Church, Walter Coleman, Elizabeth Coxhead, William Coxon, Fred W Cross, Donald Davie, Mitchell Dawson, Margaret L Eyles, Celia Fiennes, Thomas D Fosbroke, Thomas Fuller, John A Harvey, Nathaniel Hawthorne, Thomas I James, John Leland, Audrey E Lindop, Thomas Lowe, William Mountford, Candelent Price, Judge Ruegg, John Shane, Emma Smith, Mrs H Thimelby, Mrs H L Thrale, Elijah Travis, Beatrice Tunstall

WARWICKSHIRE

ALCESTER John J Britton, Dorothy Charques

ALVESTON Jacquetta Hawkes, J B Priestley

ARBURY H W Bellairs, George Eliot

ASCOTT Sheila Stewart

ASHTED Emma J Worboise

ATHERSTONE-UPON-STOUR William Thomson

BARFORD Thomas Dugard

BARTON-ON-THE-HEATH John Dover

BEAUDESERT Richard Jago

BIDFORD-ON-AVON Philip Callow, Barbara Comyns

BILTON Joseph Addison

BIRDINGBURY J Laurence Hart, Philip B Homer

BIRMINGHAM John Addison, Ted Allbeury, Walter E Allen, W H Auden, Hubert Bagster, George L Banks, Mrs G L Banks, Vera Barclay, James Barlow, Godfrey Baseley, Barrington J Bayley, Hilaire Belloc, Herbert Bennett, Bramley Berrington, James Bisset, Harold F Bradley, Charles L Brain, Michael Brassington, Noel H Brettell, John A Bridges, Walter Brierley, Herbert E Britton, John J Britton, Arthur Brockhurst, Peter Brook, Arthur H Brookes, Horace Budd, Roger Busby, Mrs B Bushnell, Michael G Butler, Paul Butters, P Button, Philip Callow, J L Carr, Barbara Cartland, Henry F Cary, Edward Cave, Peter Chamberlain, Geoff Charlton, Edward Chitham, G D H Cole, Margaret Cole, Marie Corelli, Thomas Cotterill, Marjorie Darke, O H Davies, Mary A Davis, Geoffrey Dennis, Ernest Denny, Charles Dickens, Richard W Dixon, A Conan Doyle, John Drinkwater, Andre Drucker, Albert H Duncuff, David Edgar, Edwin Edridge, Clare Emsley, D J Enright, Simon Evans, B J Farmer, Edward Farmer, Jeffrey Farnol, S Farr, Michael Field, William Field, Emily P Finnemore, E Fintan-Joyce, Roy Fisher, Sydney Fowler, Edward A Freeman, John Freeth, Leonard Galletley, Thomas H Gill, J G Gillam, Alfred J Gilmore, George Gissing, Christine Gittings, C Goodall, Gray Green, Henry Green, J C R Green, Russell Green, George Griffiths, W W Hackett, Patrick Hall, Leslie Halward, William Hamper, John Hampson, John Harrison, J Laurence Hart, Peter J N Havins, Rosa A Hayden, Alfred Hayes, Brian Hayles,

William Hazlitt, G A Henty, Mrs E Hewins, Madeline Hindsley, William G Hole, Roy Holland, G Holtham, Gerard Manley Hopkins, Harry H Horton, Arthur Hougham, Charles Hulbert, Paul Humphries, Joseph Hunt, William Hutton, Catherine Hutton, Clement M Ingleby, John Ironside, Washington Irving, Peter P Isacke, L P Jacks, B L Jacot, G E Jeffery, Samuel Johnson, Richard Jones, Benjamin H Kennedy, Charles R Kennedy (1808), Charles R Kennedy (1871), Rann Kennedy, Edward Knight, Eric Knight, Henrietta Knight, Frederick Langbridge, John Langford, Alec Lea, Robert Leach, Val Leon, Paul Lester, Mary Linwood, Charles Lloyd, David Lodge, Laurence Longbow, Yann Lovelock, Edward Lowbury, Mrs Belloc Lowndes, Gavin Lyall, B McEvoy, Louis McNeice, Alan & Frank Manford, Harriet Martineau, Eric Maschvitz, Margaret Mayo, Rosalind Miles, Paul Mills, Walter J Morgan, Stephen Morris, Brian Morse, David C Murray, Constance C W Naden, Cardinal John Newman, Clifford Nicholas, Derek Nicholls, Wallace B Nichols, Mrs C Nicholson, Edward Nicklin, Mrs D Noke, Kate Norway, Jenny Oldfield, Vera Oram, Gareth Owen, John L Palmer, Henry Parkes, William K Parkes, Leslie Paul, J Pearce, Erasmo Pelles, Max Pemberton, Henry Pettitt, William Pitt, Priscilla Pointon, Isa Postgate, John P Postgate, Enoch Powell, Norman Power, Candelent Price, Frederick Price, Miss Prickett, Brian Priestley, Joseph Priestley, Thomas Ragg, Val Ransford, Jon Raven, Charles Reade, Henry Reed, Dorothy Reynolds, William Ridler, Emma Robinson, A Rodway, Sax Rohmer, Frederick Rolfe, David Rudkin, Ernest M Rudland, Sylvia Russell, S N Sedgwick, Alfred C Shaw, Joseph H Shorthouse, John Sibley, Silverpen, C J Silverston, F B Silvester, John L Simcox, Elizabeth Smith, Gordon Smith, Raymond Speakman, John Stafford, Boswell Taylor, Josephine Tey, Mrs M H Tiltman, Norman Tiptaft, David Tipton, Nick Toczek, J R R Tolkien, Malcolm Totten, Henry Treece, Ann Treneer, Meriol Trevor, David Turner (1950), John B Twycross-Raines, Kenneth Tynan, Robert A Vaughan, J Vernal, Edgar Wallace, Rex Warner, Jane Webb, Leonard Webster, Robert Westall, Maurice Wiggin, Michael Wilding, Ronald F Willetts, Frederic W Willmore, Keith S Wilson, G Woden, Robert H Wood, Emma J Worboise, George Wyatville, John Wyndham, Richard Yates, Francis Brett Young

BISHOP'S HAMPTON Thomas Rogers

BISHOP'S TACHBROOK Walter S Landor

BURTON DASSET Anthony Cooke

CHARLECOTE James Lees-Milne, William Shakespeare

CHESTERTON GREEN Richard Jago

CHILVERS COTON George Eliot

CLIFFORD CHAMBERS John Donne, Michael Drayton, Ben Jonson

CLIFTON-UPON-DUNSMOOR Christopher Harvey

COLESHILL John Digby

COMBE ABBEY Lucy Harington

COMPTON SCORPION Thomas Overbury

COMPTON WYNYATES Henry Compton (1632)

COPELY HILL Emma J Worboise

CORELY Keith Miles, Rosalind Miles

COVENTRY Evelyn M Alexander, J A Atkinson, Reginald Bacon, Dora Barford, Richard Baxter, James B Baynard, Robert H Baynes, Josiah S Beamish, Frank Betts, Jeremy Bindman, Harold F Bradley, Angela Brazil, Nicholas Brennon, John L Brown, Philip Callow, Knightley Chetwood, Muriel Clark, Ethel M Clarke, Gertrude Clowes, Aimee M Colligan, Henry Compton (1872), J F Cramp, Gilbert Dalton, Marjorie Darke, Edward M Darling, Thomas Dekker, Michael Drayton, Maurice Edelman, George Eliot, Ralph W Emerson, Clare Emsley, Malcolm S Fellows, A E Feltham, David Findlander, Agnes Furlong, Nan Goodall, Bassett Green, Ronald Hall, Margaret Heritage, John Hewitt (1719), John Hewitt (1907), Margaret Heys, Susan Hill, E H Humberstone, Aleck Johnson, Dylis H Jones, Nancy C Keeling, George S Kemble, William H Kimbell, Edward King, Walter S Landor, Philip Larkin, Stuart Lowrie, Jessie G Marash, John Marston, John W Marston, Nora Mills, Les Milne, Maureen O'Donnell, Wilfred Owen, Charles

Payne, T Arthur Plummer, Jeremy Sandford, Fred H Shephard, John Sibree, Mark Smith, Eleanor Spence, Margaret Stewart-Taylor, Alfred Tennyson, Ellen Terry, Robert W Thom, John Tipper, Nathaniel Wanley, Humphrey Wanley, Edith Wilkinson, Robert Wright

EATINGTON Edward Underhill

EDGE HILL Richard Jago, Jan Weddup

EDSTONE William Somervile

EXHALL William Thomson

FENNY COMPTON Henry B Dudley

FOUR OAKS Kate Norway

GUY'S CLIFFE Bertie B Greatheed

HALFORD BRIDGE John J Britton

HAMPTON LUCY Thomas Rogers

HARBURY Richard Jago

HARTSHILL GREEN Michael Drayton

HENLEY-IN-ARDEN Benjamin Beddome, Robert S W Bell, Peter Brook

KENILWORTH Andrew Davies, Michael Field, George Gascoigne, William Gresley, Mary Herbert, Sir Walter Scott, Philip Sidney

LAPWORTH Edward Lapworth

LEAMINGTON PRIORS Benjamin Satchwell

LEAMINGTON SPA James Barlow, Ambrose Bierce, James Bisset, John Bonar, Emily A Browne, William Camden, Gladys Davidson, Charles Dickens, Lady Douglas, Elise Emmons, Clare Emsley, Frederick Enoch, D J Enright, Charles Graves, J Laurence Hart, John H Hawley, Nathaniel Hawthorne, Amy E Heynes, Alice James, M Forster Knight, Cordelia Leigh, Montagu Lomax, Alfred B Major, George Morley, Richard

Pryce, Kellet Rigbye, A Mary F Robinson, Frances M Robinson, John Ruskin, Arthur Sewell, Alfred C Shaw, Mary Toone, Edward T Turnerelli, Edward Wilkinson, Harrison C Wilson, Margaret L Woods, Richard Yates

LEEK WOOTTON Francis G Cholmondeley

LIVERIDGE Peter Brook

LONG COMPTON Sheila Stewart

LOXLEY George Huddesford

MANCETTER H W Bellairs

MONKS KIRBY Charles Feilding, Henry Goodere

NUNEATON A W Bellairs, George Eliot, Margaret Stewart-Taylor

PINLEY Matilda Brinkley

POLESWORTH John Donne, Michael Drayton, Henry Goodere, Ben Jonson, Philip Sidney

POOLEY Aston Cockain

RADWAY William Warner

RUGBY Matthew Arnold, G F Bradby, Rupert Brooke, Lewis Carroll, Henry F Cary, Edward Cave, Francis G Cholmondeley, Arthur Clough, Arthur B Frost, Philip Guedalla, Donald Hankey, Cyril Hare, Christopher Harvey, R D Henriques, Philip B Homer, Thomas Hughes, Richard Hull, Arthur H W Ingram, George J Kennedy, E V Knox, Walter S Landor, F L Lucas, Elinor Lyon, Gerard Moultrie, John Moultrie, Mary D Moultrie, Ole-Luk-Oie, Alfred Ollivant, Tony Petch, William Plomer, Arthur Ransome, Anne Ridler, Michael Sadleir, Geoffrey Scott, Ethel Sidgwick, John Stallworthy, John W Tomlinson, Peter Traill, Arthur Waley, Peter Whalley, Margaret L Woods, Albert H Wratislaw, Theodore Wratislaw

SHILTON Christopher St Germain

SHOTTERY Richard Hathaway

SNITTERFIELD Lady Coventry, Richard Jago

SOLIHULL Caroline Clive, Richard Jago, Cecil J Lewis, Barry Musto, William Shenstone, David Turner (1927)

STONELEIGH Chandos Leigh, Cordelia Leigh, Henry Parkes

STRATFORD-UPON-AVON Nicholas Bradey, John Brophy, Dorothy Charques, Barbara Comyns, Marie Corelli, Mrs E Gaskell, J Laurence Hart, John Huckell, Clement M Ingleby, Washington Irving, John Jordan, Thomas Lowe, Arthur Murphy, Leonard Parish, Stephen Phillips, Sir Walter Scott, William Shakespeare, Craig Thomas, Mark Twain, Nathaniel P Willis

SUTTON COLDFIELD Henry F Cary, Bernard Fell, Peter P Isacke, Rosalind Miles, John C Shannon, Richard Yates, Francis Brett Young

SUTTON PARK Edwin Edridge, Harry H Horton

TEMPLE BALSALL Edward Eglionbie

TIDDINGTON John Jordan

ULLENHALL Richard Thursfield

WARWICK George Butt, Arthur O Cooke, Richard Corbett (or Corbet), Michael Drayton, Thomas Dugard, Edward Eglionbie, William Field, Fulke Greville, Herbert Kynaston, Robert E Landor, Walter S Landor, Penelope Lively, John Masefield, John Owen, Miss Prickett, John Ryland, Philip Sidney

WOLSTON Madeleine Riley

WOOTTON WAWEN Peter Brook, Henrietta Knight, William Somervile

WROXALL Luke Milbourne

THE COUNTY IN GENERAL
Cuthbert Bede, Bernard Bergonzi, William Black, William Camden, Alfred J Church, Donald Davie, Andrew Davies, Michael Edwards, D J Enright, Thomas Fuller, Nathaniel Hawthorne, Chandos Leigh, John Leland, Paul Merchant, Miss

Prickett, John Shane, Peter Smart, Emma Smith, Mrs H L Thrale, Beatrice Tunstall, Leonard Webster, Stanley Weyman, John Wheway

WORCESTERSHIRE

ABBERLEY Joseph Addison, Mary Bromley, John Dryden, W P Hodgkinson, Gene Kemp, Alexander Pope, William Walsh

ALUM BROOK Charles H Simmonds

ALVECHURCH Godfrey Baseley

ARELEY KINGS W P Hodgkinson, Layamon

ASHTON-UNDER-HILL Fred Archer

ASTLEY Frances R Havergal, William H Havergal

BARNT GREEN Gavin Bantock

BEWDLEY John Addison, Mary Bromley, George Griffiths, Jean Marsh, Charles H Simmonds, James White

BIRLINGHAM Robert E Landor

BIRTSMORTON Charles F Grindrod

BREDON Fred Archer, John Masefield, John Moore, Tatwin

BROMSGROVE Godfrey Baseley, John Cotton, John Crane, Harold Deardon, John Fellows, Geoffrey Hill, Molly Holden, A E Housman, Clemence Housman, Laurence Housman, Robert E Landor, Thomas H P F Lowe, David Rudkin

CATSHILL Michael G Butler

CHADDESLEY CORBETT Richard Badnall

CLAINES Henry L Somers-Cocks

CLENT T Pittaway

CLIFTON-UPON-TEME George Butt, A H W Ingram, Joyce Jefferies

COVERLEY Sibella E Bryans

CRADLEY John Sibley

DOWLES J F Sayer

DROITWICH Kenneth Bird, John Cotton, Humphrey Pakington, Philip Turner

DUDLEY John Addison, T S Allen, Patrick Anderson, Richard Baxter, Luke Booker, Ben Boucher, Edward Chitham, Eustace B Cropper, Ernest Dudley, T Gough, Francis Grazebrook, Harry Harrison, Pattie Hinsull, Harold Parsons, Veronica Robinson, Ian Serraillier, John Sibley, John C Snaith, Charlotte Speke, E A Underhill

EARL'S CROOME Samuel Butler (1612)

ECKINGTON Leonard Parish, Arthur Quiller-Couch

EVESHAM Harold Avery, Elizabeth Elstob, H L Haynes, Arthur H W Ingram, Robert of Gloucester, William Somervile, Francis Brett Young

FOCKBURY A E Housman

HAGLEY Joseph Addison, Samuel Johnson, George Lyttelton, Thomas Lyttleton, Alexander Pope, William Shenstone, Lady Spencer, James Thomson, Mrs H L Thrale, Nathaniel Withy

HALESOWEN John Addison, John Byng, Joseph Hunt, James M McQueen, Jean Marsh, Samuel Rogers, William Shenstone, Francis Brett Young

HANLEY CASTLE Edmund Smith, William S Symonds

HANLEY SWAN Roger Alma

HARTLEBURY Benjamin Disraeli, Izaak Walton

HARVINGTON Arthur H W Ingram

HINDLIP William Habington

HOLT FLEET W P Hodgkinson

IPSLEY Walter S Landor

KIDDERMINSTER Richard Baxter, Cuthbert Bede, Kenneth Bird, Herbert E Britton, Herbert Broom, George Butt, Thomas Cook, Noah Cooke, Henry Garnett, Brian R Hall, Mrs H Housman, William W How, Jean Marsh, Job Orton, Peter Philp, John G Sheppard, Charles Herbert Simmonds, Stanley G Watts, Joseph Williams

LEIGH George Butt

LENCHFORD W P Hodgkinson

LOWER WICK Mrs M Sherwood

LYE Geoffrey P Adams, Noel H Brettell

MALVERN Lascelles Abercrombie, Michael Arlen, Luke Booker, Richard Cooksey, Daniel Defoe, Charles Dickens, Sydney Dobell, Ian Fearnside, Henry Garnett, Charles F Grindrod, David W H Grubb, Radclyffe Hall, Leslie Halward, Jeremy Hilton, M R James, Elizabeth Jenkins, Rosa Kettle, William Langland, C S Lewis, E R Bulmer Lytton, John Moore, Nancy Price, Lorna Rea, David Rudkin, George B Shaw, Elizabeth Smith, Henry L Somers-Cocks, William S Symonds, Geoffrey Trease, Gael Turnbull, Philip Turner, Doreen Wallace, Arthur Weigall, Walter G Whitehouse

MARTLEY C S Calverley

NAUNTON BEAUCHAMP Thomas P Wadley

ODDINGLEY David S Daniell

OFFENHAM William S Symonds

OMBERSLEY George W Gillingham

PEDMORE Deryck Grice, John J Vlii

PENDOCK William S Symonds

PERSHORE John Betjeman, Jeremy Hilton

REDDITCH Florence Allcock, Harold Avery, Ernest Denny

REDNAL John H Newman

RIBBESFORD George Griffiths

ROMSLEY Joseph Hunt, Albert J J Price

ROUS LENCH Richard Baxter

SHELSLEY BEAUCHAMP Thomas H P F Lowe

SHIPSTON-ON-STOUR Herbert E Britton

SHRAWLEY W P Hodgkinson

SNARESHILL William H Havergal

STANBROOK Laurentia McLachlan

STANFORD-ON-TEME George Butt, Lucy Cameron, Mrs M
   Sherwood

STOKE PRIOR John Toy

STOURBRIDGE Noel H Brettell, Thomas B Brindley, Paul Cushing,
   G Robert Dukes, Charles Hatton, Samuel Johnson, John M G
   McLeod, Thomas Moss, Noel Pearce, Francis Perks, John
   Reynolds, Samuel Rogers, Mrs M Routh, Robert H Wood

STOURPORT-ON-SEVERN F Easthorpe Martin

STRENSHAM Samuel Butler (1612)

TENBURY WELLS Frederick A Ouseley, Edmund Smith, Thomas
   Wright

TICKENHILL Mary Herbert

UPPER ARLEY Charles H Simmonds

WICKHAMFORD James Lees-Milne

WORCESTER Roger Alma, Elias Ashmole, Florence L C Barclay,
   Edgar Billingham, James S Borlaise, Harold F Bradley, Michael
   G Butler, Fanny Burney, Samuel Butler (1612), Thomas E Cole,
   William Combe, Arthur O Cooke, Charles Dickens, Alfred

Douglas, John Earle, Richard Edes, Celia Fiennes, Florence of
Worcester, Samuel Foote, George Gissing, Adam L Gordon,
Frederick Grice, Charles Hatton, William H Havergal, Arthur H
Winnington Ingram, Rosemary H Jarman, Edward Kelly, G A
Studdart Kennedy, Kennett Lea, David Lockwood, John Noake,
Graham Price, Susan Price, S N Sedgwick, Mrs M Sherwood,
William Smith, William Thomson, John Toy, Robert A
Vaughan, William Walsh, Izaak Walton, Gervase Warmestry,
Thomas Weaver, Fay Weldon, Mrs H Wood, Philip Worner,
Francis Brett Young

THE COUNTY IN GENERAL

William Black, William Camden, Barbara Cartland, Alfred J
Church, Augustine D Crake, Donald Davie, Thomas Fuller,
John Leland, Thomas Nabbes, Mary E Pearce, Hesketh
Pearson, John Ruskin, Edith H Scott, John Shane, Michael
Shayer, Emma Smith, Mrs H L Thrale, Ann Treneer